CAM

CAMELLIAS

THE COMPLETE GUIDE

LOGAN A. EDGAR

The Crowood Press

First published in 1991 by
The Crowood Press Ltd
Ramsbury, Marlborough
Wiltshire SN8 2HR

Paperback edition 1996

British Library Cataloguing Data

A catalogue record for this book is available
from the British Library

ISBN 1 85223 970 0

Acknowledgements
Line-drawings by Jan Sparrow.

Note   Throughout this book, the pronouns 'he', 'him' and
'his' are intended to apply to both men and women. It is
important that men and women should have equal status and
opportunities in all walks of life.

Typeset by
Footnote Graphics, Warminster, Wilts.
Printed in Great Britain by
J.W. Arrowsmith Ltd, Bristol

CONTENTS

INTRODUCTION

It has been my good fortune that, for over forty years I have been able to grow choice trees and shrubs, chief amongst these being rhododendrons and camellias. In recent years I have even had the pleasure, in partnership with others, of working and runnning a small commercial camellia nursery.

In this book my main aim has been to set out the practical knowledge I have gained over the years in order to give simple, straightforward advice and help to every grower of the lovely camellia, be he a pure beginner or a more advanced gardener. This book is essentially practical, making no pretence of going into the advanced techniques of hybridizing, of propagation by tissue culture and so on. For those who need it, this information can be found in advanced, specialist books. My aim here is to enable every one to grow better and more beautiful camellias successfully and easily.

I cannot emphasize enough that I have written a practical account of my own experience, be it right or wrong. Nevertheless, I am obviously indebted to the authors of various other books, chief among them being Stirling Macoboy's *The Colour Dictionary of Camellias*, Colonel Tom Durrant's *The Camellia Story*, *The Camellia*, published by the American Camellia Society and *Camellia Nomenclature* published by The Southern California Camellia Society. To each author I express my gratitude.

In addition I would like to express my thanks to my son, Andrew Edgar, who took and supplied all the photographs appearing in this book. I would also like to thank my wife, Doreen Edgar, for her advice on flower arranging and her persuasion in making me write this book. Finally, I would like to thank our lifelong friend, Jean Farnfield, for typing all of my ill-written manuscript, for checking proofs and for her advice and encouragement. Without her help this book would never have seen the light of day.

So, at the very end, we have the trio whose knowledge and experience dating back over forty years is frequently given in this book – namely, myself, my wife Doreen and Jean Farnfield. We are the three partners who, between us, are the Coghurst Nursery Camellia Specialists of Ivyhouse Lane, Three Oaks, Near Hastings, which started when we retired from our original occupations.

1
HISTORY AND ORIGINS

Most of us know the camellia as a beautiful and showy flowering shrub commonly planted as a garden plant, a woodlander, a conservatory plant or a container or patio shrub. Fewer of us, however, know how many species are involved in the make-up of the modern (and often much older) camellia nor where those species came from.

In 1958, J. R. Sealy published his great work *A Revision of the Genus Camellia* in which he classified eighty-two different species of camellia. However, more recently in 1981, Professor Chang published in Chinese a monograph enumerating considerably more. His work is now available in an English translation, *Camellias* (1984), by Chang Hung Ta and Bruce Bartholomew. This work recognizes some 200 species.

Later in this book the hybridization which man has engineered between a comparatively small number of these species will be referred to in more detail. Suffice it to say, at this stage, that between them these species have produced well over 5,000 different varieties and cultivars. Hence it is extremely unlikely that any one of us will have a first-hand knowledge of the majority of these. Looking through the description of many of the species enumerated by Sealy, it is interesting to note that, although the majority are described as having white flowers, quite a few are described as having yellow or yellowish blooms, whilst with one or two the flower colour is described as being 'purplish'. Accordingly, some useful colour breaks should be capable of achievement. Equally, there are several which are described as 'fragrant' or 'extremely fragrant' so that the incorporation of their 'genes' in a breeding programme in due time may provide us with blooms of many colours and fragrance the equal of the trumpet lily.

These, however, are matters for the future even though every effort is currently being made to achieve the two goals of fragrance and colour, the latter being yellow (and all its derivatives) and blue.

Having said all this I have not lost account of the fact that the average reader of a book such as this will be a practical gardener, someone who wants to grow beautiful plants to as near perfection as possible. Whilst the botanical make-up of those plants may be of some interest it is certainly not of overwhelming importance and, in consequence, I have thought it right to deal only briefly with the species involved in the make-up of the modern camellia and only briefly with the main species likely to influence their development in the reasonable future. I am well aware that there are numerous species to which I have not referred which may, in fact, play a key role in the future in the camellia breeder's programme.

Of those 200 species of camellia known to botanists, only twelve or so have made any real impact on the gardening world. Some of these are *C. japonica, saluenensis, reticulata, sasanqua, cuspidata*. Others, such as *chrysantha, lutchuenensis, granthamiana, oleifera*, although of tremendous interest and potential and although already incorporated, where possible, in some breeding programmes, have as yet made little impact on the plants we grow in our gardens, from the gardener's point of view. *C. lutchuenensis* and *oleifera* have imparted some fragrance and *C. chrysantha* may ultimately yield up its secrets to give us hardy yellow camellias and from them orange, buff, apricot and so on. As yet, the miracle has not really happened. Our scented camellias rarely, if ever, perfume the air like *Rhododendron fortunei* or one of its hybrids such as the 'Loderi Grex', nor do we appear to be much nearer the pure yellow camellia than we were before *chrysantha* was introduced.

The cultivation, breeding and selection of *C. japonica* and *reticulata* had undoubtedly been going on for over a thousand years before anyone in the western hemisphere had the opportunity or gave a thought to bringing *C. lutchuenensis* and *sasanqua* into a modern breeding programme. Such a modern breeding programme has been going on in the West only since the Second World War, whilst the breeding and selection of *C. japonica* and *C. reticulata* has been going on for well over a thousand years if we turn our eyes to the Far East.

Let us, then, look back over the centuries to try to ascertain where these plants of such great antiquity originated.

TWELVE COMMERCIAL SPECIES

Generally speaking, all camellias are native to Japan, China, Indo-China and the various islands neighbouring these countries. It would seem that, of the 200 or so species known to botanists, the following twelve are most likely to be of commercial value. They are set out below in their approximate order of importance and to show their origin and natural environment:

C. japonica It is generally accepted that *C. japonica* originated in southern Japan, the south of Korea, islands off the coast of China and the archipelago centred on Taiwan (previously Formosa).

C. reticulata Like so many beautiful plants, the species originated in the Yunnan province of China. However, although *C. reticulata* is normally listed as a species there seems to be little doubt that, apart from the 'wild form' as it is commonly called, *C. reticulata* as we know it is a hybrid involving at least two and probably several species. The *reticulata* story is a fascinating one and well worth studying by any camellia enthusiast but one beyond the scope of this book which aims to concentrate primarily on purely practical matters.

C. saluenensis Again, from the Yunnan province but coming mainly from the north and west of the *reticulata* area, so should be hardier.

C. sasanqua Native of Japan and the Liu Kiu islands. Hiemalis is probably a form of *sasanqua*.

C. granthamianum Found only in the Hong Kong New Territories.

C. pitardii var. *pitardii* Found over a wide area in the Kweichow and Szechuan provinces of China.

C. pitardii var. *yunnanica* Comes from the Yunnan and Szechuan provinces of China.

C. hongkongensis Not surprisingly it comes from the Hong Kong area.

C. cuspidata From south-west China.

C. lutchuenensis Indigenous to the Liu Kiu islands, *C. lutchuenensis* is the most fragrant species discovered so far and has mostly been used in breeding programmes directed to producing well-scented camellias.

C. sinensis var. *sinensis* (Otherwise *Camellia thea*) is of vast importance as the Chinese tea plant and is believed to be native to Yunnan.

C. sinensis var. *assamica* Very similar to *C. taliense*, a native of Assam, Indo-China, Burma and China.

Before we accept the foregoing totally, a word of warning is not out of place because so many theories exist, particularly with regard to the origins of the main species *C. sinensis* and *japonica*. We know that the famous plant hunter, Robert Fortune, introduced the tea plant from China into India but, although recorded as a wild plant in Yunnan, the modern theory is that it originated in the Irrawaddy River basin in Burma.

Equally, although *C. japonica* is generally thought of as having originated in Japan, a strong body of opinion is that it was first introduced into Japan by Chinese seafarers and, accordingly, would be a native of China.

Thus we can continue ever building new theories but as gardeners we must ask to what avail. The camellia is a plant cultivated for over a thousand years. Small wonder its origins are a matter of doubt.

Among camellia growers there is also some doubt over the pronounciation of the name itself! In fact, it was named after George Joseph Kamel by the great botanist Carl Linneas. Kamel was born in 1661 and became a Jesuit missionary and also a plant collector. The Latin equivalent of his name would be Camellus, hence the reason why, in more recent times, some insist on pronouncing the name of our beautiful plant 'Ka-mell-ia' whereas others of us are not prepared to change the habit of fifty and more years and hold fast to 'Ka-meel-ia'. For my part, I make no apology – if any of us cared to devote a little research to the matter we could come up with literally dozens of examples of accepted mispronounciation on the lines of the Kamel or Camellus example.

The introduction of the camellia into Europe is also something of a mystery. It has been said that Kamel brought it to Europe and that some of his plant material was sent to England. However, Kamel lived in the Philippines and there is no evidence that he ever visited China or Japan (where the camellia undoubtedly grew in gardens) nor that he ever returned to Europe. In addition, as camellias are not natives of the Philippines nor garden plants in Manila where Kamel set up a clinic for the poor, it is most unlikely that he ever set eyes on one of these plants! It therefore follows that the interesting stories about Kamel and the camellia which have been handed down for well over a century amount to nothing more than flights of fancy. The only incontrovertible facts we do know are that Kamel died in 1706, the year before Linneas was born, and that Linneas honoured him by naming for him the genus *Camellia* in 1735.

So if Kamel did not introduce it, who did? The more entertaining, but no doubt apocryphal, story is that the skipper of a certain merchant ship, wearying of the perilous journey to China to buy tea and the equally perilous journey home with his valuable cargo, persuaded the Chinese merchants to sell him some tea plants so that they could be planted in Europe. To this they agreed but little did our skipper know that the cunning merchants had sold him *C. japonica* plants rather than *C. sinensis*. Only when they produced beautiful flowers rather than fragrant tea plant leaves was the hoax discovered. Nevertheless, it is said that this hoax brought the camellia into Europe many years earlier than it otherwise would have been.

English garden literature reported that Lord Petre was growing *C. japonica* in his stove house at Thorndon Hall, Essex as early as 1739. By 1788 it was found to be hardy enough to stand the winter outdoors. In 1792 the camellias 'Alba Plena' and 'Variegata' were brought into England to be followed soon after by 'Incarnata' ('Lady Hume's Blush') and 'Rubra Plena'. Many others followed and new seedlings were soon producing blooms.

In 1820 Capt Richard Rawes imported to England the first *reticulata* camellia and assured his name in camellia nomenclature as did Robert Fortune later, introducing another variety with more formal flowers. This plant flowered in 1857.

Another great plant hunter, George Forrest, collected camellia seed in western Yunnan. Plants from this collection flowered in 1932 and were identified as *C. reticulata* with single blooms – often referred to as 'the wild form'. In 1958 this form was crossed with *C. williamsii* 'Mary Christian' at Nymans Garden in West Sussex, to produce the famous plant 'Leonard Messel'. In 1948 the so-called Yunnan *reticulatas* were imported into the United States following great efforts made by W. E. Lammerts and Ralph Peer. The hybridizing of *C. reticulata* on quite an extensive scale followed soon after and continues today.

The first *C. sasanqua* was imported into England in 1811 but failed to achieve great popularity, though by 1829 six distinct species had been introduced and others appeared from time to time up to the present day. In particular, *C. saluenensis* seems first to have been found by George Forrest in 1917 and to have been introduced by him at that time or soon after. Until its introduction hybrids were actually unknown but, once established, there came the beginning of the great host of hybrids we know today. There is little doubt that for all practical purposes the hybrids between *C. japonica, saluenensis* and *reticulata* are the finest hybrids available today. Other species are playing their part but not as yet to so great an extent.

The spread of the camellia from England, and probably Portugal as well, to other European countries was comparatively rapid. It is believed that the first camellia in Italy was a *C. japonica* planted at Caserta in 1760. In 1809 two red *C. japonica* were exhibited at the Ghent Flower Show in Belgium. The camellia was, presumably, in France at about the same time and in 1819 the Abbe Berlese is known to have raised a hundred plants from seed from the Caserta tree. By 1813 the camellia was growing in Germany. In all these countries the breeding of more and more cultivars continued apace, so much so that in 1846 a Concours Annuel de Camellias – the first camellia show – was held in Luxembourg when 491 plants were exhibited.

Outside Europe, the spread of the camellia proceeded: plants of *C. japonica* are known to have arrived in Australia in 1831 and it is believed that camellias planted in New Zealand in 1834 were probably imported from there. It is thought that *C. japonica* first arrived in the United States in 1797 or 1798. Others followed and by 1822 one nurseryman was cataloguing seventeen different varieties or cultivars.

In Australia, New Zealand and the United States, there began what was to become a flood of new cultivars leading ultimately to the camellia hybrids we grow in our gardens today. There is no doubt that from these three countries come the majority of the finest hybrid camellias in our gardens today. This is not to denigrate hybrids raised in the United Kingdom and other European countries. As will be noted later, some of the very best have been raised here but to find the great range of fine modern hybrids we must raise our eyes and look across the ocean to the United States and the Antipodes.

2
CLASSIFICATIONS

There is a great variation between the growth habits of the various species and even of different varieties in each of the different species. For example, C. *japonica* varies from slow compact growth to fast open growth, from almost prostrate forms to more or less fastigiate forms. In the time that a dense, slow grower like 'High Hat' or 'Cecile Brunazzi' reaches 2ft (0.6m) a fast grower like 'Juno' will have reached 5 or 6ft (1.5 or 1.8m). As a result of these different growth habits, the form of C. *japonica* varies from low spreading growth to a fine rounded bush to a tall, slender open or compact shrub.

On the other hand, C. *reticulata*, in the United Kingdom at least, tends to be leggy, favouring rather open growth. In most parts of England it is best grown indoors and some can be persuaded to bush up well in time – many of its hybrids are better and, somewhat surprisingly, some are amongst the hardiest and toughest. In general, if tried outside, C. *reticulata* seems to prefer sunnier conditions than the majority of C. *japonica* cultivars.

In the United Kingdom, C. *sasanqua* has never achieved great popularity, though it flowers from late October/November onwards. This is no doubt partly due to the fact that in colder parts of the country it is not always satisfactory as an open ground plant, but needs the protection of a wall or greenhouse cultivation. Given the latter, it is charming and frequently scented. In form, it is as variable as C. *japonica* and can be compact, low growing or tall, according to variety. It can be used successfully in milder areas for low hedges and, in general, is successful espaliered against a wall.

The species C. *saluenensis*, and most of its hybrids, are usually neat, bushy and compact although the species can vary greatly from a low dense mound to a tall open plant.

So much for the growth habit of these species. So far as leaves are concerned, and to the gardener leaves are only second in importance to flowers, C. *japonica* is clearly the outright winner with its beautiful glossy leaves of outstanding quality and substance. In fact, if it were entered in a hedging plant competition with other evergreens such as privet, laurel, lonicera, various conifers, holly, euonymous and so on, it would be a barely challenged winner. As it also bears blooms against which none of the hedging plants mentioned – or others not mentioned – would have the vaguest chance of competitive success, it remains a mystery why the camellia is so rarely used for hedging purposes. One can only assume that, despite its long history, garden architects and designers remain ignorant of its obvious capabilities and that so many who have made their contribution to camellia literature have been equally ignorant of the camellia's outstanding capability as a hedging shrub.

Whilst enthusing over the beautiful glossy dark green leaves of *C. japonica* we must not overlook the beauty and attraction of the leaves of the other species and their hybrids: *C. reticulata* with its often very large, up to 4½in (112mm) long by 2½in (62mm) wide leathery, dull green, heavily reticulated (net veined) leaf; *C. saluenensis* with leaves 1½ to 2½in (37 to 62mm) long and half as wide, dark green above and paler beneath; and *C. sasanqua* with its 1½ to 3½in (37 to 87mm) leaves of shining dark green.

The leaves of hybrids between the various species vary as much as the species themselves. Some look almost exactly like a *japonica* leaf, some like a typical *reticulata* and some, for example the beautiful 'Francie L', do not really look like a camellia leaf at all. There are always a number of exceptions to the rule. We normally refer to *C. japonica* as having deep glossy green leaves. Whilst this is generally true, if we accepted it literally we would probably have doubts as to whether the white *C. japonica* 'Gauntlettii' (syn. 'Lotus' and 'Sodegakushi') or 'White Nun' or 'Red Ensign' with their large somewhat hanging, rather dull, green leaves were *C. japonica* at all. Indeed they are and merely demonstrate one or two exceptions to the rule.

FLOWER FORMS

The typical flower form of the various species already referred to is single, as is the case with the vast majority of wild flowers. Doubling occurs as an exception and particularly in garden forms in garden cultivation.

The size of those single flowers of the original species varies considerably from about 1½in (37mm) across in the case of *C. cuspidata* to 2½ to 4in (62 to 100mm) across in the case of *C. japonica*. Excellent botanical descriptions of the leaves and flowers of the principal species can be found in W. J. Bean's *Trees and Shrubs Hardy in the British Isles* (8th edition, revised, Vol. 1). On request, *Bean*, the bible of the tree and shrub grower in the United Kingdom, can generally be found in public libraries. Its four volumes, plus a first supplement, make it expensive to buy for the man with a small suburban garden who wants to grow a few good shrubs. However, for the real enthusiast with an even smaller garden or no garden at all, it is an investment which will never be regretted. Within its pages can be found what is probably the most authentic description and details of every tree and shrub hardy in the British Isles, including a good selection of hybrids.

CAMELLIA CATEGORIES

Camellia flowers are customarily classified into six categories. Before we consider these, there are one or two phrases or words with which we should familiarize ourselves: '*imbricated*' means petals which are tapered to a point and overlap each other closely; '*petaloids*' are stamens on which the anthers have become flat and petal like; descriptions of camellia flowers often refer to '*rabbit ears*' which mean small narrow, often twisted, upright petals among the stamens or other petals and is a stage larger than petaloids; finally, '*fimbriated*' means fringed.

Single   One row of not more than eight petals and with conspicuous stamens.
Semi-double   Two or more rows of petals and with conspicuous stamens.
Anemone form   One or more rows of large outer petals around a central convex mass of intermingled petaloids and stamens.
Paeony form   The flower is a convex mass of intermingled petals and petaloids either with or without stamens. Some authorities prefer to divide the paeony form into a full paeony form and a loose paeony form, the word 'loose' in this connection meaning petals which are not close or compact in arrangement.
Rose form double   Imbricated petals showing stamens in a concave centre when fully open.
Formal double   Fully imbricated having many rows of petals never showing stamens.

Identification

Regarding these six basic forms of flowers, we delude ourselves if we think they provide a simple, clear and concise method identify-

single

semi-double

anemone

peony

rose form double

formal double

Camellia flower forms.

ing a camellia. Nothing is further from the truth! The camellia has evolved and been bred over hundreds, if not thousands, of years so we cannot expect identification to be simple.

Taking the single form of camellia, a moment's thought would tell us that there must be several different forms of a single bloom. For instance, the bloom could be trumpet shaped or, at the other end of the scale, completely flat or reflexed. But there can be variations and, in fact, the Japanese list no less than six different forms of single camellia from the formal single, then trumpet shaped to saucer (or Higo) form. Similarly with the semi-doubles they list three different forms: formal semi-double, magnolia form and doubleness.

The formation of the stamens on all blooms, other than the formal doubles (where the stamens cannot be seen), affords another aid in the classification and, of course, identification of blooms. Stamens may be columnar (the Japanese suggest four or five different forms of columnar) or they may be in ring or plum form.

Clearly, with all these aids to classification and identification the problems ought not to be too great. For example, how many saucer form singles are there with, say, ring form stamens? The answer probably is not very many, so that if we next sort out the colour involved we ought to be getting pretty close to a positive identification.

Unfortunately, anyone who believes this is heading for a bitter disappointment! The camellia is not a simple, sensibly minded flower like, say, a rhododendron. Although the latter exists in an infinitely greater number of species and hybrids which renders the task of identification infinitely more complex than it is with camellias, one can, at least, expect the average rhododendron to behave with a modicum of common sense. Take the case of the well-known hybrid rhododendron, 'Elizabeth', still one of the finest reds raised at Bodnant which is a home of fine reds. No doubt the cross has been made several times and no doubt there are several clones in existence and on the market but, nevertheless, the flower is invariably red, the shape of the bloom always much the same and the leaves pretty similar. Not so with camellias. They take a delight in producing different forms of flowers and different colours according to the environment in which they are grown.

For example, the camellia 'Joshua E. Youtz', in the forefront of its class as a formal double white for growing outdoors, is superlative at producing its large white formal double blooms which are more resistant to adverse weather conditions than any other formal double white. (In over 30 years I have never seen it bear anything outdoors other than a formal double bloom.) The well-toothed leaves with a pointed apex and somewhat columnar and small growing habit (which, incidentally, make it an admirable plant for amateur growing) ought not to be all that difficult to identify. But life is never simple. The nomenclature book of the American Camellia Society, produced by the Southern Californian Camellia Society, describes 'Joshua E. Youtz' as: 'White large paeony form to formal double'. Presumably then, the plant we grow as 'Joshua E. Youtz' is not the same as the plant known by that name in California because that is a large paeony form. But perhaps it is. Could climate have an effect on the bloom? And there is the answer: for, in the United Kingdom, grown in a conservatory or greenhouse, the 'Joshua E. Youtz' flowers with a paeony bloom but, grown outdoors, the selfsame plant is an exquisite pure formal double.

So it is with many others. For instance, outdoors, 'Grand Slam' bears large pure red semi-double to paeony form flowers. Indoors, the bloom has many more petals and an anemone centre. The situation is not made any easier by the fact that camellias quite frequently bear different blooms on the same bush at the same time. For instance, semi-double blooms can be scattered about a bush which otherwise has paeony flowers.

Others may change their blooms as the season progresses. I have three bushes of 'Hakurakuten' (syn. 'Wisley White') in my garden. This semi-double, occasionally paeony form, white flowered camellia is a most regular and reliable performer; yet, two of the three plants for the first couple of weeks of the flowering season insist on producing formal double blooms before deciding that semi-double or paeony blooms in accordance with the nomenclature book description might be more appropriate. All three plants came from the same parent. Small wonder that customers, confronted with blooms quite different from those they expected, charge the nursery which sold them either with getting their labels muddled or deliberately substituting an alternative plant of the same colour.

Size and Colour

We meet just the same problem with the size of bloom. In general camellia blooms are larger in warm conditions than they are in cold ones. It is noticeable that camellias growing outdoors in, say, Cornwall, bear bigger blooms than the same plant grown in East Sussex. Equally, a camellia grown under glass or in a plastic tunnel will bear larger blooms than the same plant grown outdoors.

Similarly, the colour of some camellia blooms is affected by the warmth of the climate in which they grow. This is particularly noticeable with many of the very pale colours. For example, *C. japonica* 'Twilight', is an exquisite pale, flesh pink indoors. Outdoors, whilst still an exquisite bloom, more often than not it appears to be white or a slightly 'off' white. The same applies to the lovely 'Erin Farmer'. Indoors it is as the book describes it, 'whitewashed and shaded orchid pink', an exquisite combination. Unfortunately, outdoors, in an average season, the orchid pink can become so diluted that one might as well have a semi-double white as often as not.

From time to time one sees colour illustrations of camellias bearing quite deep mauve blooms. It is said that a heavy, approaching clay, soil helps to cause this. That may be so, but there is little doubt that the well-known *C. japonica* 'Mathotiana', normally a fine double crimson red, though better really on a wall than in the full open, will turn a purple colour if the weather becomes cold in much the same way as we humans turn 'blue with cold'. Quite likely the same applies to *C. japonica* 'Dona Herzilia de Freitas Magalhaes' and 'Purple Swirl'.

This colour variation between indoor and outdoor plants which, no doubt, really means between plants grown in warm conditions and plants grown outdoors in most parts of the United Kingdom (which can rarely be described as warm in March/April time), is nowhere more marked than in the case of camellias with bi-colour blooms. For instance, *C. japonica* 'Adolphe Audusson Special' bears blooms outdoors of the typical 'Adolphe Audusson' red with occasional white blotches on them. It is rare indeed to see outdoor blooms more white than red and one despairs of ever seeing blooms with every variation from red, or red with a white blotch, to as much white as red in the bloom to white with red blotches, all on the same bush. Yet this is how they will often be on plants grown in the warmth of a greenhouse or conservatory.

Much the same applies with *C. japonica* 'Giganta' (syn. 'Kelvingtoniana', 'Kelvingtonii' and so on). Outdoors the large semi-double to paeony form blooms are red, occasionally marbled white. Indoors they can look like a totally different plant with as much white marbling and blotching as red.

These variations certainly cause problems for the purchaser and there is little doubt that the wisest way to buy a plant is to see it growing outdoors under conditions as far as possible similar to those in which the purchaser intends to grow it. If the plant and its flowers grown outdoors obviously stand up to the weather conditions then one can have some confidence that the same will apply in one's own garden – but the mere fact that a plant in a garden centre looks healthy, with its blooms near perfection, is no such guarantee for it may have been kept in a greenhouse up to half-an-hour before the centre opened for business.

All this may make a prospective purchaser wonder how he can ever acquire a really suitable and satisfactory plant. The answer to this is almost certainly contained in two basic rules. Firstly, choose the plant you want after seeing it growing satisfactorily outdoors in a garden, or even as shown on a TV programme. Secondly, go to a specialist nursery and either buy that plant or ask if they have a similar plant equally floriferous and hardy. No decent, self-respecting specialist nursery would sell you anything not up to the specification you have given. Equally, you can go to your local garden centre and possibly be lucky and find the exact camellia you are seeking. However, one must realize that the vast majority of garden centres are no more than retail stores buying in plants at one end and selling them at the other. The chance of finding anyone there with specialist knowledge of camellias is rare.

Whilst these are hard words, it must be remembered that there are many thousands of camellia hybrids and even the most specialist nurseries in the world deal with only a few hundred of them. Perhaps, therefore, one should not be too hard on the garden centres who offer a good selection of bread-and-butter plants which is, after all, what the average gardener requires.

The next variation in camellias which we should consider is that of growth and size. The answer to the question: 'How big does it grow?' is never an easy one. The answer depends on so many factors including soil conditions, site, age and so on. I never cease to be amused by the number of septuagenarians or octogenarians who call at my nursery to buy a rhododendron and, having found one which, for flower colour and leaf, appears to meet their requirements, ask that all too familiar question: 'How tall does it grow?' One replies: 'In average soil conditions on an average site, possibly 8 to 10ft (2.5 to 3m) in 10 to 12 years and possibly 15ft (4.5m) in 15 to 20 years. 'Fifteen feet, that's far too large' is the almost inevitable reply. The fact that the would-be purchaser could well be about 100 by the time the plant reached such a height appears to be totally irrelevant! These little anecdotes are merely intended to illustrate that age has much to do with the ultimate size of most plants and certainly with camellias. Nevertheless, some plants growing in similar conditions may only reach 5ft (1.5m) in 10 years whereas others will reach 10 or 12ft (3 or 3.5m) in the same length of time.

There are four principal factors (apart from the inherited traits of different plants) which affect growth and height. These are: the soil in which they are grown; the climate, including micro-climate, and, in particular, average warmth and rainfall; the site, for example in woodland or totally exposed; and the age of the plant or number of years growth we are talking about. It is essential that we are all talking about the same number of years' growth! We can look at each of these factors in a little more detail.

Soil

It is clearly unnecessary to say that soil varies enormously and it is not my intention at this stage to deal at any length with the various types of soil we may encounter. Suffice it to say that some soils are poor in the extreme quite apart from their physical make-up, for example, sandy, clay, rocky, etc. Other soils are rich beyond one's wildest dreams. Having never owned one of the latter, I can only say that a really poor Sussex sandstone soil, although admirably acid, even when fed with manure and fertilizers, never seems to achieve results as good as those in the richer parts of West Sussex similarly fed or even less well fed! There are, of course, compensations. Maybe the East Sussex plant is smaller but it may well be sturdier and what it lacks in height and size it may well make up for in toughness and hardiness. However, regarding 'How tall does it grow?' one can only emphasize that one highly relevant factor is the soil in which the plant is to be grown.

Climate

This will include the micro-climate, which is really a rather high-faluting way of saying that there are spots in your garden which are warmer and more sheltered than others. Most gardeners fully appreciate this and while happy to plant a native broom in the fullest exposure will choose the most sheltered area for rather tender subjects. When the temperature is low and the bitter wind makes the chill factor high, even in a small garden the difference in temperature for the broom compared with that for the rock plant could well be 5, 10 or even more degrees.

Apart from the micro-climate there are two other climatic factors of great importance, the first being the average temperature throughout the year and the other the average rainfall.

One has only to go to the west coast of Scotland or Cornwall to realize that the annual rate of growth of many, many trees and shrubs is infinitely faster than it is on the drier, colder east coast of the United Kingdom. The Romans appreciated that this division between warm and cold is also between east and west so that the dividing line runs north/south down the central mountain range, if one can call it that. The same applies to the rainfall where, in general, the east is considerably drier than the west. With a warmer average climate or, put another way, a climate which rarely gets as cold and a higher rainfall it follows that trees and shrubs such as magnolias, rhododendrons and camellias all grow faster in the climate of the west.

Site

A site may be in full exposure or in the middle of a forest or somewhere intermediate between the two. Each has its effect on the growth of plants which inhabit each particular location. The 'common' or 'wild' or 'mauve' rhododendron as it is so often called, in other words *Rhododendron ponticum*, illustrates the point extremely well. What a pity it was that *R. ponticum* was one of the first, if not the first, rhododendron to be introduced to the United Kingdom. It found conditions so much to its liking that it could naturalize itself in many different areas. One need not be a *ponticum* hater to concede that its pinky mauve flowers are not the best or even in the upper strata of rhododendron blooms for colour, form or beauty. How much more acceptable to many people the rhododendron might be had the first introduction to naturalize itself been, say, a *R. thomsonii*, a *R. decorum* or *R. nuttalli*. As it is, to far too many members of the public, the word rhododendron is synonymous with thickets of rather dreary dull leaves, struggling in woodland to reach some light and producing, occasionally, a few rather ignominious trusses of mauve flowers. That is, in fact, the habit of *ponticum* in woodland conditions. In a more open situation it is a quarter the height and three times as dense producing quite an effective display of flowers. To go to the final extreme one needs to go to one of the Scottish moors where *ponticum* has run wild. Here, its hundreds of seedlings and layers crouch close to the ground, the dense canopy formed by the whole giving shelter to each individual. It is difficult to believe that this is the same plant as the lank straggler we know in woodland conditions. It is even more difficult to believe this when one compares the two forms in flower, the woodlander having a few trusses of blooms, the moorlander a solid canopy of flower trusses so tightly packed that the whole forms a solid patchwork quilt in every shade of pink, pinky mauve, mauve and near blue or at least lavender.

When one fully considers these points one begins to appreciate how stupid is the question 'How tall does it grow?'

Age

It is hardly necessary to say that trees and shrubs normally grow taller and larger with every year that passes; what is more important is the rate of growth common to different cultivars.

For example, the tough but beautiful single rosy red flowered camellia, 'Juno', will grow to 10ft (3m) in less than 10 years while in the same length of time the lovely pale pink 'High Hat', under exactly similar conditions, will make less than half that. So it is with many different cultivars. 'Cecile Brunazzi', with its gorgeous pink blooms in colour little different from 'Donation' but finer in form, is always a mere pygmy or dwarf compared with the lovely pink 'Tiffany'. As a result, 'Cecile Brunazzi' is ideal for a container, tub, patio or small garden and 'Tiffany' far too virile for those uses but ideal as an effective shrub in the larger garden or border.

It follows that, although the number of years' growth (or, in other words, age) of a plant is an important factor in answering the question 'How tall does it grow?', an equally important factor is the plant itself. As we said at the beginning, we have to consider soil, climate, site and age and, if all these are the same, inherited traits and characteristics of each individual cultivar will determine which grows the fastest.

MODERN CAMELLIAS

Finally, we should perhaps give a little consideration to the form and size of flower of modern camellias. One answer could be that many so called 'modern' camellias are little or no different from camellias grown 150 years ago. The paeony form white *C. japonica* 'Nobilissima' is a typical example. Introduced in 1834 it is still one of the earliest flowering whites, tough and reliable. In Sussex it is an ill winter indeed if it can manage to prevent 'Nobilissima' producing enough perfect or near perfect blooms for a small arrangement on the Christmas lunch table, or a bloom for every lady guest at the Hogmanay party, together with a table arrangement. Small wonder then that, although 'Nobilissima' does not produce the largest or most exotic blooms, its popularity never wanes.

Looking at the period from about 1945 onwards, it is difficult to perceive the main aims of modern camellia breeders and hybridists. Quite clearly the quests for scent and for the elusive pure yellow camellia have been major preoccupations for a few but the majority appear to have had no particular aim other than to produce a better bloom in a bigger range of colours than existed hitherto. Every form, formal double, paeony, semi-double and so on, every colour from white through pink to deepest red and all the intermediate bi-colours and every size from the enormous blooms of 'Drama Girl' to the miniatures of 'Little Slam' and 'Little Lavender', have been produced in their hundreds, if not thousands. Many are superb but many ought never to have been named and registered.

It is often said that the Victorians' idea of a beautiful camellia was the exquisite formal double bloom and we are told that, once more, this is the most fashionable form today. I find this a little hard to believe, for as many seem to favour the enormous blooms of 'R. L. Wheeler' as seek out the miniatures like 'Little Bit' and 'Kitty'. The semi-double hybrid, 'Donation', still tops the sales list each year but this is probably due to its thoroughly deserved reputation for freedom of flower rather than any particular public preference.

Apart from those specific objectives already mentioned, namely, the pursuit of scent and the pure yellow camellia, breeding seems to have proceeded along three main lines. Firstly, the production of newer and better types of *C. japonica*, secondly, the production of hybrids between *C. japonica* and *C. saluenensis* and, thirdly, the production of hybrids between *C. japonica, reticulata, saluenensis* and such other species as *cuspidata* or *lutchuenensis* whose inclusion might appear desirable in order to incorporate one trait or sought-after characteristic or another.

In the early 1930s the first hybrid camellias were produced by J. C. Williams of Caerhays Castle, Cornwall, who crossed *C. japonica* with the species *saluenensis*. This cross produced the first *williamsii* hybrids, namely, 'J. C. Williams', 'St Ewe' and 'Mary Christian'. Soon after, at Borde Hill in Sussex, the late Col Stephenson Clarke crossed *C. japonica* 'Donckelarii' and *saluenensis* and produced the famous *williamsii* camellia 'Donation'.

It should be made clear that the *williamsii* hybrids are crosses between *C. japonica* and *C. saluenensis* only. If other species, such as *reticulata* or *lutchuenensis*, are involved the resulting progeny, though hybrids, are not *williamsii* hybrids. In the nursery it can be quite amusing to hear customers insisting that they want a *williamsii* camellia (usually because they recently heard about them in the media) when, in fact, what they are after is a hybrid camellia.

The first true *williamsii* camellias proved to be a wonderful breakthrough. They combine ease of culture, hardiness, freedom of flowers and a self-cleaning habit (in that the flowers drop as soon as they die), leaving a clean looking plant.

'J. C. Williams', with its single pale, pink blooms and floriferous habit is too well known to need description. It is still sought after, partly because it is still strongly recommended as of outstanding quality by some gardening correspondents. There is no doubt that when it was introduced in the 1930s it was an outstanding plant but that was 50 years ago and camellia hybridization since then has not stood still. Looked at critically, it does have certain drawbacks. First, it pretty quickly makes a very large, somewhat open-habited shrub, attaining 10 or 12ft (3 to 3.5m) far sooner than the average modern gardener would want. Second, there is nothing outstanding about the form of its flowers, pure well-shaped single blooms – there are dozens of single camellias equally attractive. Third, its pale pink colour, whilst very lovely, particularly in mass, is little different from many other camellias.

'J. C. Williams' was the great 'breakthrough'. In its day, it was the supreme hybrid. It is still quite a nice camellia today but whilst it is an attractive plant, particularly if one is not short of space, I do not consider it suitable for small gardens, for tubs, containers or patios. Gardening 'experts', however, continue to recommend it for these purposes, so no doubt it will continue to be planted in the future.

If one is looking for a 'J. C. Williams'-type bloom for the small garden or patio or containers, then 'Beatrice Michael' is a far better bet. Similar in colour and shape of bloom but with more substance to the petals, 'Beatrice Michael' makes but 3 or 4ft (1 to 1.3m) while 'J. C. Williams' makes 13 or 14ft (about 4m) and, in addition, produces a dense compact bush.

In 1941, only a year after the introduction of 'J. C. Williams', came another highly important event. At Borde Hill in Sussex, Col Stevenson Clarke, having crossed *C. saluenensis* with *C. japonica* 'Donckelarii', introduced the world famous 'Donation'. The plant is vigorous, with compact upright growth. Its blooms are orchid pink and large semi-double. Since its introduction, many much more attractive hybrids have been introduced with flowers of a better shape or form, petals of better substance, blooms of a better colour and so on but no one has produced a more floriferous plant. From an early age it literally covers itself annually with blossoms and, once it has attained any real size, bears so many that it is almost impossible to see if the shrub does, in fact, have leaves as well as blossoms.

I am convinced that there are several clones of 'Donation' on the market, one of which is much better than the others. Whether this can be proved or disproved scientifically I do not know, but I do know that from the practical gardener's point of view the 'best' clone is by far the best garden plant. It pays when buying to make sure that you are buying from this best clone.

Occasionally at camellia shows, conferences and garden visits one hears a colleague, overwhelmed by the colour and beauty of some new camellia, declare that as soon as he gets home he will dig up his 'Donations' and replace them with this new found treasure. If he does, he will no doubt have blooms of better texture, form and colour but he will be hard put to it to find a plant which is as floriferous or a better garden shrub than 'Donation'. After over 45 years, it still remains, in my view, one of the greatest garden shrubs ever introduced.

So much for 'Donation'. Some 13 years later yet another Sussex garden, Nymans in West Sussex, produced another 'winner' in the shape of 'Leonard Messel', the result of crossing the so-called wild form of C. reticulata with the williamsii hybrid 'Mary Christian'. Bearing an enormous crop of large semi-double blooms of deep rose colour, 'Leonard Messel' can still be considered among 'the greats'. I remember a good many years ago accompanying one of our really knowledgeable flowering shrub experts round a famous garden. His knowledge of camellias was tremendous and after we had appraised dozens and dozens of japonicas, old and new, several species and one of the biggest collections of hybrids, he said: If I could plant in my garden only two camellias, I would plant 'Donation' and 'Leonard Messel'. That was over twenty years ago but I think that, although the choice is far wider today, the gardener who chose to plant those two would not go far wrong.

Of course there have been enormous strides in the breeding of camellia hybrids (and japonicas for that matter) since those days. It is sad that the British, who made the real breakthrough with 'J. C. Williams' and 'Donation', have not been in the forefront of producing camellia hybrids since then.

We must turn to Australia, the United States and last, but by no means least, to New Zealand to locate the great hybrids of today. Each of us obviously has a very personal viewpoint in saying which hybrid he or she considers to be 'great'. If a plant does really well in my garden, perhaps as well or better than it does in Cornwall or California or, say, the North Island, I obviously consider it 'great'. If it is just average with me then my initial reaction must be to class it average however well it may perform elsewhere. Admittedly, with experience and the wisdom born of age, one can bring oneself to say: 'That is a superb outstanding plant, even though it is useless in my garden.' But I think the initial reaction is to class a plant by what it does in one's own garden, possibly the reason why I have always considered that those wonderful plants created by the great New Zealand hybridist, the late Les Jury, are amongst the greatest hybrids so far raised in the world.

I have always understood that Les discarded a great many crosses before introducing his first five plants on the grounds that the others were not up to the high standard he was seeking. I remember when I first saw them what a revelation they were: 'Elegant Beauty', 'Debbie', 'Anticipation', 'Elsie Jury' and so on, with so many outstanding plants to follow. Surely this was one of the greatest contributions to the breeding of camellia hybrids.

Meanwhile in Australia, the late Prof Waterhouse was producing some fine plants such as 'E. G. Waterhouse', 'Margaret Waterhouse' and *C. japonica* 'Janet Waterhouse'.

In the United States, too, great things were happening. Dedicated professionals such as those at the Nuccio nursery, and equally dedicated amateurs in some considerable numbers, all strove to produce the most perfect camellia. As a result, great hybrids such as 'Brigadoon', 'Freedom Bell' and 'Garden Glory' made their bow whilst with *reticulata* hybrids the results, such as 'Dr Clifford Parks', 'Lila Naff' and 'Royalty', are almost beyond compare.

In the United Kingdom the picture was not, perhaps, quite as rosy. Overcome, presumably, by their great success with 'J. C. Williams' and its many single brothers and sisters, 'Donation' and 'Leonard Messel', British hybridists seemed happy to rest on their laurels. True, in 1953, that great white single hybrid, 'Francis Hanger', made its début but, this apart, the running in general was taken on by the late Miss Gillian Carlyon. A number of her introductions have been outstanding and have deservedly been recognized by the Royal Horticultural Society (RHS) who have awarded her hybrids no less than six Awards of Merit. In East Sussex we have tried 'China Clay', 'Cornish Spring', 'E. T. R. Carlyon', 'Jenefer Carlyon' and 'Yesterday'. All have performed admirably. There seems to be little doubt that amongst them there is a plant for almost every purpose, for northern climes, for wall growing, for container growing, for the mixed shrub border and the woodland planting.

The story with the *reticulatas* is a little different. Until 1948 there were only three *reticulatas* in the Western world, namely, 'Captain Rawes', 'Robert Fortune' and the single 'wild form' brought back by Forrest. From 1948 to 1950 the Kunming *reticulatas* were introduced thanks to the great efforts made by Dr Lammerts, Ralph Peer and others.

Whilst *C. japonicas* range from slow compact growers to loose open plants of rapid growth (so that the plant in form varies from round compact shrubs and those with low spreading growth, to rounded but open taller bushes and even slender fastigiate forms), *C. reticulata* does not normally display so pleasing a form when grown in the United Kingdom. It would not be unfair to describe it as 'leggy'; a plant with a loose habit and an overwhelming desire to grow as tall as possible in the shortest possible time at the expense of side-branching and bushiness. Hence, to produce a plant of a pleasing shape requires much thought and patience and much intelligent or inspired 'pinching out' or judicious pruning. It seems to do well in sunnier situations than would be suitable for many *japonicas*. It seems to be able to thrive with even less water than an established *japonica* needs (and that is not much) but lacks the hardiness and bud hardiness needed to make a camellia a good outdoor shrub in average conditions.

One has only to see the gorgeous blooms of 'Captain Rawes', 'Robert Fortune' and the Kunming *reticulatas* grown under glass to realize that attempts to hybridize them with other species to achieve hardy, free flowering, bud hardy hybrids when grown under outdoor conditions could become a major preoccupation with many breeders of camellias. The long list of hybrids set out in the American Camellia Society's nomenclature book indicates how great an effort has been made. The variations in the resulting plants have been almost unbelievable. One of the earliest crosses was 'Salutation' introduced at about the same time as 'Donation'. For years the argument raged as to whether this plant did indeed incorporate *reticulata* blood as claimed by its raiser. To the practical gardener the answer did not appear to require highly scientific tests but I believe I am right in saying that the result of these did establish that 'Salutation' does incorporate *reticulata* blood. It is still a most useful camellia, semi-double in form and pure pale pink in colour. Although more open in growth than 'Donation', it can, with a modicum of judicious pinching and pruning, be persuaded to attain a very reasonable habit and shape and is certainly hardy enough for any normal English garden.

So many other *reticulata* hybrids have followed that their names are legion and the various types of plant and flowers are incredibly diverse. Quite a number, particularly those with *saluenensis* parentage, behave so like *williamsii* hybrids that they are best considered with them. Typical of these is 'Inspiration' (*reticulata* × *saluenensis*). This makes a fine dense shrub, free flowering in the extreme and, in addition, one of our hardiest camellias. Its individual blooms, semi-double of a rich phlox pink, are no more outstanding than the vast majority of *japonicas*. The same can be said of many others a selection of which include: 'Black Lace', a dark red double; 'Leonard Messel' with superb large semi-double rose columnar blooms in great profusion on a tough, hardy bush; 'Satan's Robe', a good semi-double oriental red; 'Tristrem Carlyon', paeony form rose pink; and 'Grand Jury', a gorgeous large, semi-double paeony form in salmon pink.

These are mostly extremely hardy free-flowering garden shrubs which thrive from the south of England well up into Perthshire and probably to Inverness. Other *reticulata* hybrids, however, come into a somewhat different category and, although easier to please and probably hardier than the original Kunming collection of *reticulatas*, nevertheless produce blooms every bit as outstanding as those illustrious ancestors. Amongst these could be mentioned: 'Dr Clifford Parks', a gorgeous large semi-double to paeony form in red; 'China Lady', a *reticulata* × *granthamiana* hybrid which produces a dense bush with outstanding *reticulata* leaves and very large semi-double rich orchid pink blooms; 'Royalty', a very large semi-double of clear bright red; 'Lasca Beauty', with clear deep pink blooms; and 'Howard Asper' of a deeper colour and enormous paeony blooms. All these have proved successful in my garden over a number of years and survived the three terrible winters from 1984 onwards with minimal damage. Unfortunately, the same cannot be said of 'William Hertrich' – although a superb plant, with a minimum of protection in the way of a porch, unheated greenhouse or conservatory (where it will produce its great deep, cherry red blooms in profusion) it has so far failed to establish itself successfully outdoors in my garden.

Finally, mention should be made of one somewhat strange but absolutely outstanding camellia, 'Francie L'. A hybrid between *saluenensis* 'Apple Blossom' and *reticulata* 'Buddha', it was raised in the world famous Nuccio's nursery in 1964. Looking at it, it is sometimes hard to believe that it is a camellia at all, for the long, strap-like leaves, a dull grey green in colour and heavily reticulated, bear little resemblance to the popular conception of a camellia leaf. In addition, in its early days, the plant tends to be leggy and lanky and possessed of an overwhelming desire to reach the heavens in the shortest possible time.

All that, however, is in the very early days. Planted against a wall it can be espaliered and trained to cover a large area if desired. One well-known specimen is reputed to embellish some 30ft (9m) of wall. Planted in the open and given a little judicious pinching and pruning to curb its somewhat exuberant spirits, it will make a fine dense bush. 'So what?' the reader may say: 'What is so different between this plant and dozens of other camellias which tend to be lanky open growers?' The answer lies in the flowers and in the plant's hardiness. Variously described as rose pink, rosy red, deep crimson rose or light red, the flowers are large to very large, semi-double with irregular wavy petals and a full 5½in (14cm) across. They are of full *reticulata* quality and when exhibited on a stand at the Westminster Show cause considerable comment. If one points out that the blooms were cut in the open from a plant in East Sussex, the majority of viewers simply do not believe it.

As a wall shrub, 'Francie L' is outstanding and seems to do equally well whether the wall faces north, south, east or west. The long branches are as easy to train as a peach tree and produce numerous laterals to ensure an abundant floral display. Grown as an open ground shrub it is generally successful, but it really needs some shelter as the very considerable weight of flowers and foliage can be almost too much for the plant in an exposed windy situation. With its 50 per cent *reticulata* blood, there is no reason to suppose it would be particularly hardy. When one sees its enormous *reticulata* blooms one certainly doubts that it could be. Nothing is further from the truth. 'Francie L', in East Sussex at least, is about the hardiest plant we grow. After each of those terrible winters, when many of the hardiest camellias suffered severe damage, 'Francie L' came through with flying colours and when many another 'hardy' hybrid lost half or more of its flower buds and produced somewhat mishapen blooms on the few that remained, 'Francie L' held her head up high and delighted us all with a great display of her 5½in (14cm) *reticulata* blooms. No one can ask for more than that of a plant!

It has only been possible to mention a few of the main *saluenensis* hybrids and *reticulatas*. There are a great many other outstanding plants from each of these main crosses. Meanwhile the quest for better camellias has continued with a number of other species being brought into the breeding programme. There have been, and still are, a number of principal objectives. Amongst these there remains the quest for a really highly-scented camellia with flowers the equal of *japonica* and *williamsii* hybrids and, of course, as easy to grow and as hardy. The self-cleaning habit of so many of the *williamsii* hybrids, by which we mean the ability or rather tendency to drop spent blooms as soon as they are over, rather than to leave them browned and dead on the shrub as so many *japonicas* do, has been another trait which hybridists have striven to achieve.

Earlier flowering camellias and later flowering ones, too, have also been targets for if the flowering season can be extended so too can the range of usefulness of the shrub itself. Accordingly, in an attempt to achieve some or one or all of these goals, use has been made of a number of other species. These include: *lutchuenensis*, a sweet-scented species from Okinawa Island; *cuspidata*, with its mass of small blooms over a long period; *fraterna* for its scented small white flowers; *granthamiana* with its large white flowers and highly attractive leathery leaves. In every case, there has been an objective to achieve. This has not always been attained but every hybridist must remember the words of the old adage: 'If at first you don't succeed, try, try and try again.' Believe me, there are plenty following that advice.

To end this chapter, mention must be made of the species *C. chrysantha*, a shrub which can probably attain considerable size and which bears large, golden yellow fragrant blooms, and the introduction of which raised everyone's hopes sky high. A native of the Guangxi province in southernmost China, it was described in 1965 and then introduced to the Kunming Botanical Gardens in China and from there to various parts of the world. It has fine, dark green leaves and bears pure golden yellow flowers 2 to 2½in (50 to 62mm) across. Unfortunately, as *Bean* so clearly points out: 'It is unlikely to thrive outdoors even in the mildest part of the British Isles.' *Bean* also sums up the current situation: '*C. chrysantha* is of interest to camellia breeders, but there is only a distant hope that a hybrid with yellow flowers adapted to the British climate will ever be raised from it.'

So one can only hope. Miracles, or near miracles, do occur. Success has been achieved more than once in crossing a lepidote with an elepidote rhododendron (originally thought to be impossible) so, perhaps, some day some dedicated hybridist will achieve the same kind of breakthrough with *C. chrysantha*, opening up the whole prospect of yellow, orange, apricot, cream and similarly coloured camellias.

3
CULTIVATION

To grow a plant successfully one must comply with that plant's growing requirements and amongst these soil is of paramount importance. We need, therefore, to clarify what we mean by soil.

SOIL AND SOIL MIXTURES

Basically, soil results from erosion caused by frost, wind and weather on mineral substances such as rock, a process which takes place over many thousands or millions of years to produce inorganic mineral particles. These are combined with decomposed vegetation and animal remains, though some soils can consist wholly or in part of one component or another. The vegetable and animal remains are broken down by micro-organisms which, as they die, also enrich the soil. In addition, water containing dissolved salts and soil atmosphere both play a part.

Soils must contain the three elements necessary for plant growth: nitrogen, phosphorous and potassium. In addition, soils must also contain trace elements such as iron, calcium, copper, magnesium and so on. Any good garden soil, by which one means a good garden loam containing humus, rotted manure or compost, would normally contain all the essential elements. These do, however, become exhausted due to leaching and use by plants so that replenishment from time to time is essential.

Every experienced gardener will understand the meaning of a reference to a pH value of 5 to, say, 7. For others it should be explained that soils are graded by reference to a scale from 0 to 14 to indicate a soil's acidity (or alkalinity). The scale is known as a pH scale with pH 7 on the scale neutral. The majority of soils, if taken over a wide area, fall into the pH 7 range. From pH 7 to pH 14 the soil becomes progressively more alkaline or limey. A soil with a pH value of 8.5 is excessively alkaline. A soil with a pH value of 4 extremely acid. Most garden centres and horticultural suppliers sell simple soil testing kits which even the most ignorant amateur can use to determine the pH value of his soil.

In its natural habitat the camellia is a slow growing tree

flourishing in temperate areas with a fairly high humidity and ample rainfall. In the wild it seems to grow best in the shelter of taller trees and shrubs and appreciates some protection from both sun and wind. It prefers a soil which is light as opposed to heavy and with a pH value between 5 and 6.5 or even 7. Such a soil, to suit camellias, must contain no lime or chalk but plenty of humus in the form of leaf mould, peat, compost or bark.

What do we do if, as a result of a soil test, we learn our soil has a pH of, say, 4.5? The answer is very simple, for although camellias prefer a soil on the acid side of neutral they are not happy on an excessively acid soil. To correct this we add a very small quantity of lime to our container mix or the area where we are planting our camellias. If, however, our tests show that the soil is excessively limey, say well over neutral 7, the cure is not necessarily quite so simple. It depends on the reason for the limeyness of our soil which may be caused by two completely different sets of circumstances. In the first case it may be because our soil has been 'limed'. By this we mean that although our natural soil may be neutral or acid, over a period of time dressings of lime have been applied to the soil in the erroneous belief that plants in general prefer a 'limey' soil.

That this is not so must become patently obvious when one considers that the vast majority of the earth's surface is, in fact, acid. As native plants clearly thrive in their own habitat it must follow that the majority of plant life prefers acid conditions. Accordingly, one may wonder why over so many years man has had this fixation with 'liming' his soil. It has often been suggested, probably quite truly, that the reason for this in the past was the obsession with growing the cabbage family. Members of this family undoubtedly prefer bags of muck and lime and because this is so it has been assumed, quite erroneously, that the majority of other plants similarly thrive on bags of muck and lime.

In such circumstances we must take positive action to neutralize this introduced enemy of the camellia – and hundreds of other trees and shrubs – and this may be achieved in a variety of ways depending on the degree of alkalinity in the soil. If the situation is severe, in other words the pH value is excessively high, we must neutralize the alkalinity by the free application of sulphur in accordance with the supplier's instructions. The introduction of acid, such as phosphoric acid into the water used to irrigate plants, might serve equally well. However, if our situation is not too drastic the addition of acid humus such as moss peat, bracken peat or acid compost may well be sufficient. The use of an acid type fertilizer would also prove extremely helpful.

The alkalinity of our soil may, however, be due to the fact that the natural soil in the area is alkaline or has a preponderance, or consists almost entirely, of chalk. The South Downs of Sussex are an example of the latter; these great green hills and valleys were once below the level of the sea and consist entirely of the remains of millions and millions of primitive crustacea.

However, if one's soil is naturally alkaline (in common with the surrounding area) then there is very little we can do to change it; indeed, any attempt to do so is certain to end in failure.

Nevertheless, we can still grow camellias. Clearly we can grow them as pot plants or tub plants to decorate the conservatory or the patio and as we will see later this can be an ideal way to grow many of the finest camellias. Apart from this, we can still grow them in our gardens although the effort and preparation needed are far greater than would be the case if we had the benefit of an acid soil.

We can grow camellias in three main ways, which we look at in more detail below.

Polythene-Lined Pits

The possibility of growing ericaceous shrubs in a chalk area was pretty remote prior to the advent of plastics and, in particular, polythene. Now, although the method is not foolproof, polythene-lined pits provide the ordinary gardener with a means of growing what is, after all, one of the most beautiful shrubs in the world – if the rhododendron is the king of shrubs, then the camellia is the queen.

The method of constructing such a pit is perfectly straightforward. It is suitable for camellias, the smaller rhododendrons, azaleas and a number of other acid loving plants. Most of these are shallow

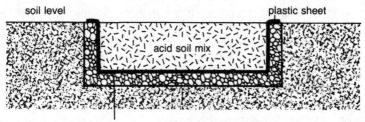

Growing in polythene-lined pits.

rooted, or comparatively so, and the top levels of soil are by far the most important. For this reason, we do not have to remove vast quantities of soil in constructing the pit.

Remove 15 or 18in (37 or 45cm) of soil from the required planting area and then line the excavation with a fairly heavy sheet of plastic, say, 500 grade, making sure that this is well tamped into the corners, existing crevices and so on. If drainage is suspect a few inches of non-alkaline rubble, broken brick, stones and so on should be laid under the plastic, topped off with finer, smoother gravel. This may entail a slightly deeper pit. A few neat punctures should be made in the plastic to allow drainage out of the 'basin'. If this is not done plants will soon be attempting to live under water. On the other hand we want to provide only the minimum number of drainage holes for, ultimately, lime-saturated water will come up through those holes and finally turn the acid compost into an alkaline one.

Having excavated and lined the pit with plastic, fill it with a mixture of acid loam, peat, leaf mould and compost. Planting then proceeds in the normal way with fertilizer and trace elements added as with any other planting.

Planting in Bags

A simpler alternative to constructing a pit, and more than adequate where only a limited number of camellias or other ericaceous shrubs are to be grown in alkaline soil, is to use the planting bag method.

The first thing is to excavate a hole where you wish to grow your camellia. The hole should be large enough to accommodate a black planting bag with a capacity of approximately 35 to 90 gallons (158 to 408 litres). In the event of difficulty in obtaining such a bag, make use of some alternative such as a bin liner, empty commercial size peat bag or anything similar made of plastic.

A layer of stones or broken brick or other 'rubble', provided it does not contain lime, should be placed at the bottom of the hole to provide drainage from the bag into the soil. The bag itself should, of course, have drainage holes for the same purpose and to prevent it becoming a swimming bath for your camellia.

Next, put the bag in the hole and part fill it with acid camellia 'mix'. Plant the camellia at the correct height in the bag and fill up with camellia compost.

Place a layer of stones or other non-alkaline rubble around the plastic bag so as to separate it from the surrounding soil.

Having gone to all this trouble anybody but a gardener might expect that life from then on would be simple. As every true gardener knows nothing is further from the truth. The snag is that, even after taking all the precautions, water from the surrounding alkaline soil will drain into the hole. It will be full of alkaline salts and will be absorbed through the drainage holes into the compost in our planting bag. In due course, our acid compost will become an alkaline compost and our camellia will deteriorate and ultimately die. The only way to avoid this is to provide drainage to get that water away but remember in doing so that the drainage must be provided below the level of the plastic bag.

Raised Beds

Planting in raised beds is a particular favourite of mine when planting in an alkaline, or a really heavy clay or ill-drained area.

Alkaline Soil

My own method is to excavate an area for my camellia of about 3 × 3ft (1 × 1m) to a depth of about 4in (10cm). The surplus soil will not be further required and should be spread elsewhere in the garden. Next, try to improve the drainage of the soil in the excavated area by forking it over or, if drainage is a real problem, incorporating stones, grit, gravel, humus or anything else available which will 'open up' the soil.

Next, prepare a good barrow load of acid compost consisting of acid loam, peat, leaf mould, bark, rotted sawdust or anything suitable which is ready to hand. Some fertilizer should be incorporated in this mix. Tip the barrow load on to the excavated area so that the depth in the centre is at least as much as the camellia's soil ball and then plant. Ensure that the soil cannot be washed or weathered away from the plant's root ball. Four lengths of rough branch about 4in (10cm) in diameter and 3ft (1m) in length will make an admirable enclosure. Alternatively, a tapered mound of soil, heavily covered with dead leaves weighed down with some thickish hedge clippings or dead branch ends to prevent the leaves being blown away, will serve perfectly satisfactorily.

On the whole, the surround of branches is the best bet. In my experience, they last for many years and by the time they finally rot away they are no longer needed, for the soil and subsequent top dressings will have found their own soil level and the branches will have unobtrusively become part of that soil. As the years pass and

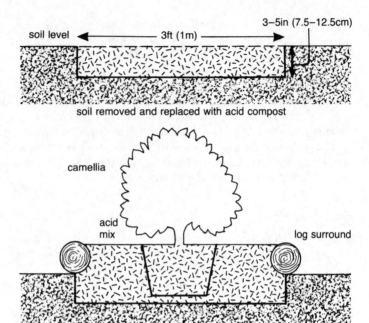

Raised beds.

lime starts to seep in, it may become necessary to give the occasional application of sequestrene but, generally, this simple method will remain satisfactory for many years.

Heavy Soil

Heavy soil may often be a badly drained soil. If we are dealing with a heavy loam it is rare to find drainage problems and correction of the undue heaviness will normally deal with any minor drainage problems at the same time. If, on the other hand, we are dealing with a heavy clay soil, such as that subsoil left on the surface by the builders of new houses, the problem may not be so easily solved.

A heavy loam needs several elements to make it ideal for camellias. We must take steps to improve its porosity so as to facilitate the passage of air and water and to increase its humus content to that of the forest type of soil beloved by the camellia.

The addition of plenty of fine grit to the area we wish to improve will provide better porosity and, accordingly, improved drainage. The addition of humus is usually essential and, when well mixed in, will 'open up' heavy soil.

Humus

Humus can consist of a number of different materials. Peat immediately comes to mind and is, of course, ideal. There are two types of peat normally available: moss peat and sedge peat. Their very names explain their origin. Both are excellent but, on the whole, moss peat is better than sedge peat as, under some circumstances, the latter can tend to 'pudge up' more than the former, but bear in mind that all peat is excellent.

As we become more environmentally conscious or 'green' there is no doubt that we should be searching for satisfactory alternatives to peat. Peat beds are no more inexhaustible than coal deposits or oil. They will not go on forever and although the use of peat obviously does not harm the environment in the same way as the use of fossil fuel does, we are using it at the rate of millions of tons a year. Once used, it is irreplaceable. We can, however, produce adequate alternatives.

Bark is extremely useful as a source of humus and properly prepared and matured is a wonderful agent in improving a heavy soil. It is normally available in three grades: coarse, medium and fine. The coarse grade is ideal for mulching flower beds and borders and serves both as a moisture-retaining mulch and weed suppressant. The medium grade is ideal for our purpose and the fine grade is mostly used in propagation mixes. There is also an extra coarse grade ideal for paths, play areas and so on.

It is not all that many years ago when bark was a by-product in the timber industry. Now it plays a more important part. The great thing about it is that it is renewable. Provided the world population is controlled timber can always be grown as a crop to meet all man's needs without the necessity of felling the rain forests or any natural forests. Bark need never run out but it is inevitable that, eventually, peat will.

Leaf mould is another natural renewable source of humus. For the woodland or forest growing plant it is the only real source. Dead leaves swept up and stacked deep will, in due course, make superb leaf mould. The only word of caution is that leaves which come from trees growing on alkaline soil can produce a somewhat alkaline leaf mould.

One sometimes reads that leaf mould should only be made from the leaves of oak and beech. This really is a counsel of perfection to which few could attain. In any case, one should bear in mind that the leaf mould consists of the canopy of leaves which annually fall on the soil and duly rot down.

Compost

Compost, like leaf mould, provides another natural form of humus. Anything of animal or vegetable origin will eventually rot down and return to the soil, from the trunks of the greatest forest trees to the leaves of herbs. Only the time factor is different. We should try to grade our basic materials for compost like with like, for we all know how annoying it is to find that although 90 per cent of the made commodity is excellent those wood prunings which we added in a moment of supreme optimism have not deigned to rot down.

There are a number of other items, such as sawdust and straw, which, rotted down, produce excellent humus. Many of these different ingredients are best mixed together in the general compost heap. The ultimate result may well be preferable and, in any case, few of us have sufficient quantities of one commodity, such as sawdust, to enable us to produce a significant quantity of humus from this one source.

Chapters and chapters, if not volumes, have been written about compost-making, so it is unnecessary to repeat it all here. Reference to any good general gardening book will provide ample information on this subject.

PROTECTION

In its native habitat the camellia is a plant which is accustomed to some protection from sun and wind. If we can provide this in our garden when planting camellias we are giving them optimum conditions.

Shade

The problem with shade is knowing how much should be provided. The climate greatly affects this so that more shade is desirable if one is growing camellias in, for example, the south of England than if one is growing them in the south of Scotland.

Camellias will grow satisfactorily in quite dense shade producing reasonable growth and adequate leaves. The trouble is that they do not produce flower buds. As the intensity of light is increased, so too will the production of flower buds be increased, so that a plant growing in full exposure may well produce far too many buds resulting in somewhat undersized blooms.

Dappled sunlight or broken shade provided by suitable trees gives ideal conditions but most of us have to make do with what we have. However, even if we do not have somewhere approaching woodland in which to garden, most of us do have areas which are partially shaded. Shade from distant trees, from the house itself or from tall walls and fences may well be all that is needed to provide near ideal conditions for many camellias. It is worth remembering that, in general, hybrids containing *reticulata* blood and second and third generation hybrids all need more sun that the average *japonica*.

If I had no other choice I would not hesitate to plant camellias in full exposure. I have done just this in the past with highly satisfactory results. The main problem is that the foliage of some varieties suffers from sun scorch. In this condition the leaves of affected plants are, at best, too light a green and, at worst, a variegated light green, yellow and white. The hybrid 'Francis Hanger' is one which suffers badly. Grown in ample shade its foliage is a fine deep green, but grown in full exposure the leaves bear more white than green. Nevertheless, it must be emphasized that the vast majority of camellias do not suffer sun scorch if grown in full exposure.

If forced to plant in full exposure, it is always worth while providing young plants which may not be very high with some shade from nearby taller plants, or even rigging up a piece of shade netting. In their first season or so, while they are getting established, this will undoubtedly help the plants thrive.

There is not much more to be said about shade. If it is very dense the camellias will grow and have fine deep green leaves but no flowers. If there is no shade at all, the camellias will grow well but have somewhat poorer foliage which, in some few varieties, will suffer from sun scorch and, if anything, will bear too many flowers. Provided we can compromise between these two extremes, we can have the best of both worlds.

Shelter

Apart from shade which provides protection from the sun there remains, of course, the question of protection from the other elements, for example the wind. Camellias just will not grow in a situation totally exposed to the full blast of the wind. If we can get them through their early stages, a group of plants may ultimately give a pretty good account of themselves as each tends to shelter the other. However, it is not usually necessary to pursue this particular experiment as there are few gardens which cannot find spots protected to some extent from the wind, for such protection can be provided by trees, shrubs, plants, buildings or fences. If the worst comes to the worst, a windbreak of hurdles, netting or something similar can quite easily be provided. Incidentally, camellias suffer far less than rhododendrons from salt in the wind. This does not mean that they are some sort of maritime shrub but it is a bonus point in their favour.

FEEDING AND FERTILIZERS

The necessary fertilizers and fertilizing programme for camellias in containers is not quite the same as for camellias in the open.

For those plants growing in the open ground, the use of fertilizers is perfectly simple. Camellias, like other plants, need nitrogen, phosphate and potash, together with a normal selection of trace elements.

It is my invariable practice when installing a camellia to mix in thoroughly a couple of good handfuls or so of one of several fertilizers in the planting hole. The quantity obviously depends on the size of the prepared hole and quality of medium to fill it, but do not overdo it. I will not refer to this particularly in planting and transplanting as I feel the addition of fertilizer at the start should be second nature.

As to the fertilizer to use, provided it is not alkaline in reaction (like nitro-chalk!) any good proprietary fertilizer, preferably organic, or part organic such as fish manure, or blood, fish and bone, is perfectly satisfactory. Two or three handfuls thoroughly mixed in to an average sized planting hole for a 18 to 24in (45 to 60cm) camellia is ample. One other point arises if bark has been added to the mix. It is a fact that soil organisms, in breaking bark down on its long journey of total return to mother earth, use up more nitrogen than they supply. Hence our soil can become nitrogen deficient in the earlier stages. To compensate for this, add a little nitrogen fertilizer. We use nitram (ammonium nitrate) at the rate of about 1½oz (40g) per 20 litres of bark.

Thus installed, the plant should have plenty of available nourishment until the next growing season. However, when watering it, Phostrogen added to the watering can will be beneficial. We have found the new Phostrogen for acid-loving plants particularly effective.

Looking at the nourishment needed by camellias in much more general terms, there are several signs of ill-health which, to the competent gardener, should be obvious. A yellowish, or poor green, colour in the leaves is almost always a sign of nitrogen deficiency. A light dressing of dried blood or ½oz (15g) of nitram in 2 gallons (9 litres) of water, applied round the roots, should soon improve matters.

If the leaves on the plant suffer from chlorosis (a paling of the leaves, becoming yellow or yellowish) the cause is almost always produced by a too alkaline soil when the excess calcium causes iron deficiency. This should not arise if proper soil preparation has been followed. However, if it does, give the plant a dose of iron Seque-strene. If the plant is not cured by this treatment (which is almost always effective), then the trouble may be a trace element deficiency. Lack of magnesium can sometimes be the culprit corrected by watering with Epsom Salts. Manganese or boron deficiency may also cause chlorosis, remedied by obtaining a little sachet of trace elements from the garden shop and watering it on. However, it should be emphasized once more that poor leaf colour is almost always a sign of nitrogen deficiency and chlorosis of too alkaline a soil. Remember, finally, that Sequestrene is not a fertilizer and that there is no point in using it occasionally, as some gardeners do, unless the plant shows signs of chlorosis.

Finally, to annual feeding. Probably the finest feed is the annual mulch of a good thickness of compost made with animal manure or even a mulch mixed with well rotted animal manure. However, if farmyard or stable manure is not available, then a dressing of fish manure, blood, fish and bone, or one of the seaweed manures, applied in March, should be given, just a handful spinkled all over the root area for a modest, say, 2ft (0.6m) plant. This should be followed in April by a light nitrogen feed of dried blood or nitram, well watered in. Do not overdo the quantity. Subsequent watering can always incorporate Phostrogen but all feeding should finish by the end of August for fear of forcing the plant to make another flush of growth which will, inevitably, fail to ripen and will be destroyed by the first severe frost.

MULCHES

The practice of mulching, or placing a layer of some suitable material over the soil covering a plant's roots, is old in the extreme. Its purpose is to conserve moisture for the plant, to prevent excessive fluctuation of soil temperature, to suppress weeds and to provide food for the plant.

In their native habitat, camellias are woodland plants growing under or among trees. Accordingly, it is inevitable that the soil around them will be mulched, the mulch consisting partly of their own discarded leaves, flowers and other plant parts and a further quantity of similar material from the trees and shrubs surrounding them.

The mulch is of the greatest importance. For instance, the camellia has a shallow rooting system so that hoeing or other similar cultivators around the plant to destroy weeds is bound to cause damage, hence mulch which prevents weeds from growing is ideal. In dry periods, unmulched soil tends to harden and pan so that watering (or rain) will run off. This is particularly true on a sloping site. The ability to keep the soil surface open so that oxygen can get to the plant's roots and water can easily penetrate is one of the most important benefits of a mulch.

Nowadays, we are far more conscious than we were some years ago of the value of insulation. In consequence, it is easy to understand that a good layer of mulching material will provide good insulation and, as a result, will prevent extreme fluctuation of soil temperature.

The slow decomposition of our mulch will provide food for the plant. This, after all, is exactly what happens in nature and is, of course, one of the basic aims of the compost heap. So there is little doubt that the best mulch for our plants is that provided by nature itself, namely, a thick carpet of fallen leaves. Some leaves we know are better when finally rotted down than others and the leaves of deciduous oak are said to be outstanding in this respect. However, as practical gardeners, we cannot be all that choosy. Sweep up all the fallen leaves on paths, lawns and elsewhere and spread them to a depth of 3 or 4in (7.5 or 10cm) or so around sizeable plants but less, of course, around small beginners. (The practice of sweeping up fallen and decaying leaves, building them into a pile and making a bonfire of them should not be permitted under any circumstances.)

Apart from fallen leaves there are many other alternatives to use for a mulch. Some will meet all our objectives, others may meet only some, but this is better than none at all. The alternatives can be organic, inorganic, dead or live material.

The expression 'dead organic' material is something of a misnomer for in nature nothing organic is ever really dead. A tree may die and fall and as a tree is dead, yet it is immediately alive, teeming with organisms intent on breaking it down to the point when it eventually becomes, once more, part of the very live soil from which it grew.

Accordingly, when we talk of dead organic material as a mulch, we use the expression only to differentiate it from living plants such as grass which, in their own way, also act as a mulch. Such material will include compost, pine needles, rotted manure, sawdust, peat, wood chippings, bark and lawn mowings. The last named are best mixed with some other material as they do tend to form a too solid mass. However, if that is not possible, they can be used just as they are and under normal circumstances will prove entirely satisfactory. If one bears in mind that anything of vegetable or animal origin which will rot down in a comparatively short space of time can be used as a mulch, it is obvious that the various alternatives are numerous in the extreme.

Earlier reference was made to inorganic mulches. The observant gardener will have noticed that in dry weather conditions the soil beneath rocks and large stones is damp. If no organic material is available, therefore, the judicious spacing of flat rocks and stones over the soil surrounding our camellias will meet several of our requirements for a mulch, namely, the suppression of weeds, the insulation of the soil and the retention of moisture. Clearly this does not mean that if we put a layer of concrete over the soil our camellias will grow well (they probably won't grow at all), though camellias do grow well alongside a paved or concrete path or drive. Here they will extend their roots underneath where there will always be some soil moisture and very restrained fluctuations of temperature.

A worthwhile experiment could also be to test the value of a layer of gravel as a mulch. It would be surprising if this proved less effective than flat rocks and stones.

There is probably no difference between a living mulch and a ground cover plant and it has been observed that camellias will grow particularly well in lawns. Whilst it is desirable to keep a small area surrounding the plant's trunk free of grass, it seems that camellia roots particularly enjoy conditions under grass. Perhaps it is the aeration of the soil which the intricate root system of grass ensures, or maybe the easy entry of water through grass, or its insulating effect or a combination of all of these. Whatever it is, there is no doubt that a camellia properly installed as a lawn specimen can be expected to thrive and thrive well.

GROUND COVER

Nature never permits bare soil but ensures that it is populated with plant life. Such plant life often presents itself as what we call weeds and we spend much of our gardening time rooting them out. Surface rooting plants like camellias, as we know, resent any but the shallowest soil cultivation due to the injury to their surface roots so that if we have no mulch as a weed suppressor we can, annually, be in for a long hard season of laborious weeding.

The alternative is to grow plants which will compete with and overcome weeds in any bare soil. There are many suitable for the purpose and as several books devoted entirely to ground cover plants are available only a very small selection will be mentioned here.

One excellent plant which will make a dense cover and suppress all but the strongest competitors, such as bracken and bramble, is the periwinkle *Vinca minor*. This is available with flowers of blue, of which the 'Bowles' variety is outstanding with white or variegated leaves and double blooms, although some of the rarer forms may be hard to come by. It thrives in sun or shade although flowers are sparse in shade and variegated forms will revert to green if not given a certain amount of sunlight. The little phlox-like flowers of the periwinkle certainly compliment those of the camellia and some charming colour combinations are easily possible.

Another strong grower, but of very different type to the periwinkle, is *Bergenia cordifolia*, well known for its early flowering, large leathery leaves and ease of cultivation. Planted in mass in front of camellias the effect is pleasing in the extreme and the large heads of pink flowers look extremely well in front of early flowering camellias such as 'Donation'.

Mention of the Saxifrage family to which the begonia belongs immediately brings to mind another member, namely, *Saxifraga umbrosa*, the well-known 'London Pride'. This spreads well, stubbornly resists weeds and has charming little spikes of pink flowers as well as most attractive leaves.

The heather family contains many members well suited to providing ground cover. *Erica carnea*, which forms dense evergreen mats and is winter/early spring flowering, is particularly satisfactory. Reference to one of the several books on heathers will suggest many more.

In discussing ground cover plants mention should be made of the ivy. Certain of the variegated leaf forms provide a most interesting and, indeed, attractive ground cover and a very effective foil to the plain green leaves of the camellia. In the conditions of the woodland garden, the common ivy *Hedera helix* is extremely useful even though it is extremely invasive. Strangely enough, it hardly ever shows any real desire to scale the trunks of camellias and even less

of rhododendrons. One sometimes hears it said that the common ivy is far too greedy in its feeding habits to enable it to be a satisfactory ground cover. This may possibly be true of plants in the open but in woodland conditions there seems to be little doubt that the ivy traps so many fallen leaves which would otherwise blow away that the extra humus derived from it at least makes up for what the ivy claims from the soil.

Having now referred both to mulches and living ground cover, perhaps one note of warning should be given which is never to remove permanently either a mulch or ground cover unless it is to be immediately replaced with an alternative. To rake away a mulch from a plant which has been long mulched or to remove a living ground cover exposes the surface soil to every severe fluctuation of temperature. The roots of our camellias are only just below the surface and, when exposed to these sudden fluctuations after months or years of being insulated from them, will suffer accordingly.

Complimentary Planting

The boundary between what is and is not a ground cover plant and a complimentary plant may, at times, be obscure but mention must be made of the greatest plant available to anyone with acid soil, namely, the evergreen azalea. This much neglected plant has everything to offer: a rugged constitution; a wide range of all the colours apart from yellow and true yellow orange; the ability to provide the most massive flower power of any plant; and in some varieties to change their leaves to orange and red in the autumn and back again to green in the spring.

They are so easy to grow if given only reasonable conditions and so accommodating that they can safely be moved when in full bloom. As the well-known pink 'Hino Mayo' regularly shows, they can be effective in bloom for six weeks and are available as near prostrate plants, such as *Rhododendron nakahari* with orange-red flowers, and as big boys, such as the late flowering 'Naomi' with salmon pink blooms and the medium-late 'John Cairns' with orange red blooms which can easily make 6ft (1.8m).

It is not generally realized that they can be clipped and shaped with shears and that in Japan, where so many of them originate, they are used for low topiary work and as little shrub hedges round flower beds in much the same way as the box was used in our gardens so many years ago.

When one goes around many of the great rhododendron gardens

in April, May and June, it is not unusual to hear the owner and his garden staff almost boast that they do not know the names of 'any of those evergreen azaleas'. Of course, there are far too many evergreen azaleas, far too many alike bearing different names, far too much hybridizing has gone on and far too many plants too much alike named and registered. The same could be said of the camellia but it is a fact that many a famous garden would have far too little colour and flower if the plantings of evergreen azaleas were taken away.

Just as the evergreen azalea is used to suppress weeds and provide flower power in the predominantly rhododendron garden, so it is ideal for the same purpose with our camellias. The choice of plants is extremely wide but, at the same time, must be carefully made. We do not want to plant 'Naomi' if we are looking for a dense ground cover plant and, if we are looking for a happy colour combination, we do not want to plant 'Hino de Giri' with its somewhat blue red flowers in front of camellia 'Adolphe Audusson' with its pure red tending to geranium red blooms.

Before we come to consider the low growing and medium growing forms, and the appropriate colours to combine with our camellias, there is one very old gardening trick in planting we can use to ensure many shrubs, evergreen azaleas and the brooms are outstanding in their results. If one is anxious to produce a fine dense dome of a plant rather than a too lanky specimen without resorting to pruning, one will peg down the plant when it is installed.

The method is quite simple. Plant the shrub in its desired position and then pull outwards and peg to the ground every branch pliant enough to submit without breaking. In the case of shrubs like evergreen azaleas and brooms most, if not all, can be pegged down. For pegs use pieces of wire, hooked ends of bamboo or other branched prunings inverted before insertion. All will serve quite well.

The reason why pegging down works is very simple. One has only to think for a moment to realize that one never sees shrubs or trees with an empty centre. Nature always ensures that the centre is filled up and it normally becomes the dominant part or, in the case of most trees, houses the leader. The practice of pegging down relies on this fact. Whilst the shrub may look a little peculiar when first installed, or may even cause a few raised eyebrows and chuckles, within quite a short time growth buds will swell to be followed by shoots and twigs all along the bare branches. The shrub will 'fill up' and will form a fine, dense mound well clad from ground level upwards. In the case of easily rooted shrubs such as the evergreen azalea, more often than not it will be found that in due course roots are formed at each point pegged down. This gives us a fine, dense bush, rooted at six or seven different points. Some of these natural layers can usually be removed without affecting the appearance of the plant, providing a useful form of increase.

Fred C. Galle's great book *Azaleas* will convince anyone that there has been far too much hybridizing of evergreen azaleas. Named plants are almost legion and it becomes inevitable that many must be as near identical as makes no difference. Out of the thousands raised, the garden centres mostly stock a dozen or so and, like so many retail shops, have no great knowledge of the plants they do have. However, there are one or two guide-lines which can be followed. If one is looking for a low growing plant, look for *Rhododendron nakahari*, late orange red, *R. nakahari* × *gumpo*, a really prostrate pink, or any of the *R. nakahari* hybrids, such as 'Wombat' and 'Squirrel', raised by Peter Cox at Glendoick Gardens. *R. nakahari* hybrids are comparatively recent and are almost always dense growing, late flowering semi prostrate plants. They are not too difficult to obtain. Among others not containing *nakahari* blood, 'Vida Brown' with late very large pink blooms and 'Rosebud' with double pink blooms are fine low growing plants.

Among the larger plants 'Hino Mayo', with sugar icing pink blooms, and 'Kure No Yuki', with white hose in hose blooms, are extremely reliable. There are many excellent alternatives best chosen by seeing the plants in bloom and creating an imaginary combination with one's camellias. It is worth bearing in mind that plenty of white is essential in almost every planting of shrubs of mixed colours. It seems to magnify yet balance the whole scene and there is no shortage of white in evergreen azaleas. Some of the pale pastel colours too are supreme and well worth seeking out. 'Hoo', also called 'Apple Blossom', in palest pink and white, 'Iro Ha Yama', white margined with palest lavender, and 'Ischi Yama', white margined with slightly deep lavender, are superb.

To prolong interest in our camellia planting some thought should be given to plants which do not compliment the camellias in flower but bloom after they are finished. There are a number of these, *Rhododendron indicum* (*Azalea macrantha*), *simsii* and *kaempferi* in their many forms, and particularly the *kaempferi* hybrids such as 'Leo', also orange, to name but a few. They provide just what is wanted in this regard, flowering on into July if carefully selected. Thus, when the camellias flower, they completely take over the scene – the evergreen azaleas with their neat little leaves provide an admirable foil, and when the camellias are finished the late flower-

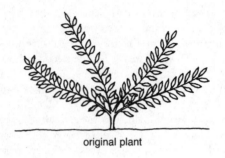

original plant

pegged all round

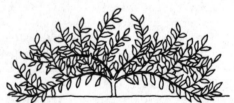

End of first season – young shoots
start to emerge from pegged-down
branches.

End of second season – the whole plant
is filling up from the centre.

Pegging down.

End of third season – whole plant
has formed a low, compact dome.

End of three seasons if the plant was not
pegged down – an open, straggly looking
shrub.

Pegging down (cont.).

ing evergreen azaleas take over to provide literally sheets of colour
of a totally different type.

PRUNING

Far too many people seem to have the idea that the camellia is a
somewhat delicate, exotic plant to be regarded almost with awe

and certainly not touched with a knife or secateurs, let alone a pruning saw. Nothing is further from the truth. The camellia is a very tough, adaptable and strong plant which responds extremely well to pruning be it light or severe.

Camellias live to a great age, certainly several hundred years. In East Sussex we have plants which we know were planted well before 1830 and which still produce many hundreds of blooms annually. Long before reaching such a venerable age they will produce branches and trunks 4 to 6in (10 to 15cm) in diameter but all too frequently these semi-mature plants have been allowed to straggle upwards, outwards and in all directions.

Anyone possessing such a plant and wanting an improvement can, with every confidence, cut it right back. Provided it is reasonably branched from low down, branches can be shortened so that the final framework is no more than 1½ to 2ft (0.5 to 0.6m) from the ground. Before long myriad new shoots will be formed and, in three or four years, a fine dense bush will have replaced the lanky old original.

In the nursery, pruning commences when the rooted cutting produces its first flush of growth. Ideally, this should be pinched back at the 'rabbit ear' stage to induce basal shoots to grow. From then on pruning continues up to the point of sale, the main object with these young plants being to produce healthy well-branched specimens. In some cases it is desirable to insert a central cane. Occasionally two or three are inserted to ensure that the soft, young shoots will grow in the right position.

Such pruning should be continued as necessary and with confidence from the point of purchase. It may seem hard, sometimes, to have to cut back long unwanted growth that the camellia has made but this must be done if an attractive healthy plant is desired. One knows from experience that this is the last thing many purchasers are prepared to do. They have bought a plant, installed it, looked after it and it has rewarded them by making growth in many directions. To cut any of it off or back after that seems like madness. What is not appreciated is that the size of top growth is controlled by the root system. If one cuts half the top growth away the root system will quickly replace it. So if one cuts back a shoot which is too long, the root system will quickly ensure that equivalent growth is produced elsewhere. It is worth remembering that the reverse situation also obtains if part of the root system is lost, as happens when an open ground plant is moved, a goodly part of the top growth must be removed because a reduced root system cannot maintain the old original top growth.

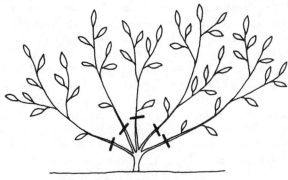

Old, worn out plant which
has out-grown its location –
cut back as shown.

After one season new growth
will appear on every branch which was
cut back.

After two seasons, strong growth
will have burst out along, and
elongated every branch, rejuvenating
the plant.

Pruning.

It follows, then, that pruning should be always with us: in the early years to produce a shapely well-branched shrub and, in later years, to maintain that good shape by reducing overcrowded branches, laterals and those that cross each other. In these later years, too, weak, twiggy growth should be removed, also those half-dead looking branches which make little growth and few, if any, flower buds. By the time this type of growth occurs our camellia grower will know enough to be able to recognize that type of growth for himself. If he does not remove it, it will probably die in two or three years' time in any event so why waste time? Always bear in mind that pruning a camellia can literally rejuvenate it.

Having travelled through the years we end where we started, namely, dealing with the big plants. Those that have grown leggy and unshapely have already been referred to. There remain those which have grown too large for their allotted space or, in other words, outgrown their welcome. Never sacrifice such old friends, rather cut them back hard, to 1ft (0.3m) or so from the ground. In a year we can start the pruning process all over again. In about three years we will have a fine bush fitting happily into its allotted space. Perhaps, this time, we will remember to keep it like that.

The best time to prune is immediately after flowering and before the new growth has begun, but further pruning, the cutting out of old unwanted wood and so on, can go on throughout the year. Of course, any type of pruning can be carried on throughout the year but where one is cutting back to induce new growth elsewhere, it is common sense to do this before new growth is made.

Finally, one should bear in mind that larger branches which have been cut back, say those over ¾in (18mm) in diameter, should be dressed, if possible, with an appropriate proprietary compound to prevent the entry of disease.

PLANTING

According to the gardening books, the camellia, like the vast majority of desirable plants, wants a moist, well-drained soil containing plenty of humus. This is something a lot of us have not got, so we must face the fact that many camellias will be installed in soil which is naturally badly drained, on clay or far too sandy.

Camellias seem to be able to adapt quite well to soil conditions which are far from ideal but that is no reason why we should test them to the limit when much can be done to improve an otherwise unsuitable site.

Pinch out at 'rabbit-ear' stage.

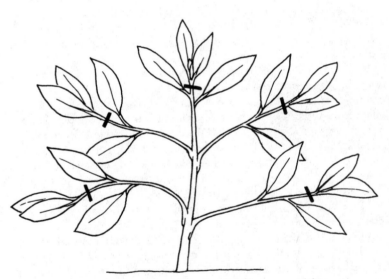

If the second flush of growth becomes unduly elongated, pinch out.

Pruning during propagation – after potting up.

A clay soil is unsuitable for camellias as it is badly drained, due to the minute size of the soil particles and lack of humus. It can be improved by incorporating plenty of grit, fine beach, better soil from elsewhere and humus in one or more of its many forms such as peat, bark, compost, sawdust and so on.

A very sandy soil can be similarly improved but here the opening agents grit, beach and so on, are omitted and in their place can be substituted better soil from elsewhere or even some clay well mixed with the original soil. The need for humus remains the same.

A well-worked good garden loam, even though near ideal, should also be improved by the addition of more humus. There is much truth in the old saying that if you spend a sum on the purchase of a plant you should spend double it on the preparation of the plant site.

The planting hole for any camellia should not be less than, say, 2ft (0.6m) wide and, for a sizeable plant, 3ft (0.9m) would be far better. The hole should be dug to a size and depth commensurate with the size of the camellia. A depth of 12 to 18in (30 to 45cm) will normally suffice and it is helpful to break up the subsoil beneath before placing a few spadefuls of prepared soil at the bottom of the hole.

If the plant is in a container as will more often than not be the case, then the correct planting depth should be arrived at before the plant is removed from the container. All too often one sees the plant knocked out of the container and then tested for depth. Depth is then found to be incorrect, so the plant is put aside while depth is adjusted and this may be repeated several times. All this should be done before the plant is knocked out of its pot. Camellias do not take well to being planted too deeply and the soil level of the root ball should never be lower than the surrounding soil level. As the prepared planting soil will certainly settle, this normally means that the camellia can be planted a little 'proud' and surrounded with mulch. In due time, it will sink level with the surrounding soil.

Unless one is dealing with a good loam fairly rich in humus already, the soil removed from the planting hole should have up to 50 per cent peat or other humus added to it. In addition, about 2oz (50g) of a general fertilizer such as fish manure or blood, fish and bone per planting hole should give good results.

If the camellia being planted comes from the open ground, then all that needs to be done is to refill the hole around the plant, tamping down lightly. When the final level has been reached, tread the soil down around the plant's original root ball. More soil will need to be added and a final treading given but do *not*, as is sometimes advocated, tread down the root ball itself. This will achieve nothing except damage to the roots.

If the camellia being planted is a containerized plant, a slightly different procedure should be followed. Tease out its roots a little; this is helpful, but a slight problem is that most containerized camellias are in up to 100 per cent humus, often peat and bark. Roots growing in such a medium can have great difficulty in making the transition to a totally different medium consisting of probably more than 50 per cent loam. These roots, however, will perfectly happily make the transition if the surrounding soil is graded to some extent. In other words, after installing the plant at the correct depth, surround it with humus, then add a 75 per cent humus/loam mix, then 50 per cent and so on until the mix is back to the original soil. Although this may sound a little complicated, it is really perfectly simple and will ensure that the containerized plant will get away in its new environment with the minimum of delay.

Often a perfectly good camellia will die after six or more months of planting. One quite often finds that it has been installed in a hole no bigger than the original container, that no effort has been made to improve the surrounding soil and that its roots are totally confined to its original container shape. The root system not having extended into the surrounding soil, and watering having been neglected, the plant has just given up the unequal struggle.

Clay Soils

All the above remarks apply equally to sandy or loamy soils made up to an acceptable standard as mentioned earlier. They do not, however, apply to heavy clay soils, where, to dig out a planting hole and fill it with a prepared soil in which the camellia is installed, sentences the plant to living in a sump.

Heavy rain, and particularly the winter rains, will fill the hole with water which cannot escape through the impervious clay sides and bottom. The camellia will literally drown – even though it is unlikely to be awash right up to the original soil level – because far too much of the root system is below water level. Of course, if the site is fairly steeply sloping, a trench dug on the lower side and filled with drainage material can alleviate the problem. However, one does not often come across a site sufficiently sloping for this to be totally successful.

Normally the answer is to plant the camellia half in and half out of the soil. Dig out a shallow hole and instal the camellia so that

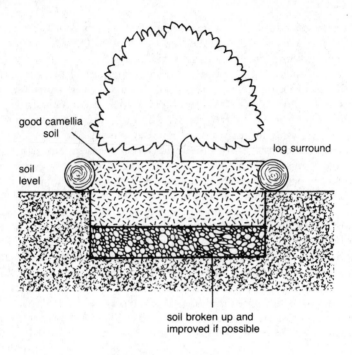

good camellia
soil

log surround

soil
level

soil broken up and
improved if possible

Planting in heavy clay and ill-drained soil.

about half the root ball is above natural soil level. The hole is filled up and additional prepared soil, humus, mulch, and so on, is placed around the camellia to protect its otherwise exposed parts. With the addition of annual mulches, the camellia will, in due time, appear to be growing on a slight mound, but grow it will and grow happily despite the clay below.

A great rhododendron expert once said that if one lifted a rhododendron, placed it on a gravel path and surrounded it with quantities of rotting bracken, it would grow and grow well. This is undoubtedly true and a very similar situation applies with camellias. It is this theory we are exploiting when, in dealing with a clay soil, we plant the camellia half in and half out.

Planting above soil level can be taken even further than this as a personal anecdote will demonstrate. I was faced with planting up camellias in a quite considerable area which was nothing less than a bog. The so-called top soil was only a few inches deep, stained brown with the unmistakable signs of bad drainage and, indeed, literally stinking when it was turned over. Beneath those few inches lay an impervious layer of clay – solid, yellow Sussex clay in some parts, solid blue London clay in others.

Apart from the physical problems of installing a satisfactory drainage system, the cost of so doing ruled it out as the area was quite extensive. Accordingly, recourse was had to planting above ground level. First the weed was stripped off the surface and an area about 4ft × 4ft to 5ft × 5ft (1.2 × 1.2m to 1.5 × 1.5m) roughly marked out and forked over in the hope of providing some drainage and aeration. A shallow ditch, about a spade's width across to a depth of the top soil, was then thrown out on to the square. Four lengths of branch, about 4 to 6in (10 to 15cm) in diameter, were laid around the square with a few small pegs driven in to prevent them falling outwards. Some better soil and humus were then worked into the loose soil thrown up from the ditch. The mix was then used to fill up to a little above the level of the top of the logs, the camellias being planted in the normal way. Anything can be used in lieu of logs to retain the top soil, such as bricks, blocks, boards and so on. (In this instance, logs were used because they were freely available on the site.)

The first camellias planted in this way were 12 to 18in (30 to 45cm) container plants. Growth has been excellent and they are now fine bushy plants about 3 × 3ft (1 × 1m). Now one can hardly see the old logs for moss growing on them and the planting sites look almost like natural mounds. Given a year or so more, they will have merged into the general area but the camellias will grow safe and sturdy on their well-drained mounds. With the good sense which plants have, they will, no doubt, have put a few roots well down to the over ample moisture which lies below.

TRANSPLANTING

In planting a camellia from a container it is not easy to go wrong. One normally has a nice root ball firmly encased in the growing medium with ample, healthy roots holding this together. Open ground plants, on the other hand, can present something of a problem. Moving a rhododendron with its mass of fibrous roots firmly interwoven with and holding the soil is child's play but the camellia, although not difficult to move, is a rather different proposition. It has a much more open, more fleshy root system and if dug out and lifted by its trunk will, as often as not, break under the weight of soil and a large part of the roots will be lost. This is the last thing we want to happen.

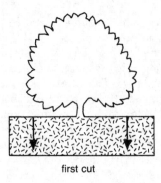

first cut

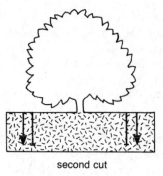

second cut

The soil is removed – forming a
trench all round.

The plant is undercut and
levers inserted.

Transplanting – method 1.

Several books explain and illustrate how shrubs such as rhododendrons and camellias should be prepared for moving by cutting
straight down with a reversed spade at the required distance from
the trunk, then removing a trench of soil back from that and then
undercutting the root ball. It is certainly arguable that this is not the
best way to prepare for a move. As the majority of gardeners work
on their own, it has to be accepted that the distance from the trunk
when the first circle of cuts is made and, in consequence, the
ultimate size of the root ball moved, is primarily dependent on the
mover's strength and ability to manoeuvre levers – that is, to get a
heavy weight out of its hole.

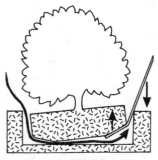

The plant is lifted and plastic or fabric is inserted, first on one side and then the other.

The plastic is tied around the whole shrub.

The shrub root ball is wrapped in plastic or fabric and lifted out, and is then ready for transportation.

Transplanting – method 1. (cont.).

That accepted, it seems far more sensible to go in with long sloping cuts so as to secure as much of the top feeder root system as possible; in other words, knowing one has got to leave some root behind, priority should be given to securing the maximum amount of surface feeding roots. Using this method it will also be found to be much easier to tease out the complete extremity of the feeder roots, thereby reducing the weight of the total root ball and helping the plant to reestablish in an alien site.

Whichever means we use to transplant (unless we are dealing with a very small plant where one can literally get one's hands under the root ball), steps must be taken to secure the roots within a

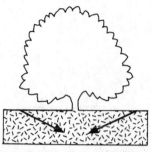

A long, sloping cut is made at the maximum possible distance from the trunk to obtain maximum surface roots.

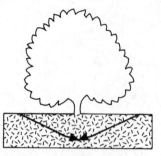

The cut is lengthened and the root ball undercut.

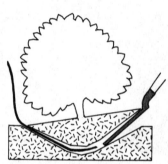

The plant is levered up and the root ball wrapped in plastic.

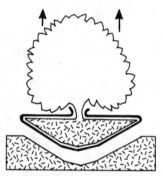

The shrub, with its root ball wrapped in plastic, is lifted out of the hole. A maximum amount of surface feeder roots is obtained for the minimum total weight compared with method 1.

Transplanting – method 2.

sheet of old plastic, sacking, hessian or something similar. To achieve this, the material must be pushed down with the hand on one side of the plant, then the plant levered on to its side and the material roughly pleated up and pushed under. The plant is then levered on to its other side and the pleated material pulled through. This is not too difficult if the material is sensibly folded or pleated when first worked under the root ball.

We now have the plant standing on a sheet of material and all that remains is to bring it up to the stem, tie it and then securely bind it around the root ball with strong string, cord, rope or whatever is to hand (old electric light flex is quite good). Having got the root ball securely encased in the material, the plant can safely be removed from the hole. If it is within the gardener's capacity it can be lifted out. The plant is now ready for transportation to another part of the garden or for a safe journey to another garden elsewhere.

The Wire Basket Method

It is unfortunate that few of us, when we instal a plant such as a camellia, give any thought to the fact that the time may come when we may want, or even worse may have, to move it. Transplanting is no easy task once the plant reaches any real size, but there is one perfectly simple remedy. This is known as the wire basket method of planting and is so easy and straightforward that it is a mystery why it is not used far more often.

Having dug the planting hole, place most of the prepared soil mixture to one side. The remainder is used to form the hole into a bowl shape. A roughly square piece of chicken wire, with a mesh of about 1 to 2in (2.5 to 5cm) is then cut from the middle of one side to the centre. By overlapping the cut edges and twisting and bending the remainder and finally firmly winding the cut ends of the wire with the remainder, a 'basket' can be formed which fits and is then placed in the planting hole.

Some more plant mix is then placed on the wire and the camellia installed in the normal way. For the sake of neatness, surplus wire netting sticking up too far out of the ground can be cut off although if one can leave a rim all round up to about 6in (15cm) deep this will prove admirable in retaining a mulch of dead leaves or other material.

When the time arrives to move the plant a sharp spade inserted outside the wire netting and continued all round and finally underneath, will ensure that the camellia can be lifted out with no fear of root damage for these are safely secured in the wire basket.

CONTAINER CULTURE

The grower produces his camellias for sale in containers. His objective is to produce the best possible plant in the shortest possible time. To continue to produce each year and every year the best possible plant is, too, the objective of the purchaser, so it is common sense to follow the grower's method.

Whilst no two groups follow exactly the same procedure or use

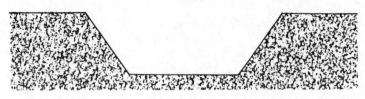

hole in ground

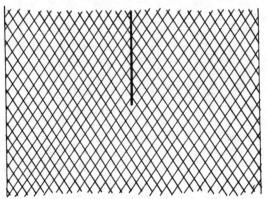

chicken wire with one cut down its centre

chicken wire bent into a rough basket form

The wire basket method.

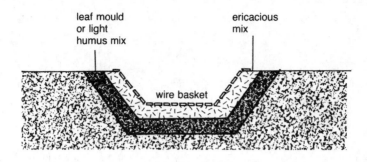

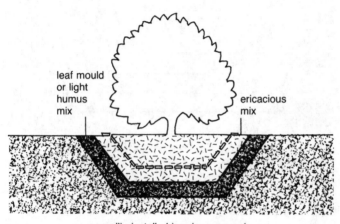

camellia installed in ericaceous mix

The wire basket method (planting).

exactly the same soil compost, all will be agreed that the primary objective is to provide the camellia's roots with adequate moisture, air, food and drainage.

There are dozens of 'best' composts and the majority are peat based but, apart from that common factor, a fairly wide assortment of other organic and inorganic materials is used.

Peat has many virtues not least amongst which is that peat from the same locale varies only slightly in character. It is possible to use peat alone as a potting compost provided it is mixed with the necessary fertilizers and so on, for peat in itself contains little or no nourishment. The difficulty, however, with pure peat is that, after

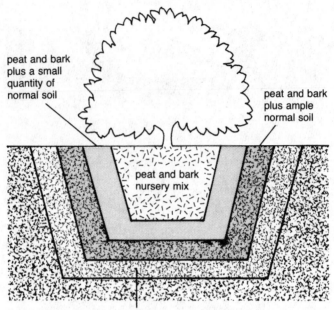

peat and bark plus a small quantity of normal soil

peat and bark plus ample normal soil

peat and bark nursery mix

normal soil plus a quantity of peak and bark for a small soil improvement

Planting a containerized plant.

a while, as it breaks down, its particles become finer and finer so that, ultimately, what started as an open friable material ends up as a soggy mass. The consequent lack of air and drainage can only harm the camellia's root system.

It is to counteract this that many varied other materials are incorporated in the compost, including bark, rotten sawdust, broken up rotting wood, grit, sand, perlite, loam and so on. No doubt innumerable combinations of such materials will give good results.

The reader may wish to experiment with some of them but if he would prefer to use a proven satisfactory compost it is doubtful if he could do better than use the following:

⅔ by volume medium grade moss peat (not sedge peat).
⅓ by volume medium grade Cambark or Forest Bark.

To this basic mixture are added the following fertilizers per cubic metre:

Ammonium nitrate or sulphate (0.3kg).
Osmocote – 16–18 month formulation (3kg) or similar slow release fertilizer.
Magnesium lime (2.4kg).
Trace elements (0.3kg).

Some of the slow release fertilizers now marketed include magnesium, lime and trace elements. Check this carefully, and if included no further addition is needed. If the camellias are intended to remain in comparatively small lightweight plastic pots for any length of time, then it may be found desirable, depending on exposure to wind, to replace about one-fifth by volume of the mix with very coarse sand or crushed grit to give added stability.

Having determined the mix, the next matter to decide is the type of container which is to be used. These are many and varied, chief amongst which are plastic pots, plastic planters, stone, man-made stone or concrete containers, half barrels and wooden tubs.

Plastic Pots

A pot eventually becomes a tub when large enough so that, to some extent, the term 'plastic pot' is a misnomer. That apart, plastic 'pots' are obtainable in sizes ranging from 1 or 2 litres in 1 litre jumps up to about 10 litres and from there in large jumps up to quite massive tubs of 1,000 litres. The larger sizes normally incorporate handles to assist in transportation.

These plastic pots are normally available in black or terracotta or sometimes green. Black is no doubt the most common. They are ideal for the person who wants or has to grow his camellias in containers as opposed to someone who wants a few impressive plants in impressive containers on a patio.

They are ideal, too, in that they are inexpensive, readily obtainable and incorporate first-class drainage holes at the bottom and bottom sides. They are the obvious choice for the enthusiast who has a greenhouse full of camellias or plants in containers or on a standing area where the plants can be moved into some protection in the severest weather. When repotting, remember to choose the larger pot at least 2 litres above the one containing the camellia. There is no problem in repotting from a 3-litre to a 5-litre pot but to do the same from a 3-litre to a 4-litre is extremely difficult.

Plastic Planters

These are really a more attractive form of plastic pot and available in various shapes, sizes and colours. Some, unfortunately, look like rather poor imitations of the real thing, others are most pleasing to the eye. Before buying, make sure that drainage holes are adequate.

Stone Containers

Under this heading we can include stone, man-made stone, concrete and terracotta. One can pay a lot of money for stone containers, in fact one can also pay quite a lot for man-made stone and 'concrete' containers.

There is no need to try to describe what is available. A visit to a garden centre specializing in good containers or a look through one of the catalogues from specialist firms is the best way to find what one wants.

Apart from plastic pots and tubs, two points should be borne in mind in choosing containers. One is that the container should not be so ornate or of a colour to detract from the camellia it is to hold and the other is that a square-sided wedge shape will be easier to deal with when repotting ultimately becomes necessary. If the container is wider in the middle than at the top it can be extremely difficult to get the plant out and recourse may have to be had to cutting downwards all round with a long thin sharp blade or sharp spade.

Half Barrels and Wooden Tubs

The genuine old half barrel produced by sawing a beer barrel in half is not seen so much nowadays but many substitutes – round, square and oblong – are available. Some quite attractive ones can be found built up of logs. Here again, the best thing is to choose one to meet one's needs at a garden centre. If made from boarding make sure that it is strongly bound with metal straps and, in any event, make sure that the wood of which it is made has either been well treated or is highly resistant to rot or both.

Potting or Repotting

The procedure for potting or repotting is first to place a layer of compost at the bottom of the container. It is arguable whether a layer of coarse stones or broken drainage material at the bottom of the container is necessary or helpful. Experience shows that drainage is perfectly satisfactory if the whole container is filled with the recommended mixture. Tamp it down lightly and continue until the plant, still in its original container, stands an inch or a couple of inches, according to container size, below the level of the top of the new one. Next, remove the plant from its old container (it should have had a good watering the previous day) and with a gentle stream of water from a hose wash off about ½in (12mm) of its old compost all round exposing the roots.

It should immediately be placed in its new container so as to avoid the fine exposed roots drying out, and filled up all round with compost which should be shaken down or carefully tamped down as the filling proceeds. A good watering follows which will normally settle the new compost still further, a final filling, a covering with mulch and the repotting is completed. A stake, normally a good bamboo will suffice, may be required for a season or so and care should be taken not to stand containers on heavy soil as this may quite soon block some or all of the drainage holes.

It sometimes happens that planting is required in a container which is considerably too large for the newly purchased plant. The best answer then is to make sure the plant's original container is amply big and the camellia not pot bound. If it is, it must obviously be repotted. One then plants the pot in the over large container, covering the rim of the pot with a little compost or mulch. The same procedure can be followd on subsequent repotting until the plant is large enough to take up its final position in the large container.

The same procedure can be followed when plants cannot be grown in the garden itself or where they have to have protection in a greenhouse or porch. Here they can be 'planted' in the garden in their pots and when mulched cannot be seen not to be growing there naturally. In any event, this plunging of plants in containers does much to minimize the need for continual watering.

Feeding

In the first place it clearly makes a difference if a containerized plant is already in a mix containing all the correct fertilizers. If so, it will normally have sufficient nutrients to cover two growing seasons when all that will be required will be the addition of a liquid feed such as Phostrogen or Liquinure to the water when watering between March and August.

If, on the other hand, the container mix only has a small quantity of general fertilizer or bone meal added, the plant will want a slightly more solid diet. In this case, use a complete general fertilizer in March followed by a nitrogen feed in April. This nitrogen feed can consist of sulphate of ammonia or dried blood. Soil in the container must be moist when fertilizers are used. If dry, water first. Never exceed the recommended quantities or severe damage, even death, will be caused to the plant.

As recommended a liquid feed should be added to the watering can when watering between March and early August. Here again, follow the maker's instructions. Only weak solutions are normally used and then only about once per fourteen days.

All feeding should cease in early August. If continued after that it can cause damage to a containerized plant causing leaves to brown and drop and this, if bad enough, will cause the ultimate death of the plant. In any event, feeding too late can produce a very late flush of new growth which, having insufficient time to ripen before the onset of winter, falls victim to the first fairly severe frosts.

Greenhouses and Conservatories

Growing in containers in these is really little different from growing any other plant which shares similar moisture and drainage tastes with the camellia.

Particular attention must be given to ventilation and shading as camellias are unhappy if the temperature is allowed to rise too high. In addition, their foliage, particularly young foliage, can be very easily damaged by sun scorch unless adequate shading in the form of shade netting or a wash on the glass is provided in good time. It is particularly annoying to leave in the house at night a number of absolutely healthy looking camellias and look in at noon the following day to find the majority marred by scorched leaves.

Watering

This is as much a problem in the greenhouse and conservatory as elsewhere. The counsel of perfection is, of course, to water the containers individually with rainwater.

Unfortunately, this is not always possible due to the lack of collection and storage facilities for rainwater or in the case of large collections the physical impossibility of regularly watering a large collection by hand.

In either of these events, recourse must be had to mains water supply. If this is more or less neutral it will be perfectly satisfactory.

If it has a high alkaline content it is possible that in time the medium in which the plant grows may become too alkaline. However, provided the plants are in an acid compost, they are perfectly alright until their next repotting when as much of the old compost as possible is removed and replaced and the new container once more filled with acid compost. (In the United States, if plants do begin to suffer as a result of continual watering with alkaline water, one method used to resolve the problem is a light dressing of sulphur which acts as an acidifying agent.)

If there is a mains water supply to the greenhouse or, equally, into the conservatory, the next question is the best way to utilize it. If only a limited number of plants are to be dealt with then a tap just inside or outside the building and a watering can may suffice. It must be assumed that this individual attention will be continued by kind neighbours or relatives if the owner goes away on holiday.

If, however, the camellia grower is a real enthusiast with a large house or conservatory full of containerized plants, then recourse to other methods is worthwhile. There are three main alternatives:

1.   Overhead spray/mist. There are a number of simple overhead spray or mist jets (cheap plastic ones are perfectly efficient) which can quite easily be connected to a mains supply. A turn of the tap results in the whole house being enveloped in a drenching mist. This is perfectly satisfactory if only one type of plant is being grown such as all camellias but may not be the answer if various *genera* with different watering needs are all grown in one house.
2.   Capillary beds. Ready-made variations of these are already available to the keen amateur from commercial sources, however, there is no great problem in designing and building one's own.

Capillary watering is based on the fact that, if a plant in a container with adequate drainage holes in the base is thoroughly saturated and placed on a medium which itself has adequate and continuous moisture, then a capillary action will be set up. This action is between the moist medium and that in the container to the extent that the plant in the container will take up all the moisture it needs, no less and no more.

The moist medium can be in the form of either capillary matting or very coarse sand but, in either case, if an automatic system is required, it must be contained in a 'tank'. This is easily made by making a wood framework about 3in (7.5cm) high and of the size required for the capillary bed. The base and sides of this bed are then lined with a single piece of thick plastic sheeting.

If capillary matting is used, arrangements must be made before the plastic is applied for a channel an inch or so lower than the main bed to run the length of one side. This need be only a couple of inches wide. After the plastic has been placed in and pinned in place, the capillary matting follows, care being taken to ensure that it is tucked well down into the channel.

Where sand is to be used as the moist medium, then after the plastic a length of perforated plastic tubing is run down the centre of the bed which is then filled with sand to about 2in (5cm) above the level of the top of the pipe.

With either method all that remains is to provide a tank with a ball valve so that its water can be kept at a constant level. These can be purchased custom made but, rather than incurring that expense, an old lavatory flush tank is ideal. The flushing gear must be removed and it will be necessary to purchase a threaded cap from a builders' merchants to seal off the old outlet flush pipe.

If the capillary bed is on the ground, the flush tank must be partially sunk in the ground when the hole housing it can be lined in wood, brick or other suitable material. If the bed is on the bench the tank can be attached to the end of that.

All that remains to be done is to tap the tank at a suitable spot, which must be below the old overflow opening, take a piece of plastic tube from there through the wood frame, through the plastic which must, of course, be sealed with sealing tape and into the channel in the matting bed or into the length of tubing in the sand bed. The tubing, like the beds, must run dead level.

Mains water having been connected, the ball cock is finally adjusted so that the water level in the tank comes about halfway up the outlet pipe opening. The final result of all this is that we shall have a constant water level in the capillary matting channel so that the raised matting will be constantly moist but not waterlogged and, in the case of the sand bed, a constant water level about 2in (5cm) below the surface of the sand.

3. Drip watering. Capillary beds are ideal for containers up to and including 9in (22.5cm). Above that size the top part of the compost in the container tends to get too dry. Accordingly, if we grow plants in the larger size containers drip irrigation is more suitable.

This consists of a length of plastic supply pipe which is tapped at intervals and a thin plastic pipe leading to each pot inserted. A small plastic drip valve is fixed to each and a plastic clip anchors the pipe so that water from the valve drips on to the container compost. Tapping the supply pipe, inserting the thin tubes, attaching the valves and clips are all extremely simple operations.

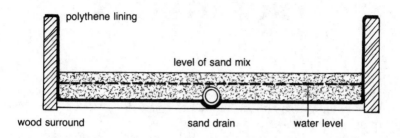

Capillary beds – sand.

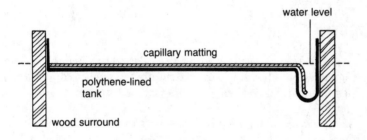

Capillary matting.

As with the capillary beds, mains water cannot be fed direct so, here again, a flush tank can be used. In this case, it must be fixed above the level of the supply pipe to give the necessary head of water to keep the system going.

One final word. Anyone fortunate enough to have a supply of rainwater can, of course, utilize this for either capillary beds or drip irrigation as neither depend on pressure to be effective. Obviously the main tanks of rainwater must be situated above the level of the feed tanks in both cases.

4
PROPAGATION

Every now and then a somewhat worried face appears at the nursery seeking advice. The cause of the worry is that 'my camellia is growing little apples' or 'my camellia has a lot of round growths on it'. These are, of course, seed pods. More often than not they will prove to be empty when opened, because (depending on what climate they are grown in) camellias require heat to set seed.

However, some, particularly in the singles, do set seed outdoors from time to time which can be collected as soon as they are ripe. In addition, seed can at times be obtained from specialist seedsmen, from the Royal Horticultural Society (members only) and from the United States.

SEEDS

The seed is best sown as soon as it is collected or obtained and for the amateur who has only a limited number of seeds to deal with, it is best planted either in small individual pots or several seeds in a larger pot.

The growing compost can consist of pure peat, peat and Perlite or a proprietary ericaceous seed compost. The pots should not be filled with more than about 3in (7.5cm) of compost and the seeds covered about ½in (12mm) deep. They should be sown with the 'eye' down as it is from here that the roots will emerge.

The pots should next be watered with a very fine rose and a piece of glass placed over the top of each. If at all possible, they should be placed in a small propagator giving a bottom heat of about 70°F (21°C) when they may be expected to commence germinating at any time from about two weeks to several months.

After two or three leaves have appeared, the seedlings should be potted up individually in a suitable potting compost and grown on in the normal way. It is generally advocated that, on potting up, the basal tap root should be pinched back by about one third to one half its length. The seedlings will respond well to a weak liquid feed at fortnightly intervals. Phostrogen used at its normal recommended rate is perfectly satisfactory.

An alternative method for those who have only a few seeds to deal with is to take a jam jar, part fill it with moist peat, insert the camellia seeds around the outside of the peat, then add more peat so that they are covered by about ½in (12mm). Next, seal the jar with cling film or plastic and a rubber band to prevent it drying out.

The whole is then put in the airing cupboard and periodically examined. As the seeds have been arranged to be visible through the glass of the jar, their germination can be easily seen. As each seed germinates, it is carefully removed, potted in an individual pot where it will, in due course, produce its leaves and will be grown on in the usual way.

GRAFTING

Whilst plants from seed will not come true to either parent as they represent new cultivars which have never before seen the light of day, all other methods of propagation are asexual. In other words, the new plants so produced are bound to be identical to the original scion or propagation wood used.

Propagation by grafting is one of these methods although it is not greatly used except for cultivars or varieties which are virtually impossible to root from cuttings such as some of the pure *reticulatas*. Its only other use is when one has a camellia, and it can be small or large, which is not, for instance, to one's liking.

There are no particular problems in grafting camellias and this can be done at most times of the year, except in the period of active growth in spring and early summer. The types of graft used are varied but the cleft graft for the big ones is usually used whereas the whipgraft is more common for small plants when both the stock and scion are usually of the same diameter.

It is felt that there are probably not a great many amateurs who will wish to do anything much in the way of grafting so that it is not necessary to go into too much detail here. The grafting of camellias is little different from the grafting of the majority of hardwood shrubs. A number of fine books on grafting or on propagation are available and can quite easily be borrowed from one's local public library.

Bark-grafting is a technique which the amateur may find easier to execute than other methods of grafting. In effect, it is not dissimilar to the well-known technique of budding.

A vertical cut about 1½in (37mm) long is made down the side of the stock which is loosened on each side. This is easy to effect in the summer. The scion is cut with a bevel on one side about 1in (25mm) long and slid bevel-side outwards inside the bark of the vertical cut. It should then be securely bound in place with plastic tape and thereafter treated like any other budded plant. Arrangements should be made to shade the graft from direct sun which might otherwise burn the scion.

Cutting Grafts

This is a fairly new technique and, it is understood, has been used with some success. One needs to take an easy rooting *japonica* cutting which is about 5in (12.5cm) long with two or three leaves. A ½in (25mm) sloping cut is made into the stem about 1½in (37mm) up from the base. Next, the scion wood is prepared. This should be about 3in (7.5cm) long with a couple of leaves at the top. The base is cut into a ½in (12mm) wedge. The scion is then inserted into the stock and secured in place with an elastic band. If the scion and stock are not identical in diameter, one side of each must be lined up perfectly.

The 'cutting' is then inserted in the propagating medium in the normal way to a depth that will cover the union by about 1in (25mm). It is then treated as a normal cutting. By the time roots have emerged from the base, the graft will have calloused. The cutting is then removed from the propagating medium and the old stock above the union cut back as close to the union as possible. From then on it is treated as a normal cutting, potted up and grown on.

This technique is reported to have been used very successfully with some of the *reticulatas* which are otherwise extremely difficult to root.

LAYERING

This is almost certainly the oldest, easiest and most certain method of propagation to produce one or two new plants from an existing one. It occurs naturally very frequently, in particular with rhododendrons and azaleas.

An extremely well-known technique, layering is best done with young wood and, of course, it must be wood which can be brought down to ground level. The soil at the point where the branch to be layered meets the ground should be improved by the addition of peat, compost and so on. The branch to be layered is then brought

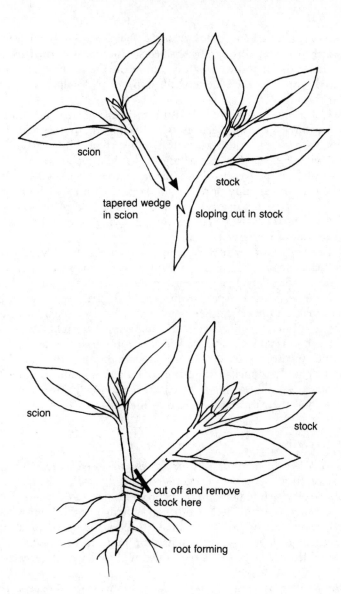

Cutting grafts.

down and notched on its lower surface with a sloping cut facing upwards part way through or scraped so as to remove the bark on the underside. It is then slightly buried in the rooting area and secured with a stick or, better still, lump of rock which seems to assist rooting.

It is then tied as upright as possible to a cane or stick and left for two or three growing seasons. Once a decent root system has formed the layer should be cut off from its original branch and left for a while to get used to existing on its own resources from its own roots as opposed to those of the mother plant. After a few months it is carefully lifted and planted. Some pinching and pruning may be necessary to form a good shaped plant and it is always far better to use a young strong growing shoot to layer than a larger but older branch.

There are a number of variations on the method of layering, all of which depend on the same principle which is the partial arrest of the sap passing along the branch to be layered at a point where roots can be formed. Apart from cutting or scraping, this can be achieved in a number of other ways such as bending the branch and pegging it into the soil, covering it and tying it upright. An acute bend will normally cause sufficient interruption in the sap flow.

Other methods used include strangulation, when the branch is wired tightly and nicked slightly above the wire, and ringing. In the latter, a complete circle of bark, about 1in (25mm) long, is removed at the part to be inserted in the soil.

Air Layering

It is said that this method of propagation was used by the Chinese many centuries ago. The necessity in this case was, and is, to grow roots on a branch which cannot be brought down to ground level. The Chinese, having notched or ringed a branch at the point where roots were desired to be formed, then anchored it in a pot (presumably having first cut it in half) or built a box around it. The reassembled pot or box was then filled with soil and, if necessary, fixed to a stout branch.

Modern air layering depends exactly on this method except that the materials used have been brought up to date.

The layer is made about 12 to 18in (30 to 45cm) down from the tip of the branch where two circular cuts are made right round the branch about 1in (25mm) apart. A longitudinal cut is then made between the two circles and the cut bark carefully removed round the entire stem. The area exposed can be dusted with a rooting

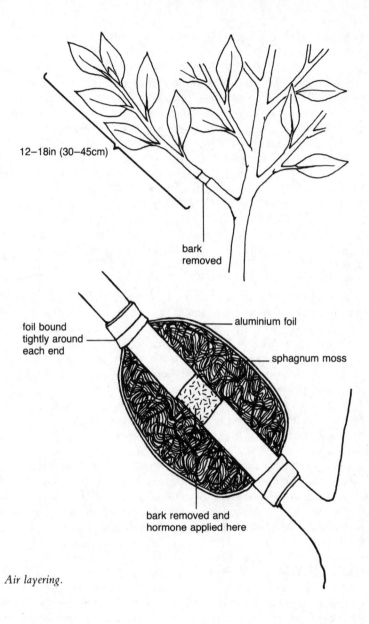

12–18in (30–45cm)

bark
removed

foil bound
tightly around
each end

aluminium foil

sphagnum moss

bark removed and
hormone applied here

Air layering.

hormone although opinions differ as to whether this is strictly necessary.

Next, a handful of spaghnum moss is dipped in water and squeezed out. Too much water remaining in the moss can be a cause of failure. The spaghnum moss is placed around the branch with one hand and a piece of aluminium foil or plastic wrapped around with the other. If the operator finds difficulty at first in carrying out both operations at once, a loose tie can be made round the moss to hold it in place thus freeing both hands to apply the foil or plastic. If foil is used, it is important to twist the foil ends firmly in opposite directions to avoid moisture loss. If plastic is used, it needs to be carefully folded lengthwise before wrapping, again to prevent moisture loss. In the case of plastic, each end must be securely bound round with insulating tape or the like, not only to prevent loss of moisture but also to prevent rainwater running down the stem and into the moss which would soon become waterlogged.

The speed with which roots are formed depends on several factors and in particular the suitability of the branch layered, for old wood can take a very long time. However, when things go well, layers taken in April or May should be well rooted by September. They should be removed as soon as possible and potted up in a potting mix having first removed the foil or plastic. The sphagnum moss and young root system are left undisturbed.

After potting they should be lightly misted every day for about two weeks and thereafter treated as any other container plant. Care must be taken not to over-water as the young roots can easily be damaged.

Many trees and shrubs, not easy to root from cuttings, can be successfully propagated by air layering. The use of aluminium foil rather than plastic makes the operation easier. If there is any fear that water can run down the branch and into the moss it is prudent to wrap the junction of the foil and branch with tape.

CUTTINGS

Propagation from cuttings is by far the commonest method used with camellias. Only a very small percentage is propagated otherwise and this only because it is extremely difficult, if not impossible, to root from cuttings (as is the case with some *reticulatas*) or else they do not grow satisfactorily on their own roots.

It is an unfortunate fact that in order to obtain a high percentage

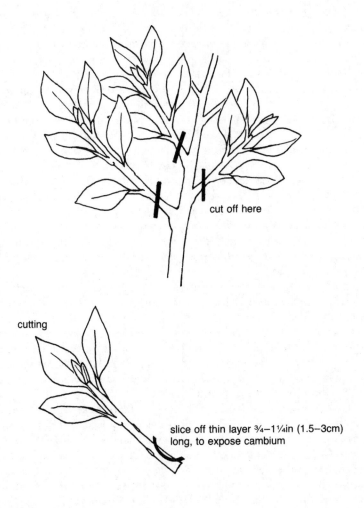

cut off here

cutting

slice off thin layer ¾–1¼in (1.5–3cm)
long, to expose cambium

Cuttings.

of rooting it is really necessary to have bottom heat in the propagation process. Without heat the percentage of rooting can be extremely small – possibly 5 per cent or less – whereas with heat 95 per cent or 100 per cent is obtainable with the easier rooting varieties. This is not to say that the skilled propagator cannot have reasonable success without heat, rather that for the unskilled novice success can be extremely difficult to obtain.

Cuttings should be taken as soon as the current year's growth is ripe. This, in a normal season, is by July. However, they are perfectly successful, given proper propagating facilities, right up to January or February.

Proper propagating facilities means a propagating bed with bottom heat (normally supplied by electrically heated cables) controlled by a thermostat and either intermittent mist, which is usually used for the earliest cuttings, or thin plastic over the bed sealed round the outside with lengths of wood to retain the moisture in the bed. There is little, if any, difference in the success rate between mist beds or plastic covered beds.

In commercial practice, a propagating bed can well be about 4½ft (1.5m) wide by any length desired. One does not want the bed wider than this because access to the cuttings in the centre becomes increasingly difficult the wider the bed becomes. The length should not exceed 18ft (6m) otherwise there is too much waste of electricity as the trays of cuttings are gradually cleared when rooted for potting up.

Propagating beds can be constructed on the bench, free standing or at ground level. The basic method is the same for all. If on the ground, a slight excavation about 3in (75mm) deep is made, to the size of the bed. This is lined bottom and sides with 2in (50mm) thick polystyrene carefully wrapped in plastic sheeting to ensure it remains dry. A wooden surround is built around the bed. (If we are building on a bench or free standing the wood surround will need to be about 6in (15cm) high; if at ground level about half that.)

Coarse sand to a depth of about 1in (25mm) is laid over the whole bed, the heating cable and thermostat installed and twice the amount of coarse sand laid on top of them. The line of misters, water supply and solenoid valve are next installed. (If we are using mist, otherwise the propagating frame is complete. If mist is not used, the trays of cuttings are set out in the sand and the whole covered with a sheet of the thinnest plastic obtainable.) Lengths of wooden lath or similar are laid on the plastic on the wood surround to create a comparatively airtight joint. In the early stages, at least, it is not important that the plastic may rest on the cuttings. If the cuttings grow out before rooting or before they can be potted up, then wire or very thin tube 'hoops' (only flat ones) are arranged to keep the plastic off the young growth.

A smaller version of such a frame can be easily made by any handyman. The only items which can be described as expenditure are the heating cable and thermostat and the cost of these is not crippling.

As a general rule, a propagating temperature in the rooting medium of about 65°(18°C) is ideal. A higher temperature of, say, 70°(21°C), may induce rooting a little sooner but it is doubtful if the small gain in time is worth the cost of the extra heating.

In fact, not every propagator relies on a thermostat; it may be sufficient to have the heat on from, say, about 5p.m. to about 8a.m. only. Accordingly, remembering to turn the electricity off and on means the thermostat can be dispensed with. An easier alternative is to use one of the many timeclocks now available which will do the switching on and off automatically.

It is doubtful whether it is worthwhile for the amateur to instal mist unless he is extremely keen and proposes to propagate a wide selection of trees and shrubs over a long period. There are, of course, a number of small propagators which provide bottom heat available to the amateur grower. With all cutting propagation, apart from bottom heat, the propagator must, above all, ensure that the leaves have a close humid atmosphere. If they dry out, all is lost. The rule is cool tops, misty middles and hot bottoms!

So much for the propagating frames. We must next consider the cuttings themselves, their treatment and insertion with the rooting medium and their management thereafter.

Cuttings are made from the half ripe wood of the current year's growth. They are the little branches which grow out from the buds in the leaf axials when the camellia puts on its growth in March/April/May time. They can be taken with secateurs in the cool of the day, normally from late June or July onwards. How soon one can take them depends on the season and no two seasons are exactly alike.

The ideal cutting has four or five leaves and is prepared to leave only three leaves. Once severed from the parent plant all cutting, in other words removal of leaves, cutting to length and wounding is best carried out by an extremely sharp blade or a single-backed safety razor blade.

Having removed surplus leaves the cutting is cut to length so as to leave about 2 to 2½in (50 to 62mm) of stem below the lowest leaf. Some methods ensure that the basal cut is made immediately below a node but this is not critical. Finally, a thin slither of wood about ¾ to 1in (18 to 25mm) long is made on one side of the cutting at the base. The object of this is to expose a larger area of the cambium layer than the small circle around the base of the cutting. As roots are made from the cambium layer, this is clearly good sense. It must be emphasized that only a very thin slice of the bark, not the wood of the cutting, is being taken. Above all, the cut

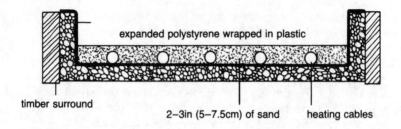

expanded polystyrene wrapped in plastic

timber surround

2–3in (5–7.5cm) of sand

heating cables

Propagating frame.

must *not* be made with a tapering slice down to a point as this will surely cause rot at the base of the cutting.

The only other type of cutting used is called the leaf, or leaf bud, cutting. It is useful if one is short of propagating material as every leaf on a shoot, short or long, provides a cutting. The tops which will have several small leaves should not be discarded as these root and grow well. These cuttings are sliced to expose cambium layers and otherwise dealt with in exactly the same way as the larger ones. Their stems may well be only 1in (25mm) long making them a little more difficult to handle and it must be remembered that having only one potential growth bud they will take an extra season to catch up in size with plants from normal cuttings. They root quite as well as the larger cuttings and occasionally even better.

Recipes for propagating mixes are legion, almost every grower, including many professionals, having their own favourite. Cuttings, as with camellia plants themselves, need moisture, air and drainage. To achieve this, peat, sand, bark grit, perlite and a host of other substances are recommended. Peat on its own, particularly if the cuttings are slow rooting, tends to become too solid and soggy so a good recipe for propagating is a mix of 50 per cent medium grade moss peat and 50 per cent fine grade Cambark. To this add a very small amount of osmacote slow release fertilizer at the ratio of approximately 1lb 6oz per yd^3 (0.75kg per m^3).

This could well be a *dangerous* recipe if bark was not used, but bark appears to have the unique ability to 'lock up' the fertilizer until it is required at a later stage by the plant. Experiments have shown that cuttings propagated in this mix with slow release fertilizer are not only better when rooted than those given no fertilizer but can maintain this superiority differential for many months after potting up. However, after much experience, we have reached the firm conclusion that no fertilizer should be added to the mix if *sasanqua* cuttings are to be propagated. This seems to apply in general to all

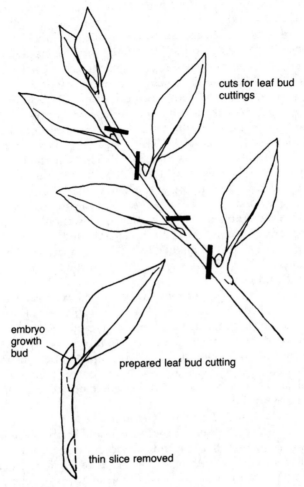

cuts for leaf bud cuttings

embryo growth bud

prepared leaf bud cutting

thin slice removed

Leaf bud cuttings.

small-leaved camellias, such as *hiemalis* and even *japonicas* such as 'Freedom Bell' or the hybrid 'Cornish Show'.

The type of container used rather depends on the number of cuttings to be struck. If these are only a few, a 4 or 5in (10 or 12.5cm) pot will suffice when they should be inserted around the rim of the pot about 1½in (37mm) apart. If more than a few cuttings are to be struck, then plastic or wooden seed trays are satisfactory.

The propagating medium should be moist when the pots or trays are filled. It should be lightly firmed down but not rammed hard. Whatever container and whatever recipe is used the procedure is the same. First place on the bench a small container of water and small container of Seradix Rooting Hormone No. 3 for hardwood cuttings. If preferred, Synergol mixed to the maker's specification can be used, in which case the container of water is not necessary.

If using rooting powder, dip the bottom 1in (25mm) of the cutting in water, shake it and dip it in the rooting powder, tap the surplus powder back into the container. Do not get rooting powder on the leaves. If Synergol is used, simply dip the cutting in the correct strength solution. With a 5in (12.5cm) nail, make a hole in the propagating medium a little less deep than the base of the cutting and insert the cutting in the hole so that it rests on the base of it. Every effort must be made to try to ensure that the rooting powder is not rubbed off the cutting on insertion. In a pot, the cuttings can go about 1½in (37mm) apart round the rim. In a tray they are usually placed about 1½in (37mm) apart in rows about 1½in to 2in (37 to 50mm) apart. About forty cuttings will fill a standard seed tray.

Once inserted, the cuttings are drenched with a solution of fungicide, normally Captan, Benlate or probably best of all Octave. Not only the cuttings but the propagating medium are thoroughly drenched and the trays or pots then stood for a short time in the shade to drain off some of the surplus liquid. The containers are then placed on the propagating beds and either the mist and heat turned on, or if mist is not used the whole bed covered with thin plastic weighted down.

The plastic should be lifted periodically and the cuttings inspected. Any dead leaves should be immediately removed. An occasional spray with a fungicide, say every two weeks or so, is a useful precaution. Under mist, this needs to be more frequent as the continual wetting of the leaves soon removes the chemical. In commercial propagation, this spraying with fungicide is carried out at fortnightly intervals using a series of different fungicides such as Octave, Rovral, Benlate and Captan to control infection.

When dealing with plastic covered beds, it is a wise precaution to arrange some shading by about the beginning of February. Although weak, there is sun in February quite often and the effect of this on a heated frame, insulated and covered with plastic, is to build up an extremely high temperature very quickly. An unshaded frame can achieve a temperature of over 100°F (38°C) with the greatest of ease. A careful watch must be kept throughout, particularly when a large number of propagating trays or pots are being used, to ensure that none of them dry out. Even in mistframes this can happen quite easily.

Heavy rooting of the cuttings should take place after about four to six months in which case they are ready for potting up. However, before removing them from their propagating trays or pots, a check should first be made to make sure that they are, in fact, rooted. A gentle pull of the cutting is sometimes enough but this is not always a true test. A cutting which has formed a sizeable callous and little or no roots can feel as though it is a rooted cutting so it is better to carry out a more reliable test than this. In trays and shallow pots, roots can often be seen poking through the drainage holes but if none is visible the tray can be held at an angle of about 60 degrees and given a sharp bang on its end on the bench. This frees the propagating medium from its container. If it is then tilted over to a little less than a right angle, one's spare hand spread out over the cuttings to prevent them falling out when upside down, one then gets a view of the bottom of the rooting medium. If plenty of roots are visible potting up can take place. If not, water the tray to settle the rooting medium and return it to the propagator.

A useful aid to have when potting up cuttings from a tray is a piece of Formica, or similar material, slightly narrower than the seed trays and a couple of inches longer. This is kept handy and when the tray is tilted as described above and plenty of roots seen, it is slid down between the bottom of the rooting medium and the tray and pushed to the far end. The rooted cuttings can then be lifted out like a large chunk of flat cake on the Formica slice. They are then easier to separate for potting up than if left in the tray.

If large pots have been used for propagating they will probably be too deep to see roots poking through the drainage holes. Give the base of the pot a sharp bang on the bench and, placing one hand over the cuttings, turn it upside down and allow the contents to come out sufficiently to see if plenty of roots have formed. The contents of the pot normally remain intact even if there are no roots to hold them. In that event, the pot is turned over, watered and returned to the propagating bed.

We all know that there are occasions when prayers, however sincere and heartfelt, are not answered. If this should happen when one turns one's pot over and the contents fall out it is not the end of the world. Any cuttings which have roots can be potted up, the remainder being replaced in the pot. If this is done, it is wise to fill the pot with fresh propagating 'mix'. This applies also when cuttings get 'stuck' and refuse to root in any normal period and consequently spend an extended time in the propagating bed. After a while it often pays to tip them out; if they have calloused heavily scrape a bit of this off and then replace them in fresh propagating mix. If this problem happens at all it always seems to happen to the cuttings which are in shortest supply and are needed the most. This does tend to reduce one's faith in the power of prayer! But here again one should not despair. Cuttings sometimes root after nine months or more on the propagating bed which teaches one the value of patience.

In potting up the rooted cuttings the growing mixture advocated earlier is used. Traditionally, cuttings were potted into a 3 or 4in (7.5 to 10cm) pot and then repotted as required. It was said that to pot them initially in a larger size was to overpot them when much of the soil in the pot would not be quickly filled with roots and would, in consequence, go 'sour'.

Whether the use of so-called 'soil-less' composts (meaning, say, peat/bark or similar composts without loam) has changed this or not one does not know but it is certainly modern practice to pot straight into 2-litre pots. The plants are then grown in good conditions on capilliary beds and make ample roots quickly, the advantage being that the plants can be grown on in these for a couple of seasons. They are then fit for sale in the popular 12 to 18in (30 to 45cm) size, and well-branched without further repotting.

When camellias are potted up after about June, it is normal to pot into a smaller container as they are unlikely to fill their pots with roots before winter. They are then repotted the following spring into 2-litre pots. For the amateur, who probably has more time to devote to individual plants than the professional grower, there is certainly no harm, and possibly some advantage, in potting up in say, 4in (10cm) pots, repotting as required in 1-litre and then 2-litre pots. He can then keep a close watch on plant growth and root growth and condition. It must be borne in mind, though, that in the growing season camellias can quickly make a mass of new roots under good growing conditions and may need repotting sooner than one might expect.

Once potted up, the growing on of the young plants follows normal container growing – they will need checking, watching, watering and so on in the usual way. They may well need a spray against blackfly and greenfly which often set up home on the succulent new growth but, apart from this, they are pretty self-supporting. The great advantage of a slow release fertilizer is that the plants will not want any feeding for two seasons.

Nevertheless, camellias do have one or two special needs assuming our aim is to produce a well-branched, attractive plant as soon as possible. Some cultivars can achieve this on their own but they are in the minority, the majority need the helping hand of the gardener.

Almost immediately after they are potted the young plants will make their first flush of growth. To be honest, some will make this in the propagating tray before they are potted which is infuriating but a reminder that nature still reigns supreme. In any event, as soon as the potted plants make their first flush of growth, or, if they've done that in the propagating trays, the growing tip with a leaf or couple of leaves should be pinched out. This is generally called pinching out at the 'rabbit ear' stage.

How much should be pinched out depends on the amount of growth made. If it is five, six or so leaves one pinches out the little growing stem carrying about three leaves. This will be the case with a virile cultivar, such as 'Debbie'. If the new growth is only two or three leaves then one pinches out only the top. For pinching out the thumbnail is the best implement. If one has been dilatory and allowed the new growth to harden, then scissors or secateurs provide a cleaner cut.

The object of pinching out is to induce the young plant to make side branches from the dormant or semi-dormant buds in the axils of the leaves lower down. One stops the terminal growth in the hope and expectation that the arrest of the growth juices will transfer them to buds which have not been pinched out. Normally this works but there are a few varieties, and 'Donation' is a typical example, where growth is only transferred to the bud immediately below the point pinched out. Here the bud will grow, determined to replace the original leader pinched out. It must be dealt with in the same way as the original leader and pinched back and back again. Sooner or later the young plant will branch out lower down.

Camellias make at least two, and sometimes three, flushes of growth a year. Each one should be looked at as being the opportunity to shape, mould and shorten shoots so as to produce a fine compact shrub. Apart from this the growing of young camellias in containers is the same as for most other shrubs.

For the gardener who does not want to incur the expense of installing bottom heat it is still possible to propagate some camellias without heat, though this is something of an expert's field. Everything which has been said before as to taking and preparing the cuttings and the propagating mix applies. They are placed in a pot, a piece of bent wire (like an inverted U) is pushed into the pot and the whole covered with an inverted plastic bag. An elastic band is then placed round the pot and the plastic bag, sealing it in position.

The pot should be well watered before the plastic is placed in position and examined occasionally to ensure it is not drying out.

If the pot can be placed somewhere where it gets a little heat from below, such as over a radiator, this is an advantage. It must be allowed ample light (the airing cupboard is useless) – light is essential because the process of plant food production depends on photosynthesis which, of course, depends on light. Until a little success and experience has been obtained it is probably wise to try this method with the easy rooting varieties such as 'Donation', 'Debbie' and 'E. G. Waterhouse'. However, choice may be limited although, to be perfectly honest, it is not worth 'having a go' with pure *reticulatas* for the success rate will be nil.

5
PESTS, DISEASES AND VIRUSES

PESTS

There are not many pests which attack camellias grown in the United Kingdom. Greenfly and blackfly can be a nuisance when they attack the young growing tips of plants, particularly those grown in a greenhouse or conservatory. Their sap sucking efforts are bound to weaken the plant to some extent and certainly mar and disfigure young leaves attacked. There are a number of deterrent dusts and sprays obtainable from garden shops and garden centres.

Scale Insects

This is a much lesser known pest whose presence is frequently unknown until it is noticed that a camellia's leaves are becoming covered with a black sooty mould. The mould is, in fact, a fungus which grows on the honey dew excreted by the insects. These are difficult to see as they attach themselves closely to the underside of leaves and twigs. Apart from the black mould, their presence can be detected during the warmer weather by the little white cocoons, about ¼in (18mm) size or less, attached to the underside of leaves. These are the young in process of hatching out.

Scale insects are quite easily controlled by spraying with Malathion (an excellent control, too, for both greenfly and blackfly so that if one is buying an insecticide specially for these pests it makes a good choice). For scale insects it is used at double the strength needed for greenfly and blackfly and it is important to thoroughly spray the underside of the leaves where the pests are to be found.

Wingless Weevils

The main pest here is the vine weevil which can cause considerable damage to camellias. Roundish holes eaten in from the edge of leaves is a good indication of damage by adult weevils. Whilst this may mar the appearance of a plant it is rarely so widespread over a plant as to cause any permanent damage. Much more of a problem is the damage caused by the small white grubs of the weevil which can infest and feed in the roots of camellias. These can cause considerable damage, particularly to young container grown plants.

It is an unfortunate fact that vine weevil is very much on the increase and commonplace in many private gardens as well as nurseries. Until a few years ago Aldrin mixed in the potting compost gave effective control but Aldrin is now banned. Fortunately, we now have another chemical on the market called Suscon Green. This is mixed with the potting compost and, correctly used, appears to give total control of the grubs.

A number of other chemicals are said to be more or less effective. The best information I have ever come across for amateurs and professionals on vine weevil control is contained in Peter Cox's superb book *The Cultivation of Rhododendrons* (Batsford, 1993).

A comparatively new biological control by certain nematodes now easily obtainable is also most effective. These can either be incorporated in the potting compost or watered on to individual pots and containers. These nematodes, or minute eel worms, are completely harmless to plants, humans, pets and wildlife. They search out and attack only certain soil-dwelling, harmful insects, chief amongst which is the vine weevil. They parasitize vine weevil larvae by entering the pests (usually through natural body openings) and bacteria carried with the nematodes are released. These multiply within the host weevil larvae and, in so doing, provide a source of food for the nematode. The nematodes feed on this and multiply and then search for other larvae hosts. The larvae die approximately two days after nematode infection.

Nematodes are extremely easy to apply via a watering can. The amount to apply is clearly set out in the supplier's instructions. For example, the small commercial packs contain about 10 million nematodes in a sponge impregnated with them, or in some other container. The sponge or carton contents are immersed in water to make a stock solution which is diluted at a given ratio in a watering can to provide the correct dosage per plant. For example, the can may hold sufficient diluted mix to treat ten plants. A little practice soon enables one to judge one-tenth of the contents for each plant. The recommended rate for the brand we use is that the carton or sponge contents will treat 1,000 2 litre pots and other sizes proportionately.

Apart from this really sophisticated method, keen nocturnal amateur gardeners can have some measure of success going round their plants well after dark with a flashlight when a number of adult weevils can be caught. (One gentleman, enraged by the damage being caused to the roots of some of his favourite containerized camellias by these pests, devised his own method of control which was to knock each plant out of its pot, submerge the whole rootball in water and pick out and kill the little white grubs with a pair of tweezers as they surfaced, presumably for air!)

Red Spider

This mite is a major pest under glass. Fond of very many plants the chrysanthemum is one of its favourites. Camellias seem to come fairly low down on its shopping list of delectable juices but they are occasionally damaged. If these little red mites are seen infesting the plants spray with an appropriate insecticide. Malathion is one of several available. Here again a biological control by a predator mite is now available.

Caterpillars

These often place young camellia leaves fairly high on their shopping list. The damage they cause can usually be differentiated from the damage caused by vine weevil as on nice young succulent leaves they will eat right up to the midrib. It is surprising that with such voracious appetites many of them are so small as to be quite difficult to find. Admittedly their camouflage helps them. When found they should be picked off and destroyed. There is rarely a sufficiently bad infestation as to require spraying. If there is, then several insecticides are available.

Other Pests

Ants can be a problem if they get into the sand of the propagating beds and there build their nests. Mice, too, can cause quite a lot of damage digging around in the propagating trays and nipping off young buds and shoots. Almost always these are field mice which have come in from the cold and so one is loathe to kill them. However, if they do too much damage and cannot be dislodged they are easy to destroy with a bit of bread on a mouse trap.

DISEASES

Flower Blight

This is one of the most important diseases of camellias in the United States. However, it is virtually unknown in the United Kingdom. It is a fungus disease which attacks the flowers as they open and ultimately turns them brown. It is spread by infected flowers and petals falling on the ground and being left or overlooked.

No doubt it is for this reason that highly self-cleaning camellias, whose blooms shatter long before they become discoloured on the bush (such as 'Margaret Waterhouse'), are soundly condemned in the United States.

Botrytis

There seem to be few plants which, at all stages of growth, are immune to grey mould. It is not an important problem for outdoor plants but under glass, particularly in damp or humid conditions, it can quickly attack flower buds and young growth. Good ventilation helps to prevent it but if this fails one of the several proprietary chemicals mixed and sprayed according to the makers' instructions will generally clear it up.

Corky Scab

This disease, frequently called oedema, is not infectious and appears as a corky looking growth on the underside of the leaves. It is said to be a problem related to watering techniques but this is by no means certain. There is no real method of control and in due course the plant normally corrects whatever caused the trouble. It is nothing to worry about.

Salt Injury

There are two forms of this. It may result from a build up of salt in the soil due to fertilizer application combined with inadequate irrigation and is more prevalent with container grown plants than open ground ones. Occasional heavy irrigation can be used to leach away the salts.

Salt injury can also be caused, strange as it may seem, by salt blown in from the sea. Fortunately camellias are far less subject to damage from wind blown salt than are, for example, rhododendrons which simply will not tolerate it. In fact in many areas, and Cornwall comes to mind as one example, camellias can be seen thriving in close proximity to the sea although they are admittedly given some sort of shelter belt on planting.

In each case salt injury is indicated by a browning of the leaves beginning at the margins and progressing inwards. If really severe this death of the tissues of the leaves causes the whole leaf to die and fall. It is usually older leaves which first show the symptoms of salt injury.

Sunscald

This has been referred to earlier and is a common cause of the yellowing of camellia foliage. Varieties vary in their ability to maintain green leaves when heavily exposed. Some are particularly bad, some particularly good.

Sunscald can normally be recognized by the fact that leaves bleach, turn yellowish and then brown. Damage is normally worst in the central portions of the leaf as opposed to salt injury which normally affects the margins. In any event, if the plant is in full, or nearly full, exposure and shows yellowing of the leaves, sunscald is likely to be number one suspect.

Plants which suffer badly from sunscald are best moved into a more shaded situation. As always, the gardener has to compromise. Too much shade will give beautiful green foliage but few, if any, flowers; too much sun will give masses of flowers but poor foliage and, with susceptible varieties, sunscald of the leaves.

Apart from the fact that it may look unsightly, sunscald appears to do no harm to the plant.

Old Age

Before leaving the subject of yellowing and discloured leaves, it is worth returning to the subject of old age. It is surprising how many gardeners fail to appreciate that evergreens are no different from deciduous plants in that they still shed their leaves. The difference is that the evergreen does not shed them all at once.

Nevertheless, camellias, in common with all evergreens, do shed some of their leaves periodically. In the case of camellias they normally shed some of their leaves each year. Before shedding, these old leaves frequently become coloured with yellow, pale green, brown and even red in mosaic patterns. This process is normal and nothing to worry about but it is surprising how often people *are* worried and bring back leaves to the nursery in a state of real worry when all the plant is doing is following and fulfilling its natural processs.

Chlorosis

Too much lime in the soil may cause the yellowing of camellia leaves. The lime causes iron and manganese in the soil to exist in a chemical form. This locks them up so that they are not available to the plant. Lack of iron is indicated when the veins of a leaf are green but the interveinal areas yellow. Manganese deficiency is indicated by dead spots on the leaves and is less common. In addition to these a general paling or yellowing of the leaves may be due to lack of nitrogen.

In the first instance, unless the plant has been regularly fertilized, it is wise to feed it with a fertilizer high in nitrogen. If this does not improve things, then it is likely that the soil contains too much lime. If the chlorosis is not too widespread and bad the plant can be fed with chelated iron. If this does not cure the problem then it must be moved to a new site.

Monocaethia Karstenii

In recent years this fungus has become an increasing nuisance with camellias just as its very close relative *Pestalotiopsis sydowiana* has been with rhododendrons.

It causes most damage at the propagating stage but may be a problem in the first year after potting up. In the cutting containers some leaves turn yellow then brown – sometimes brown straight away – and drop off. The disease rapidly spreads to other leaves and affects also growth buds and the stem. Whether rooted or not the cutting dies. The disease will rapidly spread throughout the containers. Affected leaves left in the container provide an ideal way of spreading spores from the fungus.

After much experience with this propagation curse it seems clear that many cultivars are highly susceptible to *Monocaethia* infection whereas others are highly resistant.

The fungus can also be a problem in the first year of the young plant's life when it can cause browning of leaves, leaf drop and finally death of a young plant. Young plants (like human beings) seem to be particularly susceptible if they come under stress, that is to say, if they are subjected to too much heat or too much or not enough water.

(Growers are heavily indebted to Dr Pauline Smith of the former Glasshouse Crops Research Institute in West Sussex and Dr Margaret Scott at the Efford Experimental Horticultural Station at Lymington, Hampshire, both of whom have done much work in connection with this fungal pest.)

It is said that *Monocaethia* is endemic on most adult camellias and causes them no damage. If this is correct, it is clearly difficult to obtain untreated propagating material which is free from the fungus. Accordingly, it is a wise precaution to spray plants which are to be used for propagating (commonly called stock plants) with an appropriate fungicide during the growing season.

Some propagators prefer to submerge their cuttings in a container of fungicide before inserting them in the propagating medium which has also been drenched with fungicide but one seems to get the same control results by drenching the inserted cuttings and propagating containers from a watering can. Benlate gives a measure of control but Octave is much more effective.

After potting up, it is a wise precaution to spray the young plants every month or so during the growing season with one or other of these fungicides.

Root Rot

The culprit causing this problem is a fungus called *Phytophthora cinnamomi*. The incidence of the troubles caused by it seems to be considerably on the increase and a heavy loss of plants, including camellias and rhododendrons, result from it, particularly in nurseries.

Some camellia cultivars are more susceptible than others. This particularly applies to the smaller ones such as 'Pink Perfection' (syn. 'Frau Minna Seidle'), 'Herme' and 'Pope Pius' ('Prince Eugene Napoleon'). Signs of an attack include yellowing of the foliage followed by stunting and the wilting and subsequent death of new growth. Examination of the camellia roots shows these have turned brown and rotted. New roots are sometimes formed but these in turn are attacked.

With older plants the effect of the disease may be the die back of one or more branches and the plant may survive, particularly if remedial measures are undertaken. With younger ones, an attack is usually followed by death of the plant.

High soil moisture favours the incidence and spread of root rot and, accordingly, improvement of soil drainage is of primary importance in control. Overcrowding of plants, particularly containerized plants, also appears to favour the spread of the disease.

Nursery losses can be severe and, accordingly, the addition of Aaterra to the potting up mixture has become a standard recommended practice. Young containerized plants which may have contracted the disease can often be saved provided the disease has not progressed too far, by a thorough watering with Filex applied as a drench. As usual, there are, no doubt, other equally satisfactory chemicals on the market.

VIRUSES

Both leaf and flower variegation may be due to several viral infections. These usually appear as yellow irregular blotches in the leaves and white or other variegation in the flowers. White flowers do not show any symptoms.

Viral diseases are transmitted by grafting or budding on virus infected stock. Despite what is sometimes said, the better opinion seems to be that they are not spread by insects. Perfectly healthy camellias do 'sport' at times when a plant bearing solid coloured blooms produces variegated ones. By propagating from the wood of the 'branch sport' one may obtain a camellia all of whose blooms are of the sport form. However, this does not happen all that often and it has nothing to do with viral infection. Because of this there has been much deliberate infection with virus to obtain these colour breaks, particularly in the United States. In other words, plants with solid coloured blooms are deliberately grafted on virus-infected stock to obtain this result. As a result of this it is highly likely that many of the variegated forms of solid flowered cultivars are, in fact, virus-infected. This does not mean to say that these plants, even though infected, will bear yellow mottled leaves. Some never do, some may produce the occasional affected leaf and nothing more.

In general, viral infection does no harm to the plant although yellowed leaves may suffer sunscald more easily.

There is no treatment or cure for virus infection, the only thing is to try to obtain virus-free plants. In view of what is said above about the deliberate grafting on virus infected plants, the reader will appreciate that this may be extremely difficult if not impossible. Virus-free plants can be produced by complicated procedures such as heat treatment but these are for the scientist and laboratory and far beyond the scope of this book.

Mention has already been made of salt injury and sunscald, both of which may cause some yellowing of leaves. To them may be added old age in the leaf and chlorosis as we have seen. In addition, plants may have genetic mutations causing similar symptoms or physiological problems which do likewise. Elegans comes to mind as a plant in this last category.

This gives us six causes for the yellowing of leaves quite apart from viral infection. Accordingly, it is extremely unwise to start shouting viral infection as soon as one sees yellow leaves or leaves with yellow blotches on the plant. Whilst an experienced grower may be able to sort out salt injury, sunscald, old age and chlorosis there is no way of differentiating with certainty between a virus infection and a genetic mutation, apart from complicated tests.

6
HYBRIDIZATION

THEORY

It is no exaggeration to say that in the course of half a century camellia blooms, in common with many others, have been changed out of all recognition, except in basic characteristics, due to hybridization.

To a very large extent these changes have been the result of efforts made by the amateur grower. This is particularly true of hybridization of the camellia and the rhododendron, probably due to the fact that the time lapse between producing a new plant of commercial value and marketing it in quantity has been so great.

In comparatively recent years this has changed greatly with rhododendron production. Commercial growers, such as Peter Cox at Glendoick Gardens, Perthshire, have done much valuable hybridizing and in the United States others, such as David Leach and Harold Greer, have been responsible for a flood of new hybrids. The reason is possibly the fact that propagation of rhododendrons in their thousands by tissue culture is now commonplace whereas, so far, a similar degree of success with this technique has not been achieved with camellias.

Anyone perusing the pages of the *Camellia Nomenclature* book, published by the Californian Camellia Society – which has over 150 pages devoted to cultivars of *C. japonica* alone and descriptions of most other species, varieties and hybrid cultivars – is bound to be impressed by the number of outstanding plants produced by a comparatively small band of hybridists. From the United States such names as D. I. Feathers, J. H. Asper, W. L. Ackerman and W. E. Lammerts, to name but a few, are known worldwide. The same can be said of Prof E. G. Waterhouse from Australia, Les Jury, Felix Jury and B. W. Doak of New Zealand and Miss Carlyon of the United Kingdom. In addition, of course, the names of J. C. Williams and Col Stevenson Clarke – who produced the three great plants of 'J. C. Williams', 'Donation' and 'Salutation' – will ensure that the names of United Kingdom hybridizers will live for ever.

Perhaps we should clarify what we mean by a hybrid. A hybrid is the offspring of a cross between (i) two different species, (ii) a hybrid and any species, (iii) two hybrids. When we cross the offspring of any of these crosses with either of its parents, this is known as a back cross. When we cross two of the offspring of a cross with each other, this is known as an intercross.

To be of value, rather than just a piece of fun, any cross made to produce a hybrid should have some goal in mind. It is generally agreed that there are four main areas in hybridization into which we should inject our knowledge, drive, ability and finances (be the last mentioned large or small). These are as follows:

1.   The production of new colours, particularly blue and yellow. Yellow would, of course, open the way to pure creams, oranges and so on. This is highly desirable as every true gardener yearns to grow his favourite plant in the one colour not available! Your delphinium grower will never be content with his beautiful blues and their *alba* forms. He must have reds and now that he more or less has them, no doubt wants orange and buff.
2.   The production of plants with notable fragrance. This is an understandable goal. In so many peoples' minds flowers and fragrance are synonymous. Some say that the blooms of the great hybrid *Rhododendron loderi* are too large or too floppy or have some other inane criticism but they have to admit that those great inflorescences, where each individual bloom is almost the size of a trumpet lily, combined with one of the most beautiful fragrances to be found among flowers, must amount to an outstanding plant.
3.   The breeding of plants which have greater cold hardiness. This is really the most important aim of all. For example, Europeans need plants which will not only laugh at the cold winters of so much of Europe but which will set flower buds even where sun is scanty, hold them through the cold days and open them when the warmer late spring weather comes. If we could achieve all this by breeding then most of Europe would become an area fine and suitable for camellias and there may come a time when successful camellia culture could be extended well north of Inverness.

No doubt all this will be achieved. For example, there are many areas of the United States which are too cold for camellia culture, yet more hybridization is taking place there than anywhere else. This cold hardiness, whereby camellias can become commonplace garden flowers in vast areas where they are not successful today, must be the principle objective, far more important than producing blue and orange blooms or blooms with a scent like a lily.
4.   The development of new plant forms, particularly smaller,

more floriferous plants, in keeping with today's smaller gardens. We need something which will do for the camellia what the Yakushimanum hybrids have done for the rhododendron. In any event, it is essential that the introduction of new, improved and attractive camellias continues on an on-going basis. Nobody has realized better than the rose growers that to maintain interest and to attract new devotees, there must be a continual regular introduction of new plants.

There are various lines in breeding which may achieve any one or more of these four main objectives. How one sets about obtaining a true blue camellia must be a matter for considerable informed discussion but how one obtains a yellow camellia may be easier, in theory, to suggest. It seems that that great yellow species C. chrysantha is unwilling to pass on its golden glory through interspecific breeding. If this is so, then we are bound to be thrown back on selective breeding. It was said, many years ago, that by the selective breeding of rice, namely by selecting the most cold hardy forms, crossing these and selecting the most cold hardy forms and so on, Russian scientists had succeeded in producing a strain of rice which would grow successfully as a viable crop further north and in colder conditions than had ever been known before.

Similarly, one can look at the work of that great lily hybridist, Jan de Graaf, who produced a golden *Lilium regale*. Now *regale* was always yellow in the throat and by dint of taking those with the most yellow and crossing them in vast numbers, growing or selecting the most yellow for the next cross, great patience and great effort resulted in the true golden *regale*.

Such a task may be even more difficult with camellias, for lilies can flower from seed in two to three years whereas camellias can take about three to seven. Nevertheless, there are camellias which tend to be far more yellow than others. Specifically bred to obtain a yellow colour are 'Jury's Yellow', 'Brushfield's Yellow' and 'Gwenneth Morey'. In addition, there are a number of white camellias which display a considerable yellow colouring in the centre. Such well-known varieties as the old 'Madame Charles Blard' and the somewhat new 'Lulu Belle' come to mind. When they first open the yellow colouring they display is little short of that of 'Jury's Yellow' although it may not last as long. There are a number of others which have this partial yellow caste. A large scale selective breeding programme, based on the best of all these, would, in time, almost certainly bring success and would achieve the golden camellia of so many enthusiasts' dreams.

Apart from selective breeding, the future must lie in inter-specific hybrids, and hybrids between a species and a hybrid; the simple reason for this is that there are so many species available, any one of which may have a characteristic that is really desirable to the hybridist.

Some eighty or so recognized species have been described, along with about twenty unclassified species. Of these, about forty have been introduced into the United States. Many of these must have desirable characteristics and be worthy of inclusion in various breeding programmes. In fact, there in particular, much inter-specific breeding has already taken place.

The first interspecific hybrids produced came from England when crosses between *C. saluenensis* and *C. japonica* produced the *williamsii* hybrids. The same cross has been made many times since, notably in New Zealand, Australia and the United States. They have been outstandingly successful in that they combined new colours and forms with greater hardiness and better habit.

The *williamsii* cross was an enormous success evidenced by the fact that in the United Kingdom today *C.* × 'Donation' is probably still the best selling camellia. 'Donation' is to camellias what 'Pink Pearl' is to rhododendrons. In each case one can criticize the colour, the form and so on of the flowers and yet, in the eyes of the gardening public, they reign supreme.

It was inevitable that following the huge success of the *williamsii* hybrids, when new *C. reticulatas* were introduced from China into the United States in 1948, breeders were spurred into crossing these with *C. japonica, C. saluenensis, C.* × *williamsii* and so on.

An obvious candidate for improvement was *C. reticulata*. Although it produces the largest and showiest blooms of remark-able substance, it has an open straggly habit combined with extremely suspect hardiness. On the other hand, it seems to tolerate or possibly enjoy hotter and drier conditions than most *japonicas* would favour. In consequence, any hybrid which could retain those wonderful *reticulata* blooms but combine them with improved plant characteristics such as bushiness and greater hardiness was bound to be a success. This success was achieved by breeders and still continues through breeding programmes today.

Further interspecific crosses were made following the introduc-tion of further new species (*see* Table 1 in Appendix I). Apart from cultivars of interspecific origin (first generation hybrids) it was inevitable that hybridists should also work with second and back-cross generation hybrids (*see* Table 2 in Appendix I).

It is certain that infinitely more crosses made have resulted in failure rather than success but it is the patient plodding, determination and refusal to give up of the plant breeder which finally brings its reward, though not in financial terms.

Crosses should be made with a specific purpose in view – to produce a hardier plant, for example – and, apart from the fact that it is undoubtedly interesting, there is not a great deal of point in making random crosses or growing on any old chance seed. Apart from being able to say 'I grew that from seed', nothing has been achieved unless the plant produced is an improvement on what is already available and that is unlikely with a chance cross.

Accordingly, the would-be hybridist, unless he is merely interested in growing something from seed, is well advised to decide on the goal he is trying to achieve and before wasting too much time in preliminary crosses to find out which of these have already been made. Keen fellow hybridists are normally happy to exchange propagating material or plants.

Apart from this, a lot of preliminary work is necessary to find which plants are heavy seed bearers, which are compatible and which are not. This can involve going into the subject in far greater depth than the scope of this book could justify but at the same time can be of absorbing interest. One point is that a knowledge of the chromosomes is essential to the understanding of the breeding potential of different species. Chromosomes carry the genes which determine the inheritance of plant characteristics. It is usually true to say that crossing two clones which have the same chromosome count is easier than trying to cross plants with different counts. The basic chromosome number of the camellia is $x = 15$. The largest number of cultivars are either diploid ($2x = 30$) or hexaploid ($6x = 90$) but there are others which are triploids ($3x = 45$) and other combinations.

Chromosomes can be counted but this is a task for the laboratory and not the gardener. The chromosome count is not the only problem but the mention of it is to show that random efforts at hybridizing are unlikely to bring any great success. For that, some in-depth knowledge is necessary. Much of this knowledge already exists so it should be tapped and understood before a serious start is made.

In recent years the only successful hybridizing which has been carried out in the United Kingdom has been that of the late Miss Gillian Carlyon of Tregrehan, Cornwall. However, in the Antipodes and the United States a great deal of work has been done. By joining one or more of these countries' camellia societies the door to much of that knowledge can be opened to the amateur breeder.

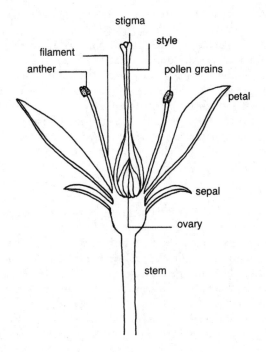

The parts of the camellia flower.

PRACTICE

So far, only theoretical matters, aims, problems, compatibility and so on have been dealt with in this chapter. We must now deal with the practical side of hybridization.

The camellia flower is bisexual, that is to say, it has both the male and female reproductive organs. The stamen is the male reproductive organ and consists of the anther which bears the pollen grains which are on a filament. The pistil is the female reproductive organ and this consists of the ovary at the base which continues into the style and ends with the stigma.

When open pollination takes place, pollen from an anther is carried by insects or the wind on to a receptive stigma. The pollen grains grow down the style and fertilize the ovule in the ovary. With the camellia, as with the other bisexual flowers, fertilization may be either by self-fertilization or cross-fertilization. In the former case the pollen comes from the anthers or one of the same blooms as the pistil; in the latter from the anthers of another plant altogether.

When seed is collected from an open pollinated plant there is no way of knowing where the pollen came from and, consequently, one knows only one of the two parents involved in the seed production process. This is, of course, useless to the hybridizer although growing open pollinated seed may be an amusing and, occasionally, worthwhile exercise. The hybridist wishes to know for sure that the pollen used to fertilize the seed-bearing parent comes from the plant of his choice.

Producing a Hybrid

This is achieved by hand-pollination by the following steps:

1.   A bud in the right condition which is to be the seed parent must be selected on the plant. A bud is in the right condition when it is swollen and about to open but not open. This is to ensure that the stigma has not already been contaminated with pollen from an unknown plant.

2.   The bud must next be emasculated, which is the process of removing the stamens before the anthers produce ripe pollen. Failure to do so may result in self-pollination. Self-pollination could still take place even though the bud was placed in a muslin or similar bag to prevent the entry of insects which might be bearing unknown pollen. To emasculate the bud it is necessary to remove the petals so as to expose the reproductive organs. The petals can be cut off with either a razor blade or an extremely sharp pair of small scissors. Whichever is used, the bud must be held firmly and a cut encircling the entire bud made at a point just above the green calyx. It must be just deep enough to remove the petals. With a pair of tweezers all the stamens are removed exposing the pistil.

3.   Place the desired pollen on the stigma of the emasculated bud. There are a number of ways to achieve this:

(a) If there is plenty of pollen the flower can be removed and taken to the stigma and lavishly dusted on.

(b) A few stamens can be removed from the pollen parent by gripping the filament in a pair of tweezers and carried to the prepared flower when the anthers bearing the pollen are wiped across the stigma.

(c) A camel-hair brush, matchstick or even one's finger can be dipped into the pollen and then dabbed on the stigma.

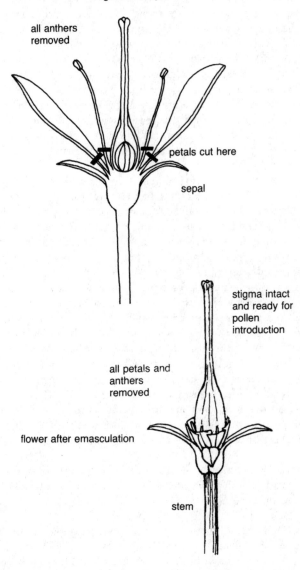

stigma and style left

all anthers
removed

petals cut here

sepal

stigma intact
and ready for
pollen
introduction

all petals and
anthers
removed

flower after emasculation

stem

Emasculation.

It is important that any instruments used in the above process are cleaned with alcohol before using them on another cross. Care must be taken not to injure the stigma but enough pollen must be placed on it so that it can be seen with the naked eye.

4. Immediately the cross has been made it should be labelled. A plastic looplock label is excellent, written with a labelling pen and hung as close as possible to the bud. There must be no room for error subsequently as to which bud was crossed. The label should bear the date the cross was made followed by the name of the seed bearing parent which is universally written first followed by a × and then the pollen parent. Other information can be written on the reverse of the label.

5. It is wise to cover the pollinated flower with a small paper (not plastic) bag which can be fixed to the twig with a twist tie. This is to prevent stray pollen being deposited on the stigma by insects or the wind. Many hybridists maintain that the chance of this happening is so small that this is not worthwhile. However, if one is making only a limited number of crosses it is better to be safe. Fertilization is completed after about ten days when the bag can be removed.

6. Assuming fertilization has been successful a seed capsule will form. When this is about the size of a marble it should be encased in a small piece of porous material such as a piece of nylon tights. A square of this tied over the seedpod allows the capsule to expand and will prevent the loss of seeds when the pod ripens and drops them. It may do something, too, to prevent grey squirrels or birds stealing the seeds as soon as they assess them to be edible.

7. It is advisable to keep a written record of the crosses which have been made, human memory being as fickle as it is. There is nothing more annoying than to find after several years that one has no recollection or record of the parents of a seedling.

The above is a complete account of the steps it is necesary to take to produce a hybrid. There are, however, a number of other matters to be borne in mind:

1. In hybridizing it is of fundamental importance to have an objective. As mentioned earlier, fragrance, cold resistance, new colours such as yellow, blue or true lavender, outstanding blooms of a new form or extreme floriferousness top the list.

2. Try to make use of the work of other hybridizers by reading all you can and possibly obtaining propagating material from them. This is well worthwhile if one is following a breeding programme such as crossing (A × B) × (B × C) particularly when one bears in

mind that a new hybrid can take anything from three to seven years to produce a bloom. In addition, much valuable information can be obtained (and it is normally readily given) as to which plants set seed easily and which do not.

3.   In the United Kingdom hybridizing should be done under greenhouse conditions. This is because a temperature of at least 60°F (15°C) is required if success in fertilization is to be obtained. In addition, most hybridizers have found that the optimum time for hand pollination is during the two weeks following the peak of the blooming season.

4.   Plenty of pollen must be used and this can be successfully stored in small airtight containers. Suitable ones can normally be begged or bought from a chemist's shop dispensing department. Equally, containers which have styrofoam moisture collecting pads (such as Alka Seltzer containers) can be used. Whatever is used the container should be sealed and placed in a refrigerator. The pollen should be warmed by placing the container under an electric lamp (about 1ft (0.3m) away) for a few minutes before use. The point of storing the pollen is to enable crosses to be made between the early flowering plants and late flowering ones. Bear in mind the advice given earlier to use plenty of pollen when making the cross. The viability of pollen from plants has been shown to be less than 10 per cent so the amount used, remembering this, is of the utmost importance.

5.   It is good practice to repeat the cross made the following day when the stigma may be more receptive. It is also good practice to make the same cross on a number of different blooms so as to obtain a greater quantity of viable seed. In addition, if it is possible, many hybridists repeat the cross in reverse using the former seed parent as pollen parent and pollen parent as seed parent. However, this will often present difficulties as many of the doubles and complex paeony and rose form doubles are known to be bad seed setters and to have pistils which are difficult to locate.

6.   Over the years much knowledge has been gained as to plants which are good seed setters or are otherwise preferable to work with. Turning to interspecific crosses, it has been found that some are better as seed parents, some as pollen parents. For example, *C. reticulata* is generally better used as a seed parent whereas *C. lutchuensis* is a bad seed parent but a reasonably good pollen parent. Much useful information as to successful interspecific crosses is contained in *The Camellia* published by R. L. Bryan Company, Columbia, South Carolina. Anyone interested in hybridizing could not do better than to consult this book.

7
BUYING CAMELLIAS

Camellias exist in many, many different forms. In colour they range from dead white through creamy white to palest pink, then through all the shades of pink from pale to deepest, not forgetting lavender pinks on the way. Opinions differ as to where rosy pink ends and light red begins but all the colours are there in the camellia, the reds giving true light reds, geranium reds, blood reds, blue reds and nearly black reds. In addition, there are many with white centres turning to palest pink approaching the outer petals and vice versa. Some, such as 'Nuccio's Pearl', 'Nuccio's Jewel' and 'Erin Farmer', to mention but a few of many, are of such ethereal beauty as to be almost unbelievable. There are whites with red margins, pinks with white margins and, of course, a great range of bi-colours, white splashed and blotched red and vice versa, pale pink splashed and blotched darker pink and vice versa, pinks blotched white and white blotched pink. What more can one ask? If one needs the elusive yellow and blues then there are many complimentary plants to provide them, the cytisus and genista for the yellows, the rhododendrons for both the yellows and blues readily come to mind.

When one is selling plants to the gardening public, it becomes clear that, apart from among those gardeners who already know about camellias, there is great confusion as to flower forms. One is often told the purchaser wants a double bloom. It is only after showing a few blooms, or photographs if it is out of season, that it becomes clear that everything, apart from a pure single, is considered to be a double in the purchaser's mind, be it semi-double, anemone, paeony, rose form double or formal double.

Hence, the first two points which the purchaser should decide upon are the colour and the floral form he wants. There are a number of other considerations: does one want an early, mid season or late flowering plant? Many purchasers will buy several plants so as to cover as long a flowering period as possible. In some countries, such as the United States for example, very early and very late flowering plants are highly rated because, by careful choice, camellia blooms can last over an eight months period. In the United Kingdom a word of caution is necessary. No doubt one can find camellias to bloom in October or November and December but with such an unpredictable climate each or any of those months could be freezing or gale or storm swept, when the poor camellia blooms are only half their normal size, battered by the weather or destroyed by severe frost. The lates do not normally suffer such extremes of bad weather but it is worth bearing in mind that a good hot spell coinciding with the flowering will mean that it is over all too soon. Camellias are just like the rhododendrons in this respect. A March bloomer will normally remain an effective flowering shrub for weeks. A late May, June, July or August flowerer, if caught by a really hot spell, can be over in a few days.

The purchaser should next get clear in his mind the purpose for which he wants camellias. Does he want one which produces a few, but magnificent, cut blooms? Are they wanted for a hedge or informal barrier? Are they to be grown indoors or outdoors, in containers or in the open ground? Are they to be in house corners or under windows or grown against or espaliered against a wall or are they to be used virtually as ground cover or trailing over low walls?

One can think of other uses but the above is a good enough selection. It is important to bear in mind that a shrub which is suitable as a large growing plant to blot out some unfortunate view would be highly unsuitable for container culture and that the reverse equally applies.

Plant form and leaf form are also important. Some camellias have what can only be described as a straggly form of growth, many of the *reticulatas* come into this category. Others are extremely compact, such as 'Cecile Brunazzi' (pink) and 'Reg Ragland' (red). Some have enormous leaves, such as 'Coronation' (white) others many very small ones such as the *sasanquas*. Some even have fish tail leaves.

For the beginner who wants one or two camellias for general garden planting or growing in containers, the best course is to find a reliable nurseryman who has a good, wide selection of plants and accept his advice. This is particularly true when one is tackling the problem of hardiness, flowering ability and geographical location. There are a number of camellias (mostly hybrids) which will grow and flower successfully outdoors in cool uplands but there are a mass which would be quite useless. A good nurseryman knows which are which.

If the purchaser is acquiring plants for outdoor planting, it is of the very greatest importance to look at as many outdoor plantings in bloom as possible. It is not generally realized that both the form and colour of camellia flowers can vary considerably on identical plants if one is grown indoors and one outdoors.

Over the years there must have been many disappointed purchasers who bought rhododendrons after seeing them only at the Chelsea or other flower shows. It often happens that, in order to get the plants to peak flowering for such shows, they have to go into hot or cold conditions. In particular, when forced open in heat their colours are not true but frequently considerably paler so that the palest pink which was chosen will flower outdoors subsequently a much darker colour.

The same situation applies with camellias. There are some which are the most beautiful very pale flesh pink indoors which, grown outdoors, are little more than off white. Quite extraordinary things can happen – half a batch of C. *japonica* 'Miss Charleston', which is a magnificent deep red, all flowered medium pink. In case a labelling error had occurred, they were put to one side and the following year flowered true.

Similarly, there are variations in flower form when, for example, a semi-double outdoors flowers full paeony form when grown indoors; or C. *japonica* 'Joshua E. Youtz', considered one of the finest formal double whites outdoors, flowers paeony form indoors.

These variations can be confusing to a novice and, here again, a knowledgeable nurseryman can be a great benefit. Of course, even he can at times be misleading, for different people have such different ideas of colour. What some call a very deep pink, others describe as rosy red or light red. Short of having a copy of the Royal Horticultural Society's Colour Chart handy and everything checked against this, there is really no answer to this particular problem. There is nothing more difficult to describe than colour.

There are a few practical points to look for when selecting a particular plant out of, say, a batch of the same plants. Examine the leaves to make sure that they look healthy but don't expect them all to be glossy dark green. Very many hybrids have dull green leaves, often reticulated, and not all C. *japonica* cultivars have glossy, dark green leaves. Some are naturally quite a light green, others are large, dull and leathery such as C. *japonica* 'Gauntlettii' (syn. 'Lotus' and 'Sodegakushi') and 'Coronation'. However, the leaves should not be a pale greeny yellow colour which generally means the plant has been starved.

Next, take a good look at the shape of the plant in general. It is a great advantage if it is branched fairly close to the ground as it means it will get off to a good start. Once planted out most camellias will naturally produce low branches from embryo buds if given good conditions. This is just as well as some seem determined not to branch low down for the first year or so. Individual taste naturally plays a part in this as many purchasers seem to prefer a few inches, perhaps half a dozen or so, of bare stem before branching begins. It is always a good sign if one can see that the plant has been cut back on some branches as it indicates good nursery practice with a view to obtaining good shaping.

It is sometimes said that it is a bad sign if surface roots are visible or if the surface of the container has a slight covering of moss or algae. None of these criticisms is true. Another suggestion, one reads in not too well informed articles, is that a good saleable plant should not have been recently repotted and that to check this the purchaser should try lifting the plant by its branches to see if it comes out of the pot. This suggestion is absolute rubbish and the would-be purchaser certainly will not be thanked by the nurseryman if he starts pulling plants out of their containers. In any normal nursery, re-potting is a continuous process throughout reasonable weather conditions. If it is not done plants would not grow on so there is always a chance that a particular plant may have been recently re-potted. As a side comment, plants should always be lifted by their containers or with hands under the root ball and never by catching hold of the plant itself. In particular, plants such as camellias and rhododendrons should never be picked up by grasping them around the stem just above soil level. Rhododendrons grown on their own roots, as most should be, and camellias tend to make a number of side branches from ground level. If a plant is grasped around the stem at the point where these branches will form, any tiny, sometimes almost invisible, buds which are starting to grow out will be broken and destroyed.

USING THE PLANTS

The modern small garden tends to have a paved area or patio nearest to the house, a modest central lawn beyond, sometimes incorporating a pool, and shrub and flowers borders around the lawn. This meets the average requirements for a sitting area, namely the patio, a recreation area, namely the lawn, and a growing area, namely the flower beds. Vegetable growing, rightly or wrongly, seems to have declined and the accent in planting is maximum effect for minimum effort and maintenance.

The camellia fits admirably into this type of garden layout. The house itself, including the garage or car port, offers great opportunities for planting. Narrowish spaces between windows will be greatly embellished by the planting of upright narrow columnar growing camellias such as 'Joshua E. Youtz' or 'E. G. Waterhouse'. Larger areas can grow the more open speading plant such as several of the *reticulatas* and their hybrids and such *C. japonicas* as 'Drama Girl' (pink) and 'Grand Prix' (red). All these will yield enormous eye catching blooms. Low areas under windows are ideal for some of the *sasanquas*, several of which tend to be trailing or low growing.

Nothing looks more effective on the patio than camellias in containers. In addition, when paving is laid, it is an excellent idea to omit the odd paving stone here and there (or half stone, according to size used) and to prepare the soil in the exposed area for planting. With an existing patio a stone should be lifted and the soil beneath improved. These gaps in the paving will provide excellent planting places for camellias which, once installed, will be largely self sufficient, particularly for watering, compared with plants in containers. For this type of planting use should be made of the small dense growing plants such as *C. japonica* 'High Hat' or 'San Dimas'.

The garage or car port are also areas where one or two or more camellias can create a vast improvement on the bare walls, empty spaces and generally utilitarian look which is all too often seen. Two or three camellias planted as an informal hedge at the back end of the car port will quite quickly make a fine barrier to break the worst of the weather driving in on the car.

When planting close to the walls of buildings there are two points to bear in mind. First, a check should be made of the eaves above. If these are very deep, and they do vary enormously, it can happen that the ground below is bone dry for several feet out from the wall. This can vary with aspect and local factors but should always be checked. Second, plants must not be installed too close to the walls of buildings for similar reasons that the ground there may be too dry for their comfort. If they are to be espaliered they should still be planted 2½ to 3ft (0.75 to 1m) out from the wall and then pinned back to it.

A short path, such as one linking a paved area to the lawn, can be greatly improved by a pair of matching camellias on each side at one end or the other or at both ends. If the scope of the garden is sufficient to enable one to create a vista, then there is no finer focal point at the end of it than a camellia, outstanding for its fine foliage out of season and for its magnificent blooms in season.

A sizeable rockery which is bound to be composed of low

growing plants can be given considerable added interest by the planting in its immediate vicinity of a late, slender, columnar growing camellia such as 'Charles Colbert' (pink) and indeed these slender, upright growing camellias are of great value as accent plants in many garden areas.

Camellias planted in the flower beds themselves are ideal. More often than not such beds back on to the boundaries of the garden where some sort of hedge or barrier is required in any event. Most medium to fairly strong growing camellias are ideal for this, providing an informal hedge in due time of whatever height its owner requires. Plants can easily be kept down to heights of 5 to 8ft (1.5 to 2.4m) by a minimum of pruning and their depth from front to back likewise restricted.

Used in this way, the dark green glossy leaves of the *japonicas* make a fine background foil to set off the contrasting foliage and flowers of the plants in front of them. As an alternative, a small bed can be set aside solely for camellias, tallest at the back, shortest at the front, with possibly a few very dwarf evergreen azaleas bordering the path or lawn.

Mention has been made of camellias used as an informal hedge or barrier when, apart from feeding, the only maintenance needed is the occasional going over with clippers to prevent them outgrowing their pre-determined space. Apart from this, camellias can be used to create a fairly formal hedge to divide one part of the garden from another. Some, such as 'Tiptoe' (pale pink) are ideal for this purpose and require an absolute minimum of clipping and maintenance.

So far, we have been considering the smaller garden and making various suggestions for that. They clearly apply equally to those who have half an acre, an acre or several acres of land but, with more space, the scope is obviously wider. For instance, a pair of camellias planted each side of the entrance porch is ideal provided there is sufficient space for them. A house in larger grounds probably will have this, whereas a semi-detached suburban residence may not.

With more space there is room for special plantings such as a rose bed and if there is room for that there should be room for planting a camellia walk. Such a walk can be most rewarding and a never failing source of interest and beauty over several months of the year.

The plants chosen must be selected with care so as to obtain complimentary and contrasting forms and colours and also a fairly even rate of growth for it does not make life easier to have a camellia which makes only 3ft (0.9m) of growth in five years planted alongside one which makes three times that. When planting such a walk it is of paramount importance to ensure that the walk is wide enough. This inevitably means that, when first planted, the space between the two rows will look far too wide. The point is that, although when planted each row may be only 2ft (0.6m) wide taking up only 2ft (0.6m) of the space from the trunk in each row, in due course each row may well be 8ft (2.4m) wide taking up 8ft (2.4m) of the path space left.

With the larger garden, too, there is more scope to use larger growing shrubs such as the camellia as accent plants. Examples are those that have very unusual shaped leaves, such as 'Francie L' (whose long narrow leaves look nothing like most people's idea of a camellia), or the single white form (possibly) of 'Kingyo Tsubaki' or 'C. M. Coates' (pink) both of which bear attractive and interesting fish tail leaves. Apart from these, others such as 'Elegant Beauty' whose young growth is pink to red, have much to offer apart from their magnificent blooms.

Large gardens often include a piece of woodland or small copse. Here the possibilities are almost limitless for such conditions are the natural habitat for the majority of camellias and very many rhododendrons. The success obtained in woodland gardening or, perhaps one should say, the speed at which one attains success is dependent, to a great extent, on the type of woodland. Beech and birch, lovely as they may look, have a great mass of surface roots which demand first choice on moisture and nourishment. They are bad neighbours whereas oaks are good neighbours. With experience, one gets to know which trees one can live with as a woodland gardener and which one cannot. When the tree canopy gets too dense, as it ultimately will, then it is the bad neighbour which must be the first to go.

The whole problem with woodland gardening is to keep a balance, and a correct balance at that, between the overhead canopy which gives shade and shelter and the light which the shrubs need if they are to grow and flower properly. Too much shade whilst beneficial in suppressing the grasses and weeds is detrimental in suppressing much wanted blooms. Too much sun whilst developing blooms also produces weeds galore and a lack of branch canopy (needed to keep off the worst of the frosts).

The aim must always be to create a woodland garden not a garden in a wood. In the latter case, the perimeter shelter of woodland is used to provide ideal conditions in a centre area which has largely been cleared. One must, above all, understand the nature of woodland, realize that it is never static and that, like all of nature, it grows and dies and replaces itself. The plants we instal must become an integral part of that cycle. They must take their proper place there to grow, we hope not to die, but to be replaced or added to by further limited plantings.

If we have space but no woodland and no copse it remains open to us to create a copse of our own. Flowering cherries, crabs, magnolias, stewartias, styrax, halesia and a host of other trees, including some native trees, can quite quickly provide shade similar to that valued so highly in a native copse. Once more, we want to concentrate on trees which are good neighbours. In this connection it is worth remembering that all members of *Leguminosae* (the pea family) such as brooms, genistas and laburnum are the best of neighbours for, with their ability to produce nitrogen, they put more into the soil than they take out.

Wherever camellias are planted it is, primarily, for the beauty of their flowers. They should be planted where they can be seen at close quarters and duly appraised and admired.

CORSAGES

The two main problems in using a camellia bloom, or blooms, for a corsage are its lack of a suitable stem and the fact that the petals are only loosely attached to the calyx. There are, however, ways by which these shortcomings can be overcome. All that is required are three lengths of thin florist's wire about 9 or 10in (22.5 to 25cms) long and a length of green florist's tape.

Next, obtain a perfect bloom, or blooms, of the chosen camellia and carefully twist this off at its stem, taking care to leave the growth bud intact below. Take one length of the florists' wire and carefully push this through the petals and calyx and then the petals on the other side. Repeat this with another piece of wire, pushing this through at right angles to the first.

The two wires are gathered together below the flower to form a stem. The third piece of wire is then bent into the shape of a hairpin and passed downwards through the centre of the flower. Make sure that this wire is well covered by petals and then tightly wind the two ends beneath the flower round the original four pieces of wire which makes a good straight stem. Finally, this stem is wrapped in florist's tape or even foil.

If a leaf or leaves are to be used, these are wired by inserting another length of florists' wire through the back of the leaf just above the petiole, over the main rib and out to the back. The two ends are then twisted around the petiole and the stem thus made bound with florist's tape or foil.

The wired flower or flowers, together with any wired leaves, are held together in the position desired and a further length of florist's tape used to wind round and secure all the 'stems' in this position.

It is a matter of personal taste whether a corsage should consist of one bloom with no leaves, several blooms with no leaves, one bloom with a leaf or leaves or several blooms with a leaf or leaves. It does not take long to make a single bloom and leaf corsage and it certainly adds a nice touch to the dinner table to have one at each lady guest's place. Not only is the thought behind this gesture appreciated but it gives the proud camellia grower a chance to show off a few of his or her flowers.

EXHIBITING

In the United Kingdom, far too few people who grow, or could quite easily grow, camellia blooms of exhibition quality actually exhibit at the major shows. In fact, the International Camellia Society has no show of its own. This is in marked contrast to the United States where a number of camellia societies hold their own camellia shows.

As the International Camellia Society has no show of its own, would-be exhibitors in the United Kingdom are largely confined to the two Royal Horticultural Society Shows which feature camellia competitions. Were it not for the Royal Horticultural Society (RHS), the situation would be poor in the extreme and it is very fortunate that the regional branches of the Rhododendron, Camellia and Magnolia Group of the RHS are so keen, active and well organized. Some local flower societies do, of course, sometimes include a class for camellias at their spring shows.

Most camellia growers try to produce superior blooms in their garden, containers and greenhouses. In some ways, in doing so, they are displaying a competitive spirit in showing that they wish to excel at what they are doing. If a thing is worth doing at all it is worth doing well, so we have all been taught. Equally, if a plant is worth growing at all it is worth growing well. There is nothing wrong in that philosophy, indeed it is one to be encouraged.

If one accepts this philosophy as being common amongst growers, and the desire to excel, to grow better blooms than next door, it is surprising that there are not more entries in the competitive classes for camellias. To grow better blooms than next door one must have better plants, for superior blooms come only from superior plants. Accordingly, if we are about to set out on the competitive trail, the first step is to select some of our best plants.

In order to produce exhibition quality blooms, preparation must commence more than a year before the show. In fact, one has to go back to the end of the blooming season in the year prior to the show because it is at this time that the plant produces new shoots and it is on these that our exhibition blooms will be produced.

From then on, every month is of importance to the exhibition grower but three periods are particularly so. These are: when the plant is producing its new wood; when it is producing its flower buds; and in the following early spring when those buds are beginning to swell, heralding the opening of the flowers.

At these times, in particular, it is essential to ensure that the plants are given ample water and ample nutrition. If the plants are short of either at these vital periods, there is no way in which they can produce blooms of exhibition quality.

Once plants have made their flower buds, consideration must be given to the question of disbudding them. Unless the buds are sparse in the extreme, disbudding will have to be carried out for it follows as a general rule that the fewer the flower buds on a plant, the larger will be the resulting blooms. However, this does not mean to say that we strip off all the flower buds apart from a few. We do not know which bud will be open as a flower at the time of the show. In other words, we have got to try to cover a fairly extended period with exhibition blooms. Flowering time, particularly with outdoor plants, remains somewhat unpredictable.

One popular way of disbudding is to leave the terminal bud and remove others which may interfere with its development. It is worth remembering that a flower which hangs pendant is much less likely to be damaged by the elements (particularly, rain, frost or sun) than one which faces upwards. This being so, it is sometimes wise to remove the terminal bud in favour of the best bud which faces downwards.

It is always difficult to say how many buds should be removed. Ideally, those which are left should be sufficiently far apart to ensure that each bloom, when it opens, is unhindered by another nearby. This obviously is a counsel of perfection. There are a number of camellias which produce long new growths and little side branches. If we disbud leaving only one terminal bud then it is highly likely that we will not have one good bloom at the time of the show, particularly if one allows for weather.

In these circumstances, the good old British compromise should be given a try. Leave the terminal bud and a couple of others. If, when the time comes, it is clear that the bloom from the terminal bud will be over before the show then whip it off and pray hard that the next in line will make it. When it becomes clear that it will, whip off any other bud which may have been left on that shoot.

Having appropriately disbudded the plants, there are still some other steps to take before they flower. As often as not, the wind will whip about terminal shoots doing nothing to enhance the beauty of our flower – in fact ensuring that it is totally ruined. Ordinary spring clothes pegs are the answer here. Peg one or two leaves of the flower branch to one or two leaves of a nearby branch and this problem is solved. Assuming that the show rules permit it, some further protection may be given to competition blooms by covering them with plastic bags and attaching them to adjoining twigs, leaves and branches with the clothes pegs.

Outdoor plants are entirely in the hands of chance so far as the weather is concerned. A cold period up to the opening of the blooms will ensure that they are small, miserly and not up to exhibition standard. Of course, all competitors are in the same boat so one can still have a good entry.

It is said that the longer it takes a camellia bloom to open, the larger it will be. In the United Kingdom, with its changeable climate and weather, this is probably something of a half truth. So far as outdoor plants are concerned, they never produce better blooms than when they have a long spell of nice warm weather right up to opening. A burst of really hot sunshine can force them out too soon and may reduce size but this rarely happens apart from those which flower later.

There is far more scope to control conditions with indoor or container grown plants. If the plants are in a greenhouse or conservatory the temperature can be easily controlled and growth forwarded or retarded, finally providing that nice long spell of warmth (not heat) right up to the time of blooming. Container grown plants on the patio or terrace can, at least, be brought into some sort of shelter to protect them from the worst of the weather, although if this is done they cannot compete as outdoor blooms.

When to cut camellia blooms is often decided by the time when one is permitted to stage under the rules of the show. This is frequently the day before, or early on the day itself, so if a journey of any length is involved then one can probably forget about staging on the early morning of the show.

It is generally best to cut one's blooms late on the day before or early in the morning before staging so as to avoid cutting the blooms after the sun has got on them. Once cut they should be kept in a cool place as long as possible before being transported to the show. Exactly how they are to be transported is no small problem for no flower is more difficult in this respect than the camellia. With only a couple of blooms to enter, travel by car is best, provided there are people available to hold each bloom carefully. Where more than a couple of blooms have to be transported, then a more sophisticated means of transportation must be arranged.

A long cardboard box filled with shredded paper or the like, into which the stem of the cut bloom may be carefully inserted, is a popular method. Many exhibitors give the packed box a light misting with clean water. This not only keeps the blooms fresh but by moistening the shredded paper a slightly humid atmosphere is created during the journey. Above all ensure that no one camellia bloom is in contact with another for if they are, the vibration of the journey will ensure that each touches and re-touches the other. This will certainly ruin both blooms. It is essential that, once packed, the blooms cannot vibrate against or bang against anything. If they do, just cross your name off the exhibitors' list!

Another method is to place some shock absorbing material on the base of the flower box and then staple or otherwise affix one's blooms onto this so that they cannot move and consequently cannot be bruised, scratched or damaged in transit. Or, completely surround the blooms with expanded polystyrene packing 'beans' or 'spaghetti'. This is so light that it cannot cause damage to the blooms in transit.

It is particularly difficult to 'time' the opening of camellia blooms, the more so with outdoor blooms. However, their full opening can be retarded somewhat by wrapping round an opening bud a small piece of foam about ⅛in (3mm) thick and tying it in position with a twist of wool or some similar soft material. To some extent this will protect the bloom from inclement weather but, more important, while in place it will prevent the bloom from opening. When removed, the bloom will expand fully quite quickly. A little experimentation with this method should be made before the show to get the tying about right.

Most show schedules have a class or classes for sprays of camellia flowers. This is to be encouraged for sprays give us far more idea of what the plant looks like in the garden than individual blooms can ever do. One or two sprays can probably be assembled in the back of the car so that none of the blooms can bang against anything, including another bloom or leaf.

There is little point in growing exhibition blooms, entering in what appear to be appropriate classes and carefully transporting and staging exhibits if it turns out that the wrong class has been entered. Your entry will promptly be disqualified. It is essential to study the various classes and equally essential to know the parentage of a number of hybrids and the categories of forms (single, paeony, double and so on) before entering one's blooms.

So that the reader may appreciate that for the beginner this may not be easy, the 1990 Royal Horticultural Society's Show schedule for the various classes in the camellia competitions, together with the relevant regulations, are set out below.

In fact, although there have been some changes over the years, these have not been great and a careful reading and construction of any new regulations as indicated here will easily simplify them.

REGULATIONS

1. **Eligibility of competitors.** The competitive classes are open to all, unless excluded by some special regulations.
2. **Exhibits must be the property of the exhibitor.** All specimens exhibited in competition must be the *bona fide* property of the exhibitor and must have been grown by him or his employees on land in his own occupation for at least the last six months before the Competition.

   Due to the risk of introducing Camellia Blossom Blight, no cut flowers imported from North America or Japan or material cut from plants so imported during the last two years may be brought into the Hall.

   In order to be satisfied that the conditions governing competitive exhibits are fulfilled, the Council reserves the right to visit by commission, before or after any Show, gardens from which flowers or plants have been entered for competition.
3. **Entry Fees.** There are no entry fees.
4. **Acceptance of entries.** All entries must be made on the official entry forms and should reach the Secretary, The Royal Horticultural Society, on or before the Tuesday, in the week preceding the Competition, though the Secretary may, at his discretion, accept a late entry up to but not after 8.30p.m. on the day before the Competition. **Exhibitors are requested to make entries in *all* classes for which they think they**

might have plant material and notify the Shows Department on the Monday before the Show of any classes in which they are not able to stage an exhibit.

The Council reserves the right to refuse any entry and in the event of any such refusal it is not required to give any reason or explanation.

5. **Exhibits must have been grown in the open.**

   Rhododendrons and other Ornamental Plants: Except where otherwise stated, the exhibits in the competitive classes must have been grown in the open. Blooms may be cut and thereafter opened under glass.

   Camellias: At the Early Competition (March 14/15) exhibits may have been grown under glass or in the open. At the Main Competition (April 11/12) exhibits must have been grown in the open except those entered for classes 63 to 72 which must have been grown under glass. Where Blooms are cut from plants growing in tubs or other containers the plants must have been standing in the open for the six months prior to the Show to qualify as 'grown in the open'.

6. **Rhododendrons: Nomenclature to be used.** All exhibits must be entered and staged in accordance with the way in which the plants are classified in the revision of the genus published by Cullen and Chamberlain [see *Notes RBG Edinb. 39* (1): 1-207 (1980) and 39 (2): 209-486 (1982)]. For species the Exhibitors may find it useful to refer to *An Alphabetical Checklist of Rhododendron Species* (RHS, 1981); the slight modifications to the revision, for horticultural use, which are contained in the list, may be used for exhibits. The classification of hybrids should contrive to follow the *Rhododendron Handbook* Part Two (1969) except that the nomenclature of species used as parents must follow the new revision.

   A Steward will be available in the Hall during most of the staging period to assist exhibitors on questions of nomenclature and classification.

7. **Rhododendrons: The meaning of 'truss' and 'spray'.** The term 'truss' means a single rachis and, therefore, a group of heads may not be shown where a 'truss' is called for. The term 'spray' means a single stem or branch.

8. **Rhododendrons: Variant.** The term variant is used in this schedule to include the botanical ranks sub-species, varietas, and forma.

9. **Cultivars of Camellia japonica** should be shown in accord-

ance to the classifications given in regulation 10 except where a class for a specifically named cultivar exists.

10. **The Classifications of cultivars of Camellia japonica.** For the purposes of the Competition and Show, cultivars of *Camellia japonica* are classified into six groups conforming to the following definitions:

Single – Flower with usually eight and not more than nine petals.

Semi-double – Flower with two or more rows of petals; stamens conspicuous.

Anemone-formed – Flower flat, with one or more rows of larger outer petals, and a central convex mass composed of petaloids and stamens intermingled.

Peony-formed – Flower deep and rounded, with several rows of outer petals, and a central convex mass of twisted petaloids and stamens.

Rose-formed – Flower with imbricated petals, showing stamens in a concave centre when fully open.

Formal-double – Flower with many rows of fully imbricated petals, never showing stamens.

Camellia japonica is considered to include *rusticana* where applicable.

11. **Camellias:** Flowers in which the petals show any evidence of flecking are not eligible to be shown in classes for self-coloured cultivars. For the purposes of this Schedule 'Self-coloured cultivars' include both cultivars with a single uniform colour, and those where one shade of a colour merges into another shade of the same colour, such as *Camellia japonica* 'Spring Sonnet'. 'Variegated cultivars' include those with blotches, spots, flecks or stripes of white or of a contrasting colour.

12. **Camellias – Blooms and sprays.** In classes calling for blooms, each species or cultivar is to be represented by one bloom with a leaf or leaves. Specimen vases will be provided. The term 'spray' means a small branch. In no case may a spray exceed 18in (45.72cm) in height from the top of the vase. Green earthenware vases 6in and 9in (15.24cm and 22.86cm) in height will be provided for sprays. No other method of staging blooms or sprays may be used.

13. For the purposes of these competitions, plants such as *Cornus kousa*, Davidia and Euphorbia, grown for their ornamental bracts, are eligible as flowering plants in bloom if their bracts are fully expanded even if their florets are not open.

14. **Number of entries allowed.** An exhibitor may enter and stage any number of exhibits and be eligible for any number of prizes in any class, provided that in each exhibit all the species, cultivars or hybrids, as the case may be, are different from those in his/her other exhibits in that class. Note: While a species and its sub-species are regarded as distinct, as are two sub-species of the same species, different forms of the same species are not permitted, except where otherwise stated.

15. **Time for staging.** Exhibits may be staged between 2 p.m. and 10 p.m. on the day before or between 7 a.m. and 9.45 a.m. on the first day of the Competition.

16. **Steward to advise exhibitors.** For the Main Camellia and Rhododendron competitions and the Heather Competitions a steward or stewards will be in the Hall between 8.30 a.m. and 9.45 a.m. on the first day of the Competition, to advise exhibitors in regard to the appropriate class for any exhibit and the steward's decision on all matters of classification will be final.

17. **Exhibitors' Passes.** Only exhibitors and such assistants as may be required for the arrangement of exhibits will be admitted before the Competition is open to the public. Exhibitors' passes will be posted on receipt of entries.

18. **Vases.** The Society will provide earthenware vases 6in, 9in and 11in (15.24cm, 22.86cm and 27.94cm) in height, and 4in (10.16cm) diameter bowls; no others may be used, except where otherwise stated in the Schedule.

19. **Labelling.** All exhibits should be labelled with the names of the plants, typed or written in block letters. The label for a hybrid should bear (in addition to the name) the parentage, when known. For this purpose small cards will be posted to exhibitors on the receipt of their entries and no other labels should be used. Where the name of a cultivar is unknown the label should bear the words 'NAME UNKNOWN'.

20. **Exhibit cards.** Cards corresponding to the entries will be obtainable from the Steward in the Hall. Competitors will be responsible for the placing of these cards and must satisfy themselves that the descriptions of the exhibits on the cards are correct.

21. **Additional support of sprays.** The use of canes, wires or any other means of additional support above vase top level is not permitted except in the case of natural climbers.

22. **Protests.** Any protest must be delivered in writing to the Shows Department by 1 p.m. on the first day of the Competition.

23. **Alteration of exhibits.** After judging has taken place, no exhibit or part of any exhibit may be altered or removed until 5 p.m. on the day when the Competition terminates, except with the permission of the Secretary.

24. **Prizes may be withheld.** Any prize may be withheld or modified if the exhibits are considered undeserving of the prize offered.

25. **Cups.** The winner of a challenge cup will be entitled to hold it for one year and will be responsible for its return in good condition.

26. **Payment of Prizes.** Prize-money will be paid during the month following the Competition.

27. **Liability for loss.** All exhibits, personal property, etc., will be at the risk of the exhibitors and the Society will not be liable for compensation for loss or damage by theft, fire, water, accident or any other cause whatsoever.

28. **Usual regulations apply.** The competitions will be subject to The Royal Horticultural Society's usual rules and regulations except on points where, under this Schedule, they obviously do not apply.
(See *Regulations for the Society's Exhibitions* and *The Horticultural Show Handbook.*)

Non-Competitive Displays

Amateurs and nurserymen are also invited to stage non-competitive displays.

The Society's medals will be available for award for such exhibits. Application for space should be made on the forms used in connection with the Society's Flower Shows and should reach the Secretary not later than the first post on Tuesday of the week preceding the Competition, on which day notices will be sent to all applicants notifying them of the space allotted to them.

From the above, it is clear that for those interested in displaying camellias, Regulations 6, 7, 8 and 13 are not applicable. However, they are included here in case our keen camellia grower, having achieved success in the competitive classes with his blooms, decides to move on to other spheres such as rhododendrons, several of the

Cornus family, davidias and many others whose 'flowers' are in fact bracts surrounding an insignificant bloom.

Reverting to camellias, some of the above regulations are of particular importance. Regulation 2 which deals with the possibility of introducing camellia blossom blight – a virulent disease in the United States but virtually unknown in the United Kingdom, is of the utmost importance. Regulation 5 deals with camellias at the early competition and the main competition.

It must be noted that the regulations are strict as to which plants have to be grown in the open or under glass in order to be eligible. To the camellia grower this is absolutely essential for, however good one's outdoor blooms may be, they cannot possibly equal blooms from the same cultivar grown under glass. With freedom from frost, complete protection from wind and rain and a temperature which is bound to produce the largest possible blooms, an open competition between indoor and outdoor blooms is about as fair as competing a high-bred racehorse against a Clydesdale in a flat race!

In consequence, for the vast majority of us it is pointless to enter our blooms for the early competition unless we can afford them glass protection or some protection approaching it. However, having said that, our would-be competitor should not be put off because he does not own an architect-designed conservatory or even some sophisticated greenhouses. Just a little protection in a small plastic tunnel or small 'lean-to' perhaps only 1m (3ft) deep from a wall and only 2m (6ft) high can provide sufficient protection to put one's blooms in the first prize category.

I remember one lady who, a few years ago, used to enter, and quite frequently win, the class for the camellia 'Souvenir de Bahuaud Litou'. She told me more than once that she owned only a small greenhouse in her back garden in an exposed Midlands town, which could accommodate only two or three camellia plants. However, her understanding and care of her plants in her own particular circumstances ensured that, as often as not, she beat the largest gardens and best growers in the country. I shall never forget the look of quiet pleasure on her face when I asked her how she had fared and she replied 'I've done it again.' Anybody prepared to study the needs of his plants and to meet them can 'do it again' and join the first prize winners, however humble his 'glasshouse' may be.

So much for the early competition. The main competition is a somewhat different kettle of fish. Apart from Classes 63 to 72 (for which the plants must have been grown under glass) all exhibits must have been grown in the open. Blooms from plants grown in tubs or other containers will only qualify if those plants have been standing in the open for the six months prior to the show.

Carrying on from Regulation 5, the next important regulations are Regulations 9 and 10. The latter deals with the classifications of cultivars of *Camellia japonica*. The definitions given in Regulation 10 are the *only ones* we must comply with.

Regulation 11 is important as it deals with classes for self-coloured cultivars. Flowers showing any evidence of flecking are not eligible to be shown in classes for self-coloured cultivars but the term 'self-coloured cultivars' does include blooms where one shade of colour merges into another shade of the same colour. *Camellia japonica* 'Spring Sonnet' is given as an example of an eligible cultivar. This is possibly not the best example of what is intended as although the *Camellia Nomenclature* book describes it as a bloom of pale pink with deeper pink margins, Stirling Macoboy in the *Colour Dictionary of Camellias* describes it as pale pink with irregular mauve pink petal edges. No doubt 'Spring Sonnet', like so many camellias, can vary extensively but I must say after growing a good many plants for a good many years that they usually produce very definite mauve pink petal edges in considerable contrast to the main body of the flower which is very pale pink. Probably there is more than one form of this particular cultivar. Variegated cultivars are also defined in Regulation 11.

Regulation 12, which deals with blooms and sprays, makes it clear that in classes for blooms only one bloom with one or more leaves can be shown, whereas 'spray' means a small branch which may not exceed 45–72cm (18–28in) in height from the top of the vase. Specimen vases for blooms and green earthenware vases for sprays are provided by the Society and no other method of staging blooms or sprays may be used.

Those who may wish to enter and stage more than one exhibit in any class should peruse Regulation 14 extremely carefully and note, in particular, that different forms of the same species are not permitted in a class except where otherwise stated.

Regulation 19 dealing with labelling should also be carefully complied with. In the case of camellia cultivars, the fact that the label bears the words 'name unknown' does not appear to count against the bloom as a potential prize winner.

'Donation'

'Primavera'

'Tricolor'

'Elizabeth'

'Red Dandy'

'Bob Hope'

'Jury's Yellow'

'Reg Ragland'

'Nuccio's Pearl'

'Little Lavender'

'Betty Sheffield Supreme'

'Royalty'

'Grace Bunton'   'Tomorrow'

'Waterlily'

'Glen 40'   'Beatrice Michael'

'Kelvingtonii'

'Mrs D. W. Davis'

Competitive Classes

These must be carefully studied. It will be found that in the early shows prior to the early camellia competition in March (where most entries are grown under glass) there are classes where camellias may be entered. In every case, very properly, the competitor must solemnly declare that any material he enters has been grown on his land and been in his possession for at least six months. The Council of the Society reserves the right to visit gardens from which competitive material has been entered either before or after the show.

In the earlier shows there is a note which states that those exhibits which must have been grown in the ground and open air may be protected from frost for a few days prior to the competition.

Before looking through the competition classes it is worth noting that, apart from the cash prizes which may be won, there are a number of challenge cups which the winner holds for a year. For camellias entered in shows in the United Kingdom, the Leonardslee Bowl is offered for the best exhibit of twelve cultivars of camellias where one bloom of each is shown in Class 25 of the main camellia competition in April each year.

The exact date of each show, and as a result each competition, must obviously vary slightly from year to year. Taking 1990 as a typical example, the first show was 30–31 January with competitive classes for ornamental plants from the open. If one grows only camellias for competitive purposes then there were only three classes open, namely:

Class 4   A flowering tree or shrub other than a rhododendron or hamamelis in bloom, one vase.
Class 6   A tree or shrub with variegated foliage, one vase.
Class 7   A tree or shrub including camellias and rhododendrons grown under glass in bloom, one vase.

To be fair, Class 6 is something of a long shot but there are a few camellias with variegated foliage, such as 'Golden Spangles' and *C. sasanqua* 'Variegata', which are worth a try.

Apart from Class 7, exhibits must have been grown both in the ground and in the open air. Frost protection for a few days prior to the show was permitted.

COMPETITIVE CLASSES
for
ORNAMENTAL PLANTS FROM THE OPEN
to be held on
January 30 and 31 1990

Unless otherwise indicated, the prizes will be:
First Prize, £2; Second, £1.50; Third, £1; Fourth, 50p.

Class 1. Three ornamental trees and/or shrubs of different genera, in bloom, one vase of each.
First prize, £4; Second, £3; Third, £2; Fourth, £1.

A competitor may not enter in Classes 2 to 4 any plant which he or she is exhibiting in Class 1.

Class 2. A rhododendron in bloom, one vase.

Class 3. An hamamelis in bloom, one vase.

Class 4. A flower tree or shrub, other than a rhododendron or hamamelis, in bloom, one vase.

Class 5. A plant other than a tree or shrub in bloom, one vase.

Class 6. A tree or shrub with variegated foliage, one vase.

In classes 1 to 6 all exhibits must have been grown in the ground in the open air. They may, however, be protected from frost for a few days prior to the Competition.

Class 7. A tree or shrub including camellias and rhododendrons grown under glass in bloom, one vase.

Class 8. A pot, pan or vase of bulbs grown under glass or otherwise, in bloom.

The next show took place on 20–21 February and comprised competitive classes for ornamental plants from the open. Here there were only two possible classes suitable for the camellia grower, namely:

Class 4   A camellia in bloom, one vase.
Class 10   A tree or shrub grown for its foliage.

The March show on the 13–14 March included the early camellia competition. The classes were comprehensive, numbering no less than forty-six so there was something for everyone.

The competition schedule was as follows:

EARLY CAMELLIA COMPETITION

(For Camellias grown under glass or in the open
see Regulations 2 and 5.)

**Tuesday and Wednesday
March 13 and 14 1990**

DIVISION 1   SPRAYS
(*See* Regulation 10 and Notes on Hybrids on Page 60.)

> In this Division, except where otherwise stated, the prizes will be:
> *First Prize, £3;   Second, £2.25;   Third, £1.50.*

Class 1.   Japonica, any three cultivars, one spray of each.
First Prize, £6;   Second, £4.50;   Third, £3.

Class 2.   Japonica, any semi-double cultivar, one spray. (*See* Regulations 9 & 10).

Class 3.   Japonica, any anemone-formed or peony-formed cultivar, one spray. (*See* Regulations 9 & 10).

Class 4.   Japonica, any rose-formed or formal double cultivar, one spray. (*See* Regulations 9 & 10).

Class 5.   Japonica, a small flowered cultivar with blooms measuring not more than 3in (7cm) in diameter, one spray.

Class 6.   Reticulata and its hybrids, any three, one spray of each.
First Prize, £6;   Second, £4.50;   Third, £3.

Class 7.   Reticulata or its hybrids, one spray.

Class 8.   Saluenensis, one spray.

Class 9.   Any species other than japonica, reticulata or saluenensis, one spray.

Class 10.   Any three hybrids, one spray of each.
First Prize, £6;   Second, £4.50;   Third, £3.

Class 11. Any three × williamsii hybrids, one spray of each.
First Prize, £6; Second, £4.50; Third, £3.

Class 12. × williamsii, any single-flowered cultivar, one spray.

Class 13. × williamsii, any semi-double cultivar, one spray.

Class 14. × williamsii, any peony or rose-formed or formal double cultivar, one spray.

Class 15. Any hybrid or species not eligible for classes 1 to 14, one spray.

DIVISION II   BLOOMS

> In this Division, except where otherwise stated, the prizes will be:
> *First Prize, £1.50; Second, £1; Third, 75p.*

SECTION A   CULTIVARS OF CAMELLIA JAPONICA
SUB-SECTION 1   SINGLE CULTIVARS
(*See* Regulations 9, 10 & 12)

Class 16. Any three single-flowered cultivars, one bloom of each.
First Prize, £3; Second, £2.25; Third, £1.50.

Class 17. Any single-flowered white cultivar, one bloom.

Class 18. Any single-flowered self-coloured cultivar other than white, one bloom.

Class 19. Any single-flowered variegated cultivar, one bloom.

SUB-SECTION 2   SEMI-DOUBLE CULTIVARS
(*See* Regulations 9, 10 & 12)

Class 20. Any three semi-double cultivars, one bloom of each.
First Prize, £3; Second, £2.25; Third, £1.50.

Class 21. Any semi-double white cultivar, one bloom.

Class 22. Any semi-double self-coloured cultivar other than white, one bloom.

Class 23. Any semi-double variegated cultivar, one bloom.

SUB-SECTION 3   ANEMONE AND PEONY-FORMED CULTIVARS
(*See* Regulations 9, 10 & 12)

Class 24.   Any three anemone and/or peony-formed cultivars, one bloom.

Class 25.   Any anemone or peony-formed white cultivar, one bloom.

Class 26.   Any anemone or peony-formed self-coloured cultivar other than white, one bloom.

Class 27.   Any anemone or peony-formed variegated cultivar, one bloom.

SUB-SECTION 4   ROSE-FORMED AND FORMAL DOUBLE CULTIVARS
(*See* Regulations 9, 10 & 12)

Class 28.   Any three rose-formed and/or formal double cultivars, one bloom of each.
First prize, £3;   Second, £2.25;   Third, £1.50.

Class 29.   Any rose-formed or formal double white cultivar, one bloom.

Class 30.   Any rose-formed or formal double self-coloured cultivar, one bloom.

Class 31.   Any rose-formed or formal double variegated cultivar, one bloom.

SUB-SECTION 5   MIXED TYPES OF CAMELLIA JAPONICA

Class 32.   Any six cultivars, one bloom of each.
First Prize, £6;   Second, £4;   Third, £3.

Class 33.   Any three cultivars, one bloom of each.
First Prize, £3;   Second, £2.25;   Third, £1.50.

> Note: An exhibitor may enter in Class 32 and Class 33, but may not enter the same cultivar in both classes.

Class 34.   Any cultivar, one bloom, shown by an exhibitor who has not won a Prize at an R.H.S. Camellia Competition since 1985.

SECTION B

Class 35. Any three hybrids, one bloom of each.
First Prize, £3; Second, £2.25; Third, £1.50.

Class 36. Reticulata any three, one bloom of each.
First Prize, £3; Second, £2.25; Third, £1.50.

Class 37. Three reticulata hybrids of which one parent is × williamsii or saluenensis (parentage to be stated), one bloom of each.
First Prize, £3; Second, £2.25; Third, £1.50.

Class 38. Any reticulata hybrid of which one parent is × williamsii or saluenensis, (parentage to be stated), one bloom.

Class 39. Any single flowered reticulata, one bloom.

Class 40. Any semi-double flowered reticulata, other than those eligible for Class 38, one bloom.

Class 41. Any reticulata not eligible for Classes 38, 39 or 40, one bloom.

Class 42. Any three × williamsii, one bloom of each.
First Prize, £3; Second, £2.25; Third, £1.50.

Class 43. Any semi-double × williamsii, one bloom.

Class 44. Any peony or anemone-formed × williamsii, one bloom.

Class 45. Any hybrid other than of reticulata or × williamsii, one bloom.

SECTION C

Class 46. Any yellow species or hybrid, one bloom.

This is an extremely comprehensive list of classes and anyone who grew two, three or more camellias was bound to find several classes in which he could enter provided he had competition class blooms.

In this connection let us be clear from the outset that it is virtually useless to enter plants grown in the open against blooms from plants grown indoors. Regulation 5 clearly states that, at the early competition, exhibits may have been grown under glass or in the open. In consequence, for all practical purposes, camellia-growers needed only to concern themselves as potential competitors in the early show (apart from Division II) if they had blooms to enter which had been grown under glass. Division II catered for those who do not possess glasshouse facilities. A perusal of the various headings shows that there was something for everyone in every form of *Camellia japonica* (single, semi-double, paeony and so on).

Once more the note to the schedule of classes should have been carefully perused and particularly the fact that *reticulata* camellias includes various hybrids. The note on *Camellia × williamsii* is particularly important as it clearly states that these are hybrids between *C. japonica* and *C. saluenensis*.

Anyone involved in the propagation, growing and selling of camellias cannot but be impressed by the ignorance demonstrated by so many of the gardening public as to what is a *williamsii* camellia. This is probably due to the large number of ill-informed articles and advertisements for *williamsii* hybrids. From these one is almost certain to gain the impression that the only camellia worth trying in any conditions less than perfect are these. One way and another we have managed to get ourselves into a rather stupid situation with *williamsii* hybrids. The great breakthrough – the cross between *japonica* and *saluenensis*, leading as it did to famous plants such as 'J. C. Williams' and 'Donation' – should never be forgotten and all honour should be paid to those who achieved those landmarks. Life, however, does not stand still and other species have since been incorporated in producing camellia hybrids.

The introduction of other species such as *C. reticulata* has widened our horizons of camellia breeding and achieved results which could never have been achieved had our breeding remained confined to *C. japonica* and *saluenensis* crosses. Surely it is high time we came to realize that the *williamsii* hybrid is but a part of camellia hybrids as a whole, that in some instances the original *williamsii* hybrids have been superseded and will be more and more as the years roll on and hybridizing becomes more and more sophisticated.

Whilst it may still be necessary to be precise and specific for competition schedules, in my view the time has long since been reached when camellias should broadly be categorized under their species name (for example, *japonica* or *reticulata* and so on) or as hybrids. One must certainly bear in mind that there are a number of camellia hybrids apart from *williamsii* hybrids. In making these remarks, I fully appreciate the necessity in a competition schedule to use phrases such as *williamsii* hybrids and so on in order to be precise in defining eligible blooms. One has a very similar thing with rhododendron classes such as 'any hybrid of which one parent is *yakushimanum*'.

One must be alert in choosing the classes in which to enter competition blooms. For example, Class 10 calls for 'any three hybrids' whereas Classes 11 to 14 call for *williamsii* in various forms. Whilst 'Innovation' or 'Donation' could be included in Class 10, only 'Donation' could be included in Class 13.

In Class 45, any hybrid other than of *reticulata* or × *williamsii* opens the door to the little ones, those lovely *cuspidata* hybrids such as 'Cornish Snow', 'Cornish Spring' or the larger flowered but rarely grown plants such as 'Bonnie Marie' (*C. cuspidata* × *C. saluenensis*) × *C. japonica* of delicate pink or, returning to the smaller flowered ones, 'Freedom Bell', a bright red, very free flowering semi-double whose parentage is unknown, or 'Tiny Princess', a delicate pink miniature semi-double/paeony form achieved by crossing *C. japonica* 'Akebona' with 'Fraterna'.

Class 46 (for any yellow flowered species or hybrid) is, of course, open to anyone fortunate enough to own a plant of *C. chrysantha* and who has been able to flower it. For lesser mortals the practical choice would seem to be between 'Jury's Yellow', 'Brushfield's Yellow' and 'Gwenneth Morey'.

Next we must turn to the main camellia competition (for camellias grown in the open and under glass).

Regulation 5 makes it clear that exhibits must have been grown in the open except those entered in Classes 63 to 72 which must have been grown under glass. Where blooms from containerized plants are entered those containers must have been standing in the open for six months prior to the show.

The schedule for the main camellia competition was as follows:

MAIN CAMELLIA SHOW
(For Camellias grown in the open and under glass
see Regulations 2 and 5.)

Tuesday and Wednesday April 3 and 4 1990

DIVISION I SPRAYS FROM THE OPEN
(*See* Regulations 10 and 12 and Notes on Hybrids.)

Except where otherwise stated, in this Division the prizes will be:
First Prize, £3;   Second, £2.25;   Third, £1.50.

Class 1. Any six, one spray of each.
First Prize, £15; Second, £9; Third, £6.

Class 2. Any three, one spray of each.
First Prize, £6; Second, £4.50; Third, £3.

Class 3. Japonica, any three cultivars, one spray of each.
First Prize, £4.50; Second, £3; Third, £2.25.

Class 4. Japonica, any single-flowered cultivar, one spray. (*See* Regulations 9 & 10).

Class 5. Japonica, any semi-double cultivar one spray. (*See* Regulations 9 & 10).

Class 6. Japonica, any anemone-formed or peony-formed cultivar, one spray. (*See* Regulations 9 & 10).

Class 7. Japonica, any rose-formed or formal double cultivar, one spray. (*See* Regulations 9 & 10).

Class 8. Japonica, a small flowered cultivar with blooms measuring not more than 3in (7.5cm) in diameter, one spray.

Class 9. Any reticulata, one spray.

Class 10. Saluenensis, one spray.

Class 11. × williamsii, any single cultivar, one spray.

Class 12. × williamsii, 'Donation', one spray.

Class 13. × williamsii, any cultivar other than a single or semi-double cultivar, one spray.

Class 14. × williamsii, any cultivar other than a single or semi-double cultivar, one spray.

Class 15. Any other hybrid of, or descendant from, saluenensis, one spray.

Class 16. Any species or hybrid not eligible to be shown in Classes 3 to 15, one spray.

DIVISION II   BLOOMS FROM THE OPEN
(*See* Regulation 5.)

> Except where otherwise stated, in this Division the prizes will be:
> *First Prize, £1.50;   Second, £1;   Third, 75p.*

Class 25. Any twelve, one bloom of each. Entries in this Class may include cultivars of japonica.
First Prize, The Leonardslee Bowl;   Second, £6;   Third, £3.

SECTION A

SUB-SECTION 1   SINGLE CULTIVARS OF CAMELLIA JAPONICA
(*See* Regulations 9 & 10)

Class 26. Any three single-flowered cultivars, one bloom of each.
First Prize, £3;   Second, £2.25;   Third, £1.50.

Class 27. Any single-flowered white cultivar, one bloom.

Class 28. Any single-flowered self-coloured cultivar other than white, one bloom.

Class 29. Any single-flowered variegated cultivar, one bloom.

SUB-SECTION 2   SEMI-DOUBLE CULTIVARS OF CAMELLIA JAPONICA
(*See* Regulations 9, 10 & 12)

Class 30. Any three semi-double cultivars, one bloom.
First Prize, £3;   Second, £2.25;   Third, £1.50.

Class 31. Any semi-double white cultivar, one bloom.

Class 32. Any semi-double self-coloured cultivar other than white, one bloom.

Class 33. Any semi-double variegated cultivar, one bloom.

SUB-SECTION 3   ANEMONE AND PEONY-FORMED CULTIVARS OF CAMELLIA JAPONICA
(*See* Regulations 9, 10 & 12)

Class 34.   Any three anemone-formed and/or peony-formed cultivars, one bloom of each.
First Prize, £3;   Second, £2.25;   Third, £1.50.

Class 35.   Any anemone or peony-formed white cultivar, one bloom.

Class 36.   Any anemone or peony-formed self-coloured cultivar other than white, one bloom.

Class 37.   Any anemone or peony-formed variegated cultivar, one bloom.

SUB-SECTION 4   ROSE-FORMED AND FORMAL DOUBLE CULTIVARS OF CAMELLIA JAPONICA
(*See* Regulations 9, 10 & 12)

Class 38.   Any three rose-formed and/or formal double cultivars, one bloom of each.
First Prize, £3;   Second, £2.25;   Third, £1.50.

Class 39.   Any rose-formed or formal double white cultivar, one bloom.

Class 40.   Any rose-formed or formal double self-coloured cultivar other than white, one bloom.

Class 41.   Any rose-formed or formal double variegated cultivar, one bloom.

SUB-SECTION 5   MIXED TYPES OF CAMELLIA JAPONICA

Class 42.   Any six cultivars, one bloom of each.
First Prize, £4.50;   Second, £3;   Third, £2.25.

Class 43.   Any three cultivars, one bloom of each.
First Prize, £3;   Second, £2.25;   Third, £1.50.
Open only to those who have not won a prize in this competition in the last three years.

Class 44.   Any cultivar, one bloom.
Open only to those who have not won a prize in this competition in the last three years.

DIVISION III MISCELLANEOUS
(*See* Notes on Hybrids.)

Class 45. Any three, except japonica cultivars, one bloom of each.
First Prize, £3;   Second, £2.25;   Third, £1.50.

Class 46. Reticulata, any three cultivars other than those descended from saluenensis, one bloom of each.
First Prize, £3;   Second, £2.25;   Third, £1.50.

Class 47. Any single-flowered reticulata, one bloom.

Class 48. Any semi-double flowered reticulata, one bloom.

Class 49. Any anemone-formed or peony-formed reticulata, one bloom.

Class 50. Any rose-formed or formal double reticulata, one bloom.

Class 51. Any reticulata cultivar of which one parent is saluenensis (parentage to be stated), one bloom.

Class 52. Any three reticulata cultivars of which one parent is saluenensis (parentage to be stated), one bloom of each.
First Prize, £3;   Second, £2.25;   Third, £1.50.

Class 53. × williamsii, any six hybrids, one bloom of each.
First Prize, £4.50;   Second, £3;   Third, £2.25.

Class 54. × williamsii, any three hybrids, one bloom of each.
First Prize, £3;   Second, £2.25;   Third, £1.50.

Class 55. × williamsii, any single-flowered cultivar, one bloom.

Class 56. × williamsii, 'Donataion' on bloom.

Class 57. × williamsii, any semi-double cultivar other than 'Donation', one bloom.

Class 58. × williamsii, any anemone-formed or peony-formed cultivar, one bloom.

Class 59. × williamsii, any rose-formed or formal double cultivar, one bloom.

Class 60. Saluenensis, one bloom.

Class 61. Any yellow species or hybrid, one bloom.

Class 62. Any species or hybrid not specified above, one bloom.

DIVISION IV RESTRICTED TO PLANTS GROWN UNDER GLASS OR OTHER PROTECTION

Except where otherwise stated, in this Division the prizes will be: *First Prize, £1.50; Second, £1; Third, 75p.*

Class 63. Japonica, any three single flowered cultivars grown under glass, one bloom of each.
First Prize, £3; Second, £2.25; Third, £1.50.

Class 64. Japonica, any three semi-double cultivars, grown under glass, one bloom of each.
First Prize, £3; Second, £2.25; Third, £1.50.

Class 65. Japonica, any three anemone-formed and/or peony-formed cultivars, grown under glass, one bloom of each.
First Prize, £3; Second, £2.25; Third, £1.50.

Class 66. Japonica, any three rose-formed and/or formal double cultivars, grown under glass, one bloom of each.
First Prize, £3; Second, £2.25; Third, £1.50.

Class 67. Japonica, any semi-double cultivar, grown under glass, one bloom.

Class 68. Japonica, any anemone-formed or peony-formed cultivar, grown under glass, one bloom.

Class 69. Japonica, any rose-formed or formal double cultivar, grown under glass, one bloom.

Class 70. Any three reticulata cultivars, grown under glass, one bloom of each.
First Prize, £3; Second, £2.25; Third, £1.50.

Class 71. Any reticulata cultivar, grown under glass, one bloom.

Looking through the above schedule, the remarks made earlier as to the various regulations dealing with blooms, sprays and flower forms (single, formal double and so on) apply equally here and must be strictly complied with.

Class 15 can raise difficulties: 'any **other** hybrid or **descendant** from *saluenensis*' [author's stress]. This presumably means a

NOTE For the purposes of these Competitions:

(1) RETICULATA CAMELLIAS include:

(a) the species and its wild forms; hybrids between *C. reticulata* and *C. japonica* including *C.* × *heterophylla* and its cultivar 'Barbara Hillier', *C. reticulata* cultivars of Chinese origin and their progeny;

(b) Hybrids between *C.* × *williamsii* including 'Barbara Clark', 'Black Lace', 'Brian', 'Dr Louis Pollizzi', 'Francie L.', 'Grand Jury', 'Inspiration', 'Leonard Messel', 'Phyl Doak' and 'Salutation'.

(2) *C.* × *williamsii* covers the hybrids between *C. japonica* and *C. saluenensis*, and includes any seedling of *C.* × *williamsii* provided that no species other than *C. japonica* or *C. saluenensis* is involved in the parentage.

(3) *C.* 'Vernalis' and *C.* 'Wabisuke' are regarded as being of hybrid origin.

saluenensis hybrid other than *saluenensis* × *japonica*. 'Cornish Snow' (*saluenensis* × *cuspidata*) or 'Sylvia May' (*cuspidata* × *saluenensis*) may be appropriate here but it is difficult to follow what is meant by a 'descendant from *saluenensis*'. If this means a variety of *saluenensis* then something like 'First Flush' should be appropriate.

Class 16 offers many possibilities. For the outdoor grower the many hybrids such as 'Leonard Messel' and, indeed, any hybrid other than *C.* × *williamsii* would probably offer the best chance.

Class 25 comprises any twelve blooms. This really will sort out the sheep from the goats for one needs quite a collection to be able to pick twelve competition class blooms at one time.

Division II, Section A covers the various forms of *Camellia japonica* – single, semi-double, anemone and paeony, rose form and formal double – so there is scope here for any grower of one or two *japonicas*.

When deciding what can be entered in Division III, Miscellaneous, a careful study must be made of the note defining what is eligible as a *reticulata* camellia for the purposes of the competition. From this it will be seen that a number of *reticulata* hybrids are, in fact, eligible.

Finally, Division IV is restricted to plants grown under glass or other protection. Of the ten classes, eight are for *japonicas* and two for *reticulatas*.

No apology is made for dealing with the show schedules in some detail for it is only after reading through them that it must be apparent that *any* grower of camellias who can produce a few good quality blooms can find a class in which to enter them and may be surprised to learn that there is no great competition in that class. The more who enter, the better the competition, so it is up to every camellia grower to have a go.

FLORAL ARRANGEMENTS

There are four main areas in which a knowledge of floral arranging of camellias is either necessary or useful. First, sprays of camellia blooms are often included among the classes in camellia competitions. It is a great plus if such sprays are exhibited to their best advantage and this can only be achieved if the exhibitor has a reasonable working knowledge of floral arranging.

Second, at some shows there are classes, or at least a class, for a floral arrangement of camellias.

Third, with competitive work still in mind, camellias with their wide range of colours, subtlety of their variations of colour in shade and tone and almost infinite variations in form, offer a most useful ingredient for a floral arrangement to be entered in a competition.

It is surprising that when so many exotics are used in floral arrangements in the United Kingdom, most of which have either been produced under heat in this country or imported from abroad (in either case acquired at fairly considerable expense), the tough and easily produced yet exotic blooms of the camellia are not more often included. Perhaps the problem is one of supply for those who do not grow their own.

Though nothing to do with competitive work, a floral arrangement of camellias, tastefully executed, is a most lovely adornment of the home or decoration of the dinner table. Many a non-gardening flower arranger, not originally entirely sympathetic to the idea of spending time and money on acquiring camellias, has been known to change his or her outlook when those selfsame plants started producing sufficient blooms for some to be included in floral decorations.

Camellias vary considerably in their usefulness as cut blooms. Some, such as the lovely single white *williamsii* 'Francis Hanger', have little to commend them for they either fall as soon as picked, fail to open properly or shatter the moment they are open. Others such as the old white *japonica* 'Nobilissima' are good tempered in the extreme, lasting well when cut and opening well from part open buds. A knowledge of what to use as a cut flower and at what stage of development to cut the bloom is of the utmost importance.

If a camellia when cut persistently fails to open properly or browns or shatters too soon, one can be reasonably sure that this is the plant's habit and it is pointless to try to use it time after time as a cut bloom. Fortunately these traits apply to only a minority of camellias, the majority, if properly treated, being suitable in the extreme.

Having cut the blooms, the next matter to deal with is the problem of an air lock developing in the stem or of the cut bloom failing to suck up sufficient water to open, or keep, its bloom in pristine condition.

Even a non-flower arranger hears many and varied suggestions as to the best method: split the stems; dip the end of the stem in boiling water; burn the end over a gas jet or in the fire; just put xyz tablets in the water; bash the stems with a hammer ... and so on. No doubt each of these treatments is efficacious with certain flowers but it is doubtful if all are equally effective in the case of camellias.

Whichever method is used, remember that when cutting blooms for decorative display or flower arranging, do make a point, if at all possible, of combining cutting with pruning. Cut the stem which needs pruning back rather than one that does not. This sounds too obvious to be worth stating but, all too often after the cutting has been done, it is realized that a better result all round could have been achieved if a little more thought had been given to the best place to cut. The same applies when taking cuttings for propagation.

The camellia certainly has one great advantage for cutting in that its leaves never wilt. In fact, they can last in good condition from six weeks to six months, according to temperature and so on. Some experts accentuate their glossy foliage by giving them a light smear of clear vegetable oil – preferably without the garlic dressing! In addition, when one has sizeable plants to deal with, camellias have another great advantage in that they produce long, sweeping branches which can be cut more or less from inside the camellia bush. If cut just as the flowers are about to open, one or two can be of great assistance in building up the larger arrangement.

One could continue to sing the praises of the camellia as a cut bloom for many pages, but this is not possible due to lack of space. An excellent discourse on the subject is set out by Neil Treseder, an acknowledged expert on the floral arrangement of camellias, in his book, *Growing Camellias* (Nelson, 1975).

8
CAMELLIA LISTINGS

There are so many different camellias – species, varieties, hybrids, cultivars and so on – that there would be no problem in filling a complete book with nothing but descriptive listings. Whether the compiler had first-hand experience of each one would, however, be another matter. The longer the list, the more likely it is that many descriptions are copied from someone else's book or catalogue.

To my mind, this is a situation to avoid. Even though my own personal experience may be contrary to other growers, or even contrary to the vast majority of other growers, it is surely about my own experience that I am really entitled to write. To do otherwise is the same as copying someone else's book or writings.

Hence the camellia lists which follow reflect a very personal view. It is a view no doubt coloured by personal preference, likes and dislikes, by the soil and conditions in which I grow, by the climate I have to enjoy and suffer and a dozen and one other such factors. Nevertheless, it is a view born of experience and not one arrived at by slavishly copying someone else's work. The latter view, unfortunately, is far too prevalent in gardening articles, pamphlets and even books.

So much for the basis on which the following lists are compiled. Next, what do these lists seek to cover? First, a list of *japonica* cultivars which, in my opinion, for one reason or another, are worth describing because they are worth growing. Always remember that it is just my opinion and the vast majority of camellia enthusiasts may disagree. Equally, though, they may agree!

It follows then that in the list of *japonica* cultivars, as with the list of other species and hybrids, I have attempted to include plants which are outstanding for very different reasons. Such reasons may include the desirability of describing in, say, each colour, plants which cover each floral type – single, semi-double, paeony, etc. It is also important to describe outstanding garden plants as well as plants which produce outstanding blooms and, possibly most important of all, the plants described should be plants which are available commercially in the United Kingdom. To describe rarities which no one can acquire or buy always seems to me to be a meaningless overindulgence.

CAMELLIA JAPONICA

The following list of *C. japonica* cultivars is, then, my own preference.

'Aaron's Ruby'
Introduced in the United States in 1954. The growth of this camellia is slender, but vigorous, and of a slightly pendulous habit. The medium to large semi-double to anemone form flowers are of a bright metallic red. Petals are intermixed with petaloids around a mass of golden stamens. It has a long flowering season, being usually classed as E-L.

'Adelina Patti'
Named after the famous singer and introduced into the United Kingdom from Japan in 1889. This is a wonderful single camellia bearing exquisite pink blooms, the petals being edged with white. Despite the 100 years since its introduction it is still often seen among the competition blooms at the main camellia competitions and is still among the prize-winners. Although usually classed as M-L, I find it quite often opens some blooms very early in the season. Although not one of the most vigorous growers, making a more modest bush than some, it is of easy healthy growth.

'Adolphe Audusson'
A French-bred camellia released in 1877 this remains one of the greatest camellias and, arguably, the greatest red of all time. The dark geranium red, large semi-double blooms are borne in profusion on a medium growing bush of compact growth. It is an easily satisfied plant which we invariably recommend as a 'beginner's red'. Suitable for the beginner it undoubtedly is, but its blooms would grace the plantings of the most skilled and knowledgeable connoisseur. It is a 'must' for every grower of camellias.

'Adolphe Audusson' exists in two other forms, 'Adolphe Audusson Special', reputedly a predominantly white bloom, blotched red, and 'Adolphe Audusson Var.', a variegated form of 'Adolphe Audusson', of red spotted white. In practice, these two cultivars could well be merged into one. As with most variegated forms of camellia, the amount of blotching greatly depends on weather and growing conditions. 'Adolphe Audusson Special' varies from a red self, when it is indistinguishable from any other 'Adolphe', to the nomenclature description of 'a predominantly white "Adolphe Audusson"'. The predominantly white bloom blotched and gashed red normally requires greenhouse conditions or good hot weather to make its appearance in any numbers. Outdoors, in average conditions, it tends to be predominantly red blotched occasionally with white.

As 'Adolphe Audusson Var.' behaves in just the same way, it follows that according to situation (under glass or outdoors etc.) and weather (cold, warm or hot) its blooms vary from plain red to red blotched white to occasionally predominantly white blotched red, which are exactly the variations we get with 'Adolphe Audusson Special'.

'Alba Plena'

Introduced into the United Kingdom from China in 1792 this medium sized formal double white remains the double by which all other double whites are judged. It is of fairly slow compact bushy growth and suffers bad weather conditions outside as well as most double whites. There are several other forms of this fine old camellia, chief of which is 'Fimbriata' in which the edge of every petal is heavily fimbriated. In other respects it is just like the type.

'Alba Simplex'

There would seem to be little doubt that any single white *japonica* camellia is entitled to be called 'Alba Simplex'. However, life is rarely as simple as that with the result that the name 'Alba Simplex' is reserved for a medium to large single white which opens flat. The name 'Devonia' is reserved for more trumpet shaped white blooms, 'Rogetsu' normally has very large single white flowers and so on.

Whichever single white one goes for the great thing is to get a free blooming, well shaped plant. In my view, 'Snow Goose' is outstanding in every respect. It is very free flowering, opening almost flat and has all the necessary virility to make a fine dense bush. The flowers occasionally bear a pink fleck.

'Althaeiflora'

This dark red, medium paeony flowered camellia was certainly in the United Kingdom by 1824 so it has a long history behind it as a garden plant. It is reliable and free flowering in the extreme and the blooms are more frost resistant than many. Its dark glossy foliage is a picture in almost any position and it will put up with poorer positions better than most. It usually flowers mid-season. In some collections it appears to be very similar to 'Blackburnianum' – another very old plant.

'Ama-no-kawa' ('Milky Way')

There is probably more than one plant living under this name as one reads various descriptions of the bloom. It has been traced back to 1877 in Japan and arrived from there in the United States in 1930.

In the plant I know, the flowers are white (they are all white in the several different descriptions one can find, which is one blessing) and medium sized semi-double. I first saw this plant some 20 or 30 years ago at Wisley. Nearby was another white, namely, 'Hakurakuten', otherwise known as 'Wisley White'. Amongst all the white camellias there, these two were outstanding for one simple and extremely valuable reason. The weather prior to my seeing them had been appalling but they had withstood frost, wind and rain better than any other white camellias there. And so, although 'Ama-no-kawa' does not bear the largest blooms it does bear excellent blooms in great profusion once established and when its competitors have been written off by inclement weather it flowers happily on.

There is an excellent plant of this cultivar at Windsor Great Park which from time to time is greatly admired.

'Ama-no-kawa' makes an outstanding dense shapely bush with a spread as wide as it is tall. It makes a fine subject, too, for the patio or container culture. It flowers mid-season.

'Angel'

Produced in the United States in 1953 this large white semi-double camellia bears blooms with a profusion of notched and fluted petals and a slight golden tinge in the centre of its cupped blooms. It is a plant of vigorous compact growth. On occasions I have seen its blooms faintly washed flesh pink as though its angel's wings were momentarily caught in the sunset rays. It flowers mid-season and is a fine plant.

'Annie Wylam'

Raised in the United States in 1959 I would place this outstanding camellia in the absolute front rank. Its medium to large paeony blooms are of clear pink, shading to pale pink or white in the centre. The many, slender, petaloids do much to enhance the quality and attraction of the flower.

The plant is of somewhat slow but nevertheless vigorous growth making a fine dense upright bush flowering early to late.

'Annie Wylam' is one of those camellias which bear blooms of such delicate, ethereal beauty that one would be bound to think that the first sign of inclement weather would see it off. Nothing is further from the truth. 'Annie Wylam' is a fine, strong camellia and the strength, quality and staying power of its flowers belies their delicate appearance. I would never be without it.

'Arajishi'

Easily traced back to 1877 in Japan, and probably many years before that if one had the time to carry out further research, 'Arajishi' (or 'Arejishi' as it is also known) was introduced into the West in 1891. The name reputedly means 'Restive Lion' but, whatever its true meaning, 'Arajishi' is a gorgeous red of full paeony form with golden stamens exulting amongst a mass of frilled petaloids. Its leaves are almost as easily distinguishable as those of 'Francie L', being extremely long and deeply toothed or serrated.

It tends to make very long flexible shoots and branches, ideal for tying in on a wall or fence to create an espaliered plant. Grown in the normal way as a border or woodland plant it seems to need a more open position than some to set its flower buds freely. It is a vigorous, healthy bush and basically flowers mid-season.

'Auburn White'

This large white semi-double camellia was imported from Japan to the United States in 1900. It makes rather slow compact growth.

The flowers of 'Auburn White' are of excellent quality though possibly no better than many other semi-double whites. It is, however, outstanding and worthy of mention here as being one of the very last camellias to come into bloom. If one wants a late camellia – here it is.

'Augusto Leal de Gouveia Pinto'

A Portuguese plant dating back to 1890, it is a sport of 'Mathotiana'. It bears large double coral pink blooms, sometimes faintly flushed with lavender. Each petal is bordered in white so that the mature bloom is quite exquisite. It normally flowers mid-season but such is the delicacy of its colouring and the susceptibility of the flowers to damage from wind and rain that it is only really satisfactory for most of the United Kingdom if grown in the glasshouse or conservatory. In those conditions words like 'outstanding' and 'exquisite' simply fail to describe it.

'Berenice Perfection'

For those who love the pastel shades, 'Berenice Perfection' is out of this world. The medium to large formal double flowers are normally described as pale pink with a deeper pink margin, but this description is about as informative as it would be to say that Michelangelo's David is a statue of a young man with a sling! With 'Berenice', Nuccio's attained perfection, introducing it in 1965. It flowers mid-season on a vigorous, somewhat columnar, upright bushy plant.

To the camellia grower it is a never ending surprise that so many of the very delicate looking blooms, such as 'Annie Wylam', 'Berenice Perfection', 'Tomorrow Park Hill' and others are, in fact, among the toughest, both in bloom and plant growth.

This is certainly true in this case and, in addition, whilst 'Berenice Perfection' has that ethereal pastel beauty so many of us love, it, nevertheless, has sufficient colour to be an effective outdoor plant. It cannot be stressed too often that the palest pastels which are perfection under glass are little more than off white or, even worse, a dirty white when grown outdoors in the testing climate of the United Kingdom.

'Betty Sheffield'

Introduced in the United States in 1949, 'Betty Sheffield' is a medium to large semi-double to paeony form camellia, basically white, blotched and striped red and pink. It flowers mid-season on a strong, dense, compact bush. It may take a year or so longer than some to commence flowering but, thereafter, flowers regularly and freely.

Few camellias have given rise to as many sports as 'Betty Sheffield'. In all there are over a dozen. It is, perhaps, a little unfortunate that in extolling the praises of many of these, the value and beauty of the original 'Betty Sheffield' is often overlooked.

Chief amongst the many sports one can mention are: 'Betty Sheffield Blush' with pale pink blooms and variegated deeper markings; 'Betty Sheffield White', a white bloom which normally comes true; 'Betty Sheffield Pink', a deep pink form of the original 'Betty Sheffield'; 'Betty Sheffield Supreme', the greatest of the clan 'Sheffield'. It is a large bloom, white with a deep pink to red border on each petal. The width and colour of the border varies considerably but, whatever the variation, the bloom is lovely in the extreme.

Where there is a rose there is always a thorn and, in the case of this rose, it shows a more than willing desire to revert at the drop of a hat to 'Betty Sheffield Pink' or some other form of 'Betty Sheffield' far less desirable than 'Betty Sheffield Supreme'.

For this reason, every reputable grower warns his customers that 'Betty Sheffield Supreme' may continue 'Supreme' with white petals bordered in red and pink but that it is highly likely that it will revert to plain pink, white blotched red, plain white or some other combination of red and white.

It is unfortunate that although 'Betty Sheffield' seems more than ready to change to, say, a deep pink self, once having done so it rarely seems to have the same desire to change back to the 'Supreme' form.

'Bienville'

This medium to large formal double white has incurved petal edges which do something to enhance the bloom. Apart from this, it is a healthy compact growing plant with no fussiness, flowering early to predominantly mid-season. It was bred in the United States in 1961.

'Blaze of Glory'

Introduced in the United States in 1965 this is a really eye-catching, large anemone form of brilliant, blazing red blooms showing a few golden stamens amongst the petals. It flowers early to mid-season on a compact plant very suitable for container culture.

'Blood of China' syn. 'Victor Emmanuel'

A deep salmon red, medium-sized, semi-double to loose paeony form. Although introduced in the United States in 1928 it is still deservedly popular and flowers late in the season. It rather seems that there may be more than one form of this camellia in gardens and on the market. Although both have somewhat similar flowers, one is an extremely dense slow growing shrub which shows little inclination to flower for a good many years. The other is a less dense, much faster growing plant which flowers at a relatively early age and regularly and well thereafter.

'Bob Hope'

Probably the darkest black red to date. Introduced by the famous Nuccio nursery in 1972 it is a large, semi-double to paeony form flower and blooms mid-season. Growth is compact and slow, making it an ideal container plant.

'Bob's Tinsie'

Another Nuccio success. These brilliant red, miniature to small anemone form blooms are irresistible to all camellia growers who like miniatures. Introduced in 1962, 'Bob's Tinsie' is a comparatively small growing plant with leaves in keeping with its miniature blooms. It likes sun, flowers mid-season and tends, ultimately, to make a bush taller than wide.

'Brushfield's Yellow'

A medium-sized bloom of anemone form in which antique white-guard petals surround a double centre of pale primrose yellow petaloids giving the whole bloom the appearance of a pale yellow camellia. True it is not the long sought after yellow camellia which, so far, has evaded every hybridizing effort but, until that is achieved, 'Brushfield's Yellow' is a very good substitute. It was raised by an Australian, the late Keith Brushfield, and introduced in 1948. It flowers medium to late and is excellent for the open garden or a container.

'C. M. Hovey'

Propagated in the United States in 1853, this medium to large formal double camellia of brilliant red colour is a 'must' for any collection.

It is a reliable, free-flowering plant blooming mid-season and makes a strong, compact bush. In fact, there are not all that many formal double reds around and 'C. M. Hovey' is still, undoubtedly, amongst the best.

'C. M. Wilson'

Introduced in 1949 this is one of the many 'Elegans' sports with similar wavy leaves and dense, rather low, habit. The flowers are light pink anemone centred, shading paler towards the perimeter. It flowers mid-season and bears good, large blooms. Like all the 'Elegans' family it is an excellent container or patio shrub.

'Can Can'

This beautiful Australian cultivar is a sport of 'Lady Loch' and bears medium-sized paeony blooms. The spectacular blooms are pale pink with ruffled petals, finely edged with lavender pink. Introduced in Australia in 1961 it flowers mid-season.

'Cecile Brunazzi'

An outstanding plant for small gardens and container culture. Introduced in the United States in 1957 it bears in profusion large, semi-double flowers of light pink not dissimilar to the colour of 'Donation'. Growth is slow and densely bushy and the plant blooms mid-season.

'Cheerio'

An excellent white striped and flecked red camellia, it bears medium-sized semi-double blooms in profusion. Growth is extremely compact, making it excellent for a container or small garden. It flowers mid-season and was introduced in the United States in 1947.

'Cheryl Lynn'

This lovely medium-sized formal double, sugar pink camellia has much to commend it. Its blooms are beautiful in the extreme and have the added bonus for the United Kingdom that they shatter when over. Growth is graceful and spreading and the blooming period mid-season. Introduced in the United States in 1965.

'Christmas Beauty'

A tall slender plant with weeping branches. Ideal for training on a wall or fence although with a little judicious pruning it is perfectly satisfactory in the open ground. It bears large semi-double blooms with fluted petals of bright red and its outstanding dark, shining foliage sets off the blooms to perfection. Introduced in the United States in 1958, 'Christmas Beauty' starts to flower early but normally continues over a long period.

'Clarise Carleton'

One of the earliest red paeony form camellias to bloom and so is a 'must' for every collection. It normally commences flowering outdoors in February and may well continue into May.

The bush is dense and upright with dark, rather narrow but deeply notched, leaves. 'Clarise Carleton' was a 1965 introduction in the United States.

'Colonial Dame'

This large semi-double to paeony form to formal double white is occasionally blushed pink and flowers mid-season. Introduced in the United States in 1955, it produces vigorous, slender, somewhat open, growth.

'Conrad Hilton'

This white sport of 'High Hat' has a certain something which places it high up in the camellia list. Introduced in the United States in 1955 it bears medium-sized paeony form blooms in early to mid-season. 'High Hat' is, of course, a pale pink sport of 'Daikagura' and, from time to time, 'Conrad Hilton' will bear blooms with the faintest hint of pink. As with the others of its family, 'Conrad Hilton' is slow growing, producing a dense compact bush which makes it ideal for container culture.

'Contessa Lavinia Maggi'
One sometimes wonders whether this old Italian camellia introduced as long ago as 1860 will ever be surpassed as a formal double bi-colour. It is a medium-sized formal double with pale pink and carmine stripes on a white ground and remains the most popular striped formal double camellia in the United Kingdom. It is a strong, upright grower with large rounded leaves and sometimes sports pure red flowers which, when propagated, are known as 'Contessa Lavinia Maggi Rosea', itself a very fine camellia.

However, although the striped form frequently sports red, the red form rarely, if ever, sports striped. As a result, if red flowers appear, the sport branch should be cut out. Enormous old bushes are sometimes seen in which half the plant flowers striped and the other half of the bush flowers red.

'Daitarin' (or 'Dewatairin')
Also known as 'Hatsusakura', this is an outstanding large, rose pink, single camellia with a mass of petaloids in the centre. It was introduced in Japan in 1941 and is early flowering on a strong, vigorous, rounded bush.

'Dear Jenny'
Bears superb large, semi-double to paeony form, pure white blooms on a vigorous compact growing plant. It was introduced in the United States in 1959 and flowers early to mid-season.

'Debutante'
Well known as a parent of several outstanding hybrids, such as 'Debbie', in its own right 'Debutante' is equally well known for its prolific crop of light pink, medium-sized full paeony blooms. True it may need to reach a certain size before it commences flowering really freely but once started it certainly keeps it up. It is a strong, vigorous, upright grower, with rather light green leaves. It was introduced in the United States in 1905.

'Dona Herzilia de Freitas Magalhaes'
The camellia with the longest name is, in fact, Portuguese and released in 1952. It is normally a medium-sized semi-double to anemone form red camellia, very worthy but not terribly outstand-

ing. However, if it can be grown on a clay or shale soil it produces distinctively purple blooms and it is for this that it is famous. It flowers mid-season and is named after a descendant of the explorer, Magellan.

'Drama Girl'

Some of the largest blooms that one can grow outdoors, they are literally enormous semi-doubles of deep salmon pink. They last a long time. 'Drama Girl' flowers mid-season and was introduced in the United States in 1950. It makes long, drooping branches which means it is an ideal subject for a wall or fence. Grown as an open ground shrub, it is perfectly satisfactory but needs some regular judicious pruning. It will then produce a fine compact plant.

'Dr Burnside'

Introduced in 1962 in the United States we have grown and extolled its virtues for many, many years – long before it was really introduced to the United Kingdom market. As a garden plant, we have found it completely reliable producing dark red, semi-double to normally full paeony, blooms with just a few yellow stamens showing. It is a fine, rounded bushy grower with quite bold dark green leaves. It is suitable for both open ground and container culture. It flowers mid-season to late and is as fine a dark red as one could want. We rank 'Dr Burnside' as the best all round dark red to date. Of its competitors which we grow, 'Midnight' must come a close second then 'Bob Hope' for its even darker blooms and, finally, 'Wildfire' – more beautiful but we would like to see a little more vigour here.

'Duc de Bretagne'

Introduced by Van Houtte in 1846 this fine old camellia bears a profusion of medium-sized double blooms, light red, with a tiny white fleck on the edge of each petal. It flowers early to mid-season and is tough and reliable. In the past, we have exported a number of plants to Brittany where they take pleasure in planting it to honour their local duke – the Duke of Brittany.

'Elegans'

It is over 150 years since this camellia was first introduced and it remains as popular today as in those far off days. When Chandler introduced it in the United Kingdom in 1831 it is highly doubtful if he foresaw that it was due to become the parent of a large number of famous sports and seedlings.

'Elegans' flowers mid-season to late and bears a huge crop of large deep pink anemone form flowers with notched petals and, occasionally, a few white petaloids. It has a dense spreading habit as do its progeny. Its wavy, somewhat lax, leaves are distinctive. An excellent container plant.

'Elegans Champagne'

There are good 'Elegans' sports such as 'Elegans Splendour', pink fading to white frilled edge, but the most recent is 'Elegans Champagne'. Introduced in the United States in 1975 as a sport 'Elegans Splendour' it has a fine large paeony flower with large white outer petals around a cream centre of petaloids. This is yet another Nuccio introduction and flowers early to mid-season.

In general, all the 'Elegans' sports are dense, comparatively low growing plants ideal for container culture or the open ground. They are tough, vigorous and hardy.

'Elegans Supreme'

Although a sport of 'Elegans', this is a totally different flower, large anemone in form with wide deeply serrated petals of deep glowing pink to salmon pink. It was introduced in the United States in 1960 and flowers early to mid-season to late.

'Elizabeth le Bey'

A large, loose, paeony bloom of deep rose pink with erect central petaloids. Introduced in the United States in 1948 it has a long blooming season and the added advantage of vigorous, spreading, pendulous growth.

'Ellen Sampson'

Very popular in Australasia, 'Ellen Sampson' was produced in New Zealand in 1938. It makes a fine container or border plant bearing large, semi-double blooms of carmine pink with two rows of large waved petals and a centre of gold tipped stamens. It blooms mid-season to late.

'Emmet Pfingstl'

This is a variegated form of 'Joseph Pfingstl' with dark red and white flowers, the form varying from semi-double to loose paeony. It blooms early to mid-season and was introduced in the United States in 1950.

'Emperieur de Russie'

A fine old camellia with imperial scarlet blooms of medium to large paeony form. Growth of the plant is quite slow and very compact, with fine, dark green leaves which set off the blooms to perfection. It was introduced in Belgium in 1856 and flowers mid-season.

'Erin Farmer'

A most beautiful camellia with large, semi-double to paeony form flowers, white, flushed orchid pink, amongst deeply fluted petals and heavy golden stamens. It was introduced in the United States in 1962, flowers mid-season and makes a fine bush.

If it has a fault, it is that, in some seasons, the pink flushing outdoors is too pale and fails to stand out sufficiently. Given some protection the lovely pastel shaded blooms are seen to perfection.

'Extravaganza'

This might almost be called the ultimate in variegated blooms. In 'Extravaganza', they are large to very large anemone form, white, vividly and profusely striped and marked light red.

Introduced in the United States in 1960 it has vigorous, compact, upright growth and flowers mid-season. It can sometimes produce pure red blooms on a 'sport' branch. If this does occur, be sure to cut them out.

'Faith'

A large flowered, semi-double to anemone form, rose pink camellia with slightly variegated white petaloids. It makes a handsome upright, well branched shrub, fine as a specimen on its own or as the centrepiece to a mixed camellia planting. Introduced in the United States in 1956 it flowers mid-season.

'Fimbriata' (syn. 'Fimbriata Alba')

See 'Alba Plena'.

'Finlandia'

A fine white with medium-sized semi-double blooms with swirled and fluted petals and a beautiful wide centre of golden stamens. It is a sturdy, healthy grower of medium, compact growth. It flowers early to mid-season and was imported from Japan to the United States in 1940, when it immediately sported 'Finlandia Variegated', where some petal edges are lightly streaked with crimson. It quite often does flower pure white for a season or so.

'Finlandia' has produced at least six other variants including

'Finlandia Blush', 'Finlandia Red', 'Sunset Oaks' and 'Monte Carlo'.

'Furo-an'

This old Japanese cultivar bears medium-sized, soft pink, single blooms, reminiscent of a wild rose.

It flowers mid-season from an early age. A sizeable bush of 'Furo-an' covered with its dainty flowers is, indeed, an enchanting sight. It makes a moderate, dense bush and is an excellent choice for anyone seeking a lovely single, pink, *japonica*.

'Gauntlettii' ('Sodegakushi', 'Lotus')

Can be traced back to 1879. Some authorities say 'Sodegakushi' is the prior name, others give 'Gauntlettii', whilst the nomenclature book lists it under 'Lotus' as it has been known under that name in the United States for many years!

Whichever name should have priority is probably not all that important for here we have this great white, large semi-double, of water lily form. It makes a rather open branched shrub, with very large easily recognizable leathery leaves. It has been used as a parent and tends to pass on the large, leathery leaf as in the hybrid 'Exaltation'.

'Gauntlettii' needs careful placing in the garden as its glorious blooms are easily marred by inclement weather. In addition, if the weather or its situation is too cold, they may open only to a cup-shaped form. In a greenhouse or conservatory it is, of course, perfection. Its flowering peaks mid-season.

'General Leclerc'

Produced in France in 1950, this is a fine, large, deep red, semi-double to loose paeony form flower which blooms at its best at mid-season. The bush is medium sized and compact.

'Glen 40'

It is said to be synonymous with 'Coquettii', but if that is true then the 'Coquettii' which we have grown for years must be something else for there are distinct differences.

'Glen 40' was introduced in the United States in 1942 and has achieved popularity worldwide as one of the most profusely blooming *japonica* cultivars there is. It is a deep red, medium to large semi-double to rose form double, blooming mid-season to late. Growth is slow and compact, which means it is entirely suitable for container culture for many years.

There seems to be no reason why 'Glen 40' does not appear to have achieved in the United Kingdom that high degree of popularity it holds in its native home and the Antipodes.

'Gloire de Nantes'

Although approaching its hundredth birthday, having been produced in France in 1895, 'Gloire de Nantes' remains an outstanding camellia for its early flowering habit, sometimes commencing as early as November in the United Kingdom. Its growth is only moderate, very compact and upright yet strong. Its medium-sized, semi-double, rose pink blooms are produced in profusion making it highly satisfactory as a container shrub although it is equally good in the border.

'Granada'

This vivid red, large semi-double to paeony form camellia has, for a very long time, been a favourite of ours. It is strange that only comparatively recently have its virtues been recognized in the United Kingdom leading to its 'introduction'. 'Granada' was raised in the United States in 1968 and flowers mid-season. It makes medium growth with fine broad, rounded, dark green leaves.

'Grand Prix'

Another superb brilliant red, bearing very large semi-double flowers with irregular petals. It was introduced in the United States in 1968 by Nuccio and flowers mid-season.

It is a vigorous grower which tends to make long spreading branches which render it an ideal plant to train on a wall or fence. With a little judicious pruning it will, equally, make a fine open ground compact plant.

'Grand Slam'

Yet another Nuccio introduction, this time in 1962 and yet another outstanding red. The very large flowers outdoors are semi-double to paeony form. The rich red flowers are superb in any form. 'Grand Slam' flowers mid-season to late on a strong growing bush with superb large, dark green leaves which show off its blooms.

'Guest of Honour'

There has been criticism of this camellia in the United Kingdom on the grounds that it is a shy bloomer. For those who have so criticized it, no doubt, it has been shy but our experience is quite different as we find it a free flowerer on an extremely strong bush.

For those who want a strong, rapid, but dense grower, this is it. Its large to very large, semi-double to loose paeony form flowers are of rosy salmon pink. Introduced in the United States in 1955 it flowers mid-season.

'Guilio Nuccio'
Another Nuccio introduction in 1956 and an absolute winner. This outstanding semi-double bears blooms of glowing salmon red of great quality. It flowers mid-season. Growth is vigorous but can tend to make a spreading, rather than an upright, bush. If one searches long enough, one will almost always find a fishtail leaf or so among the foliage emphasizing one of its parents, namely, 'Kingyo Tsubaki', the 'Fishtail' camellia.

'Guilio Nuccio' is considered by many to be the finest *japonica* camellia raised to date. There is a great deal to support this view.

'Hakurakuten' (syn. 'Wisley White')
This is a superb white, not only for its large, purest white, semi-double blooms, but for the fact that it will come out of its corner fighting, even smiling, after an appalling spell of weather, so bad as to persuade most plants to defer their blooming until the following season!

Introduced from Japan in 1929, 'Hakurakuten' makes a sturdy, upright bush with fine leaves. It flowers early and, grown outside, often starts the season by producing formal double flowers.

'Hatsuzakura'
See 'Daitarin'.

'Hawaii'
A beautiful 'Elegans' sport with large paeony flowers, its petals almost white, shading to pale pink. They are so fimbriated and crimped as to make the flower look like some beautiful tutu.

Introduced in the United States in 1961, 'Hawaii' is one of the last camellias to flower. Growth is low and dense, making it, like all the 'Elegans' family, eminently suitable for container culture.

'High Hat'
A lovely light pink sport of 'Daikagura'; unlike the last named, it flowers very early. Its large blooms are paeony form and more resistant to the weather than many. It was introduced in the United States in 1945 and makes very slow, dense, upright growth. Highly suitable for container culture.

'Ice Queen'

A 1965 Australian introduction which, outdoors, is a medium-sized semi-double white with a small, but telling, centre of golden stamens. Under glass, it develops its flat cartwheel form. It is a plant of smallish leaves and dense, rounded shape, flowering mid-season.

'Iwane-shibori'

Listed in Japan in 1877. It is a mid-season medium semi-double, quite often showing a few petaloids, rose red and white. A most attractive camellia and a slow grower, it is very suitable for container culture.

'J. J. Whitfield'

This 1950 United States introduction is a medium-sized paeony bloom of bright deep red on a moderate upright bush. It flowers from early (often very early) to mid-season.

There is a variegated form listed in the nomenclature book as 'J. J. Whitfield Var.', of dark red, blotched white.

It may be that 'J. J. Whitfield' sports very freely, for my own experience is that in the nursery about half the plants flower pure red and the other half red blotched white. The variegated form is very attractive.

'Janet Waterhouse'

The late Prof Waterhouse named this cultivar after his wife and introduced it to Australia in 1952. The flowers are medium-sized, formal double, of purest white which stands the weather quite well. They are borne on a slow growing bushy plant with outstandingly good, dark green, foliage.

'Janet Waterhouse' flowers mid-season and, because of its habit, is a fine plant for a container or a focal point in a formal garden.

'Jean Clere'

The 1850 Australian cultivar, 'Aspasia MacArthur', has given rise to a considerable number of sports – at least nine, possibly more. Amongst the most famous of these are 'Lady Loch', 'Can Can', 'Margaret Davis' and 'Jean Clere'.

The gorgeous 'Jean Clere' is a medium-sized, full paeony form bloom of red, tellingly edged with white. In fact, it is the exact reverse of 'Margaret Davis' which is white, edged with red.

It flowers early to mid-season and makes rather slow, medium bushy growth.

'Jean Lynn'

A medium-sized semi-double to paeony form flower of white, striped and flecked carmine.

It flowers mid-season on a compact plant and is reliable in every way. Introduced in Australia in 1941, it has produced one or two sports of which the light pink 'Nancy Bird' is a worthwhile plant.

'Jingle Bells'

This miniature bears small crimson anemone flowers on a bush of good upright growth. It is very free flowering, given plenty of light, and is a sport of 'Tinker Bell' flowering early to mid-season. Introduced in the United States in 1959 by Nuccio.

'Joshua E. Youtz'

With almost all flowers, one hears of some outstanding variety or cultivar in comparison with which all others should be judged. For instance, we are told that red rhododendrons should be compared with 'Jean Marie'. Equally, we are told that the lovely old camellia 'Alba Plena' is the criterion in comparison with which all other double whites should be judged. Others suggest 'Mathotiana Alba' as the criteria and yet others say that 'Margarete Hertrich', that wonderful, many petalled, formal double which is acknowledged to be among the élite, should control the test.

However much one may argue points of beauty, of whiteness, of bloom, of healthiness and a hundred and one other characteristics, in the end we come down to personal choice, the choice which everyone is free to make for himself, and so in our nursery we make no excuse for our choice, which is that 'Joshua E. Youtz' is the greatest all-round double white that we grow.

Outdoors, 'Joshua E. Youtz' is a large formal double of purest white, one which defies the winter weather, the gales and storms and which, in due time, opens its pristine blooms as though it had just been born rather than fought its way through six or more months of ghastly autumn and winter. And what beautiful blooms they are. Whiter than white, fully double, large and perfect in size and form and very much more resistant to bad weather than any other formal double whites which we grow.

'Joshua E. Youtz' flowers early to mid-season. It is slow growing and makes a bushy but very upright shrub, ideal for container culture and equally at home as an exclamation mark in the shrubbery.

It was reputedly brought from Japan to the United States in 1915 and to be synonymous with 'White Daikagura' (although we have certain reservations about that). Grown indoors it usually assumes its less attractive paeony form.

'Julia France'
Introduced in the United States in 1958, 'Julia France' is a poem of beauty and simplicity. It is a superb, large, semi-double with fluted petals and large foliage. In colour it is an exquisite silver pink, so lovely as to make one catch one's breath. It makes a fine shrub of vigorous upright growth.

'Juno'
This has a number of synonyms but we are too long in the tooth to stick out our necks and suggest those which are truly the same plant for there really are several large, single, rosy red camellias around.

Suffice it to say that, whatever the competition under various names might have to offer, the 'Juno' we grow (it came originally from the late Lionel Fortescue at the Garden House Buckland Monachorum) will always hold its own.

Once it reaches a couple of feet or so high, it is free flowering in the extreme. From early in the camellia season to mid-season, it is covered with large, single blooms, 4in (10cm) or more across, set off by a superb boss of yellow stamens.

Although described as rosy red, we have a large plant of it growing alongside a large plant of 'Adolphe Audusson' and close scrutiny may disclose colour differences. Looked at from a modest distance, however, it is difficult to say, from the colour point of view, which plant is which.

'Juno' is not really a plant for the timid. Clothed with dark, glossy, green foliage, it is extremely strong growing and will make a fine, large, dense bush to block out any unwanted view, whilst plants like 'High Hat' or 'Cecile Brunazzi' will make only 3 to 4ft (0.9 to 1.2m).

'K. Sawada'
This is a fine, large, white formal double to rose form double, flowering mid-season. It is a vigorous grower, making a fine rounded bush. Introduced into the United States in 1940.

'Kelvingtonii' (syn. 'Kellingtonia', 'Monstruoso Rubra', 'Giganta')
It is also known by half a dozen other names! This camellia was imported to the United States in 1840 when it was named 'Magnolia King'. Each country taking it on seemed to give it another name. In

Italy it has always been 'Monstruoso Rubra' and we brought it in the United Kingdom forty years ago as 'Kelvingtonii'. Its correct name is 'Giganta' but old habits die hard!

'Giganta' is a large semi-double, anemone form to paeony form, raspberry red marbled white. It flowers mid-season on a rather open, almost weeping, bush which benefits from a certain amount of judicious pruning during its first few years to build up a bushy branch framework.

'Kick Off'
Another Nuccio introduction of 1962, this is generally the earliest bi-colour. It is a medium to large, flat, paeony form flower, frilly pale pink, marbled and striped deeper pink. It is a vigorous plant which flowers over quite a long period.

'Konronkoko'
This was brought from Japan to the United States in 1930 and still remains a highly popular camellia in the very dark red (some call it black red) range. Bearing medium-sized double blooms, it is reliable and very free flowering on a vigorous rounded bush.

'Kramer's Supreme'
Reputedly fragrant, we find this camellia needs the benefit of a greenhouse or a really warm summer to set flower buds freely. A brilliant turkey red, it produces large paeony form blooms quite often starting in December outdoors.

For the reasons of bud setting, flowering period and fragrance (a beautiful carnation scent indoors) it is really better to treat this as a greenhouse shrub, although one should hasten to add that it is fully hardy outdoors. Introduced in 1957 in the United States.

'L'Avvenire' (syn. 'Lallarook', 'Laurel Leaf')
An original 1854 Italian introduction whose name means 'the Future', it is a medium, formal double bloom, soft pink, sometimes with white marbling. The degree of white marbling on a bush varies very considerably from season to season.

After a year or so of white marbling on 90 per cent of the blooms, our stock plant flowered plain pink for at least four years but, last year, decided to be a marbled beauty again!

'L'Avvenire' flowers mid-season to late and makes slow, compact growth. Its leaves reputedly resemble those of the laurel — hence one of its alternative names.

'Lady Clare'

This was introduced from Japan in 1887 as 'Akashi-Gata' and is probably the easiest of all camellias to recognize and name for it is unique in making a great, round, spreading bush. It bears large, semi-double pink flowers with a barrel of white stamens and sometimes petaloids.

It is a strong grower and flowers mid-season.

'Lady de Saumarez'

A sport of 'Tricolor', it was introduced by the Caledonian Nursery of Guernsey in 1920 and named after the local de Saumarez family. We grow from a second generation plant of the original introduction and our 'Lady de Saumarez' is solid red, not red spotted white, as is often described.

In view of the apparent disagreement as to whether the self red is 'Lady de Saumarez' or 'Tricolor Red' we are pleased to note that the supplement to the 8th edition of *Bean*, dealing with the 'Tricolor' sports, states: ' "Lady de Saumarez" with self-coloured carmine pink flowers is the best and most stable.'

Whatever its correct name, the light red form of 'Tricolor' is a fine plant being very free flowering on a compact, upright, rounded bush with rather undulated edges to the leaves. It flowers early to mid-season.

A final thought: if 'Lady de Saumarez' is in fact a red spotted white form of 'Tricolor' what is the difference between it and 'Lady McKinnon', described as a rich crimson, mottled white, form of 'Tricolor'?

'Lady Loch'

Another sport of 'Aspasia MacArthur', introduced in Australia in 1898, 'Lady Loch' is light pink, edged white in a medium-sized formal double to paeony form bloom.

It flowers mid-season on a rather slow growing, compact bush.

'Lady McCulloch'

A very old camellia but not to be underrated for its medium-sized semi-double blooms, light pink with a darker fleck, and borne in profusion on a vigorous shapely bush. Flowering mid-season, it tends to sport, producing full pink or light red blooms.

'Lady Vansittart'

Imported from Japan in 1877 this camellia remains highly popular, flowering mid-season to late. It is a medium-sized semi-double with somewhat undulating petals of white, flushed and marked rose pink.

Its foliage is rather holly-like. It is slow growing, making a dense, rounded bush excellent for container culture.

'Laurie Bray'

The medium to large soft, pale pink, semi-double to paeony blossoms with ruffled petals are borne in great profusion and regularity on a dense rounded bush. A most reliable camellia produced in Australia in 1955.

'Lily Pons'

This 1955 United States introduction is quite different from any other white camellia we grow. The flowers are single and occasionally semi-double in form, with long, lily-like or tongue-shaped petals, flaring out from a delicate centre of greenish stamens with golden anthers.

It makes slender growth and needs a little early pruning to make a good compact bush and is at its best mid-season.

'Little Bit'

A little miniature charmer of anemone to paeony form, red and white in colour, looking for all the world like a carnation.

It was introduced in the United States in 1958, flowers mid-season and makes a nice compact bush.

'Lulu Belle'

A lovely, large, semi-double to loose paeony form white with a distinct creamy, yellow centre. It has particularly fine, almost reticulated, foliage on a somewhat slow growing, upright bush. Introduced in the United States in 1909, it flowers early.

'Madame Charles Blard'

This is a fine old French camellia introduced in 1920. It bears medium-sized white paeony blooms, with a distinct yellowish centre for the first few days. These are borne over a long period commencing mid-season.

It tends to make long, almost weeping, growth which makes it an excellent subject for a fence or wall. A good dense bush can quite easily be attained with a little judicious pruning for the first few years.

'Madame Martin Cachet'

Not to be confused with 'Madame Cachet' which is basically white to pale flesh pink, 'Madame Martin Cachet' is a favourite of ours. It flowers freely and early, producing medium-sized, light rose pink flowers of paeony form which greatly resemble pink carnations.

Introduced in France in 1920 it is a healthy, strong growing camellia which we find utterly reliable.

'Madame Victor de Bisschop' (syn. 'Le Lys')

A medium-sized semi-double to paeony form camellia with a centre of creamy stamens and, at times, petaloids. It weathers better than most whites and flowers mid-season.

An old camellia introduced in Belgium, it remains, deservedly, popular. It makes a good compact bush.

'Magic City'

A fine medium-sized fire red, marked, moired and variegated white paeony form bloom, flowering mid-season.

Introduced in 1965 in the United States it makes a vigorous, upright bush. As with so many variegated camellias, the grower should not be too upset if, every now and then, he gets all red blooms. Just have patience and, sooner or later, the white markings will appear again.

'Maiden's Blush'

This is a medium-sized formal double with incurved petals of palest flesh pink, flecked and marked deeper pink, flowering early to mid-season.

It is a lovely camellia and outstandingly hardy and weather resistant. Imported from Japan in 1900, 'Maiden's Blush' makes a good, strong, compact bush.

'Man Size'

The name is, of course, a typical example of man's perversity for 'Man Size' is, in fact, a very charming miniature anemone form bloom in purest white. Introduced in the United States in 1961 it flowers mid-season and makes a good medium-sized upright shrub.

'Margaret Davis'

Yet another 'Aspasia' sport, appearing in 1961, 'Margaret Davis' is a beautiful medium-sized, informal double white with picotee petals edged brilliant rose or vermilion. This edging may be the finest line or a broad band and varies from season to season. It flowers mid-season and is a rather slow growing, compact plant.

This is a highly popular and successful plant for, unlike 'Betty Sheffield Supreme', which is as likely to turn to pure pink as to be red with a white border, 'Margaret Davis' can normally be relied on to produce its true flowers.

'Margarete Hertrich'

This medium-sized formal double white is of superb shape, fine substance and is made up of many small notched and perfectly imbricated petals. It always appears to have more petals than any other formal double camellia.

Introduced in the United States in 1944 and flowering mid-season, it makes a shapely, vigorous, compact bush.

'Maroon and Gold'

Aptly named, as this is a small, maroon coloured paeony form flower, with sumptuous golden stamens flowering mid-season to late. Introduced in the United States in 1961 by Nuccio it is a fine, vigorous, upright growing plant.

'Mathotiana'

This large double camellia is crimson, sometimes with a purple cast, particularly if the weather turns cold. It flowers mid-season onwards and makes a vigorous, compact bush.

'Mathotiana' has many names and was known in Europe in 1840 when it was exported to the United States. Although perfectly satisfactory as an open ground shrub, its blooms are only seen to absolute perfection under glass or at least with wall protection.

'Mathotiana Alba'

It is generally accepted that 'Mathotiana Alba' is no relative of the last named 'Mathotiana'. 'Mathotiana Alba' is a superb large, formal double white which makes vigorous, upright growth.

Unfortunately, it does have a tendency to succumb to bad weather to the extent that frost or rain may mark and brown its supreme double white blooms more than most.

For this reason it is best grown under some protection. Given this, it is superb. It was introduced from Belgium in 1858 and named after Monsieur Mathot of Ghent. It flowers medium to late season.

'Mathotiana Rosea'

This is a fine, large, formal double clear pink sport of the last named. It has some of the virtues which 'Mathotiana Alba' lacks in that, above all, it is weather resistant and not normally marked by adverse conditions. For anyone whose idea of a camellia is the old large, formal double pink Victorian bloom, this is a must and, when one has had a good look at it, who can possibly say that our Victorian forebears were wrong?

Yet another sport of 'Mathotiana Alba' is the famous 'Souvenir de Bahuaud Litou', an even paler form than 'Mathotiana Rosea'. In most respects, all three are similar but, of the three, we find that only 'Mathotiana Rosea' can be classed as an all-round outdoor garden shrub. Whilst the other two grow well and flower well outdoors, their susceptibility to weather damage makes it clear that, in most areas of the United Kingdom, they are better with a little protection. 'Mathotiana Rosea' was introduced in the United Kingdom in 1875 and 'Bahuaud Litou' in France in 1908.

'Mathotiana Supreme'

As a garden plant we rank this as supreme as its name in the 'Mathotiana' clan. It is a large semi-double to paeony form, with irregular petals interspersed with stamens in superb red.

It buds well, it flowers well, it makes a very healthy, shapely plant, flowering mid-season to late. What more could one ask? It was introduced in the United States in 1951.

'Mattie Cole'

A beautiful large single, rose carmine flower, early to mid-season. There is something which makes this an outstanding camellia. It is difficult to say what it is. Perhaps it is the darker veining on the large blooms. Perhaps it is the fine boss of golden stamens and petaloids. Who is to say, but it certainly has something which takes it out of the usual run of singles.

Flowering early to mid-season, it was introduced in Australia in 1955 and tends to make slender, spreading branches although no one can fairly criticize the shape of the ultimate shrub.

'Melinda Hackett'

It is arguable that we have far too many anemone to paeony form pinks, but everybody must want a few. If so, the choice of 'Melinda Hackett' with large medium pink flowers could not be bettered. It is free flowering, hardy and consistently good on a moderate sized, bushy plant.

Introduced in the United States in 1960, it flowers early to mid-season.

'Midnight'

We rank this second only to 'Dr Burnside' in the really dark reds. It is a medium-sized semi-double to anemone form bloom, borne in great profusion on a healthy compact plant.

Introduced by Nuccio in 1963, as with all of their introductions, it is outstanding. It flowers mid-season and as a shrub makes vigorous, compact, upright growth.

'Midnight Serenade'

This is probably the best single darkest red. The flower is medium to large, the bush dense and upright. It flowers freely mid-season to late and was introduced in the United States in 1973.

'Miss Charleston'

One of the greatest semi-double to paeony form reds in existence, 'Miss Charleston' produces huge, deep red blooms with a high centre. Introduced in the United States in 1961 it flowers mid-season to late.

To us, it is one of the greatest camellias – full stop! We make no apology for this for 'Miss Charleston's' flowers are superb. They are produced over a very long season and those produced at the very end after almost all camellias have finished flowering are as large and as perfect as those produced in the middle of its flowering season. Added to this, it makes a medium-sized, compact bush, fit for any use be it container, border or woodland planting.

'Miss Universe'

This is a medium to large paeony form, white camellia. It is free flowering and vigorous in growth, at its best in mid-season.

'Miss Universe', although not as consistent as 'Lady Clare', frequently insists on making a prostrate plant just like 'Lady Clare'. However, give it an inch and it will take a mile and, rather than producing a wholly worthwhile prostrate plant like 'Lady Clare', it will on occasions revert to a more popular form.

Since its introduction to the United States in 1960, 'Miss Universe' has been a consistently good bloomer, selected from amongst many others as a really fine camellia.

'Monte Carlo'

This light pink sport of 'Finlandia' has much to commend it. Like 'Finlandia', it is of rugged constitution and flowers consistently and well, its blooms being more weather resistant than many.

Introduced in the United States in 1950 it produces medium-sized blooms, semi-double with rather fluted petals on a medium-sized, compact bush. It flowers early to mid-season.

'Moonlight Bay'

A most beautiful pale pastel bloom. The large semi-double pale, orchid pink blooms are slightly tubular in form which adds to their attraction. 'Moonlight Bay' was introduced in the United States in 1982 and flowers early to late on a vigorous, upright, bushy plant. It is one of those camellias which seems determined to be a trouble free and healthy plant from the moment it is propagated.

'Mrs D. W. Davis'

This is a very large semi-double in blush pink. In fact, it is so large that blooms on the lower part of the plant tend to go down to the ground. For this reason, it is best to grow it under cover.

Introduced in the United States in 1954 it flowers mid-season on a dense growing bush.

'Nagasaki' (correctly 'Mikenjaku')

Imported from Japan to the United Kingdom in 1889, 'Nagasaki' has had a somewhat trying time so far as its name is concerned. Like so many of these old Japanese introductions most people who grew it appear to have decided on a new name for it. Hence its list of synonyms (ten or more) is not really surprising.

Under any name, 'Nagasaki' is a great camellia, strong, healthy and weather resistant. It produces its large semi-double flowers of rosy red marbled white in varying degrees in mid-season. They are set off to perfection by the fine, dark, glossy leaves of this slow, but dense, growing shrub.

Like so many variegated camellias, 'Nagasaki' is not consistent in producing 'marbled white blooms'. In some seasons 90 per cent or more of its blooms are 100 per cent red. In others, the majority may be marbled white. It depends very much on the temperature when the buds were forming and, additionally, on site, soil and so on.

'Nobilissima' (syn. 'Fuji Yama')

This very old cultivar was introduced from Japan in 1834 and still remains popular, particularly in the United Kingdom.

It is one of the earliest *japonicas* to bloom, normally producing highly decorative, medium-sized paeony form flowers by Christmas (or before, in East Sussex). They are white in colour with yellowish shadings in the centre.

'Nuccio's Gem'
In most areas this is a plant for the greenhouse, not because it is not hardy but because, in most of the United Kingdom, it fails to set buds freely and if it does flower outdoors fails to produce the superb spiral-shaped arrangement of the petals on its perfect formal double bloom of which it is capable and for which it is famous.

Introduced by Nuccio in the United States in 1970, it flowers mid-season.

'Nuccio's Jewel'
Another Nuccio success introduced in 1977. This jewel is a medium-sized, paeony form bloom of white shaded and washed in orchid pink towards the perimeter.

It makes slow, bushy growth which makes it ideal for container culture and flowers mid-season to late. A very lovely camellia.

'Nuccio's Pearl'
Another 1977 introduction from Nuccio, as much a pearl as their 'Jewel' is a jewel.

This pearl is an elegant, medium-sized, formal double, flowering fairly late in the season. In colour it is a breathtaking blush white or palest pink with the petal edges washed orchid pink, the colour progressively increasing as the perimeter is reached.

'Nuccio's Pearl' makes vigorous, compact growth.

'Onetia Holland'
This is a most reliable plant which bears very lovely large, loose paeony form, white flowers. It is not a particularly large grower and has the advantage of flowering mid to late in the season. It was introduced in the United States in 1954.

'Paolina Maggi'
This fine old formal double white was introduced in Italy as long ago as 1855. It makes a fine, big shrub and is of excellent constitution. It is said that, if you look long enough, you will always find a pink stripe on a bloom somewhere. Some say you'll find one on every bloom but this is something of an exaggeration. 'Paolina Maggi' flowers mid-season.

'Paul Jones Supreme'
A large, semi-double which bears flowers of white to blush white, spectacularly striped with carmine. Introduced in Australia in 1968, it flowers mid-season on a rather slow growing bushy plant.

'Pensacola'
The blooms of 'Pensacola' are usually described as large paeony to anemone form but in the United Kingdom it is normally a fine large anemone form of dark red. There are not too many camellias of this colour and form and, accordingly, it is outstanding in any collection. It makes vigorous, upright growth and flowers mid-season. Introduced in the United States in 1956.

'Pink Clouds'
A large, loose paeony bloom of cream pink marked deeper pink which, as the flower ages, changes to a somewhat lavender pink. It is very lovely at all stages.

It flowers mid-season on a plant of vigorous, compact growth. Introduced in the United States in 1953.

'Pink Perfection' (syn. 'Frau Minna Seidel')
There is no doubt that the correct name of this cultivar is 'Usu Otome'. It was brought from Japan to the United States in 1875.

It is a small formal double of pale shell pink and over the years has retained great popularity as a flower for the buttonhole or for personal adornment. It is a vigorous, bushy grower and flowers over most of the season.

'Prince of Orange'
The name may make one think of an old cultivar for among them there are so many princes, princesses, dukes, counts, countesses, ladies and so on. In fact, 'Prince of Orange' was produced in the United States in 1950 and so named on account of its deep orange red, large paeony to anemone form flowers.

It is a plant which makes vigorous, compact, upright growth. We find it a little slow to set flower buds for the first year or so but, after that, it is a reliable bloomer in mid-season.

'Purple Emperor'
The nomenclature book and other writers insist that 'Purple Emperor' is merely another name for 'Mathotiana'. Having obtained stock of it from an impeccable source and, in addition, having compared notes with one or two other independently

minded growers, I can only say that either the nomenclature book and others are mistaken, or that a number of us are growing the wrong plant or that there is more than one clone or cultivar bearing that name. The last would seem to be the most likely explanation.

The plant which several of us grow as 'Purple Emperor' is outstanding and a far better garden plant than 'Mathotiana', which really needs the advantage of a wall to be seen at its best.

Our 'Purple Emperor' is a large formal double, occasionally paeony form flower of deep crimson, sometimes having a purple cast, particularly in cold weather.

The bush is vigorous, making strong, compact growth, the leaves a lighter green than 'Mathotiana'. All in all, 'Purple Emperor' is a fine, indeed outstanding, red camellia.

'R. L. Wheeler'

For those who want a really large, reliable, hardy outdoor bloom, this is it. The blooms are rich rose pink, semi-double to anemone form, frequently with white petaloids among the golden stamens. They are usually described as enormous.

'R. L. Wheeler' has large attractive foliage and vigorous bushy growth. It is a plant of outstanding splendour and very popular.

Flowering early to mid-season it was introduced in the United States in 1949. There is also a variegated form which bears white blotches on the petals but otherwise is the same as the original.

'Red Dandy'

This is a fine red, usually described as brilliant orange red. It is a large semi-double with irregular petals flowering mid-season to late.

It makes vigorous upright growth and may be found to be a little shy flowering in its earlier years. However, like all good things, it is well worth waiting for and from then on will flower regularly.

It was introduced by Nuccio in 1975.

'Red Ensign'

A semi-double crimson Australian, it has something a little different about it. The large leaves are more leathery than most *japonicas* and it makes excellent growth.

Introduced in 1955 it flowers mid-season.

'Reg Ragland'

Ideal for container culture this is a small grower, but bears large to very large semi-double flowers with a mass of yellow stamens. It is a very fine, clear red and flowers over a long period. It was introduced in the United States in 1954.

'Rubescens Major'

A fine, reliable old variety, introduced in France in 1895, it has enjoyed nearly a century of popularity.

It is a large formal double bloom, rose red, veined crimson. It is extremely free flowering and a really reliable performer, making strong, bushy, compact growth. It flowers mid-season.

'San Dimas'

An outstanding, dark red camellia with large semi-double blooms and an arresting circle of yellow stamens. Introduced in the United States in 1971 it is a most excellent plant with medium, compact growth flowering early to mid-season.

When so many reds, be they dark or light red, are produced and where so many of these are so similar to others in colour, shape, habit and growth that one begins to wonder whether it would not be best to stick to 'Adolphe Audusson' and call it a day, it is refreshing to find one so totally different from the majority as 'San Dimas'. A most excellent camellia.

'Saturnia'

Yet another bright red semi-double, it is included here because of its extremely vigorous, upright growth and spectacular display of perfect semi-double blooms in mid-season. It was introduced into the United States in the late 1800s.

'Serenade'

A very popular medium-sized paeony form flower of creamy white, 'Serenade' makes rather slow, compact, upright growth. It is a fine camellia, flowering rather late, and was introduced in 1957 in the United States.

'Shirodaikagura'

Also known as 'Daikagura White', this is a fine paeony to formal double form white borne on a compact, upright bush flowering early. It was introduced from Japan to the United States in 1895.

According to the nomenclature book, 'Joshua E. Youtz' is just another name for 'Daikagura White'. We do not accept this as, to the best of our knowledge, we grow plants of each and there are distinct differences between the two.

Even the nomenclature book gives different descriptions. For example, it is stated that 'Joshua E. Youtz' is: 'White, large paeony form to formal double. Slow compact growth. E. (Japan to US 1915)', whereas 'Shirodaikagura' is given as: 'White medium loose paeony form, medium compact upright growth (Japan 1895 Yoko Hama)'.

It is surprising that two descriptions of two identical plants, indeed the same plant, should be so diverse.

'Silver Anniversary'
A superb semi-double white with golden stamens borne on an extremely healthy, vigorous, compact shrub. A wonderful gift for a silver anniversary, especially when one notes that it was a Nuccio introduction in 1960. 'Silver Anniversary' flowers early to mid-season.

'Silver Waves'
The nomenclature book lists no less than eleven *japonica* cultivars whose name begins with silver. Some are better than others and 'Silver Waves' must definitely be classed amongst the best. This large to very large semi-double white with wavy petals is a fine plant. Yet another Nuccio introduction in 1969 it makes vigorous, bushy growth and flowers early to mid-season.

'Snow Goose'
Probably the best selected form of 'Alba Simplex', 'Snow Goose' opens its pure white flowers almost flat. The occasional petal may bear a pink fleck.

Its strong, vigorous and extremely compact growth and free-flowering habit make this a most desirable plant. It flowers mid-season.

'Souvenir de Bahuaud Litou'
See 'Mathotiana Rosea'.

'Speciosissima'
There are not all that many pure carmine red camellias in the classical large anemone form. Introduced in Australia in 1862, 'Speciosissima' is one of these. It starts to flower early and continues over a long period. It makes vigorous, compact growth.

'Spring Sonnet'
A sort of 'Herme', 'Spring Sonnet' can be anything from semi-double to informal paeony to informal double in form. The

bloom, in its most captivating form, is pale pink with an irregular mauve pink petal edging. However, like so many camellias, it does not necessarily come the same colour every time any more than the same form. Nevertheless, even though the mauve pink edging may, sometimes, be lacking, the bloom is still a lovely one.

'Spring Sonnet' is not the most virile or strong growing camellia. It flowers mid-season and was introduced in the United States in 1952.

'Taro-an'
Supposedly syn. 'Yoibijin' – or so we are told. This is an early, soft pink single, with large round petals, heavy stamens and trailing habit. It flowers early and was introduced from Japan in 1936.

'The Czar'
This light crimson, semi-double, flowers extremely well and is sun resistant. Its slow, sturdy growth makes it an ideal container plant. Its true origin has never been located but it was found growing on an estate in Australia in 1913. It flowers mid-season.

'Tickled Pink'
An unusual camellia of fluorescent pink medium to large loose paeony form with large fluffy outer petals. It makes vigorous, upright growth and flowers early to mid-season. Introduced in the United States in 1959.

'Tiffany'
A large to very large, gorgeously ruffled, loose paeony to anemone form flower in light orchid pink to deeper pink at the margins.

Tiffany makes very strong, bushy, upright growth and flowers early to mid-season. At first a little shy to set flower buds, it flowers well once it has attained 2 or 3ft (0.65 to 1m) in height. Introduced in the United States in 1962

'Tinker Bell'
This is a prolific little plant, bearing small anemone form flowers white striped pink and rose red, not dissimilar to 'Little Bit' and looking for all the world like a carnation. 'Jingle Bells' is the red sport of this cultivar. Both are vigorous, upright growers. 'Tinker Bell' is a Nuccio introduction of 1958 and 'Jingle Bells' of 1957. They flower early to mid-season.

'Tomorrow'

With 'Tomorrow' we start looking at some of the loveliest varieties or sports of any camellia. 'Tomorrow' is a strawberry red or deep rose pink large paeony to informal double flower with crimped petals, flowering mid-season to late. It produces vigorous, slightly open, pendulous growth and was introduced in the United States in 1953.

'Tomorrow Park Hill'

A nursery favourite. A plant we would place in the first half dozen camellias of our choice. 'Tomorrow Park Hill' is a large informal double, shading from pink outer petals to a softer central colour with some white variegation. We find it unbelievably lovely. It needs to be seen for words cannot adequately describe its charm or beauty.

With us it tends to flower late on a strong growing but somewhat pendulous plant. All in all, it tends to look a delicate flower. Nothing could be farther from the truth for it is one of the toughest one can grow. It can almost bring tears to one's eyes to see a bloom of such beauty and perfection emerge from a really hard winter.

It was introduced in 1964.

'Tomorrow's Dawn'

This was a 1960 United States introduction and, again, very lovely. In this cultivar, the blooms are soft to light pink shading to white at the petal edge with some white petaloids. In other respects, growth and so on, it is similar to 'Tomorrow' and flowers mid-season.

There are a number of other 'Tomorrow' variants such as 'Tomorrow Crown Jewel', pure white with an occasional fleck of red, 'Tomorrow Leanne's', a delicious coral red with an occasional streak of white, 'Tomorrow Variegated', strawberry red, blotched irregularly with white, and 'Tomorrow's Tropic Dawn', white with some red rays, the whole flower ultimately fading to blush.

All are very good and, no doubt, others will, in due course, appear.

'Tricolor'

This is so old and so well known that it would be a shame to omit it even though in its colour and form it has, arguably, been super-seded several times over.

'Tricolor' was imported from Japan in 1832 under the name 'Eko Nishiki'. However, 'Tricolor' it has always been with us, so 'Tricolor' it shall remain. It is a medium semi-double, early to mid-season flowerer, white streaked carmine. There are several forms around, some being a basic pink rather than white.

It makes vigorous, compact, upright growth and is extremely free flowering and dependable.

'Twilight'
A flower of ethereal beauty of palest blush pink, shading to white. It is a large formal double bloom on a plant of vigorous, compact growth, flowering mid-season.

Like so many of the extremely pale pastel shade camellias, it is really better grown under protection where its delicate beauty can be fully appreciated. Outdoors, that pale, ethereal, flesh pink can be virtually lost so that we are left with a large, slightly off white, formal double.

A Nuccio introductuon in 1964.

'Victor Emmanuel'
See 'Blood of China'.

'Ville de Nantes'
This is a French introduction of 1910 and is a sport of 'Donckelarii'. It is a medium-sized semi-double, dark red blotched white. What makes it unusual and particularly attractive to some growers, is the intricate fringing of the petals.

It blooms mid-season to late on a fairly well-branched shrub which we do not find all that strong growing.

'Warrior'
This medium to large semi-double to full paeony form flower is brilliant red, making it an outstanding plant. Growth is slow and compact making it a good container plant.

Another Nuccio introduction of 1960 it flowers early to mid-season.

'White Nun'
A beautiful, very large, semi-double pure white with fine yellow stamens borne on a bush of vigorous, upright growth and well furnished with large, somewhat leathery, leaves.

Introduced in the United States in 1959, it flowers mid-season.

'Wildfire'
A superb, dark orange red on a medium-sized, semi-double bloom. It is one of the finest of the very dark reds.

The plant makes moderate but healthy growth and flowers early to mid-season. It was a Nuccio introduction in 1963.

'William Honey'
This is a fine plant for those who want a variegated flower. It is a medium to large anemone to paeony form bloom in white striped and flecked carmine. It has a high centre of petaloids and stamens and flowers mid-season to late on a vigorous, bushy plant with slightly pendulous growth. Introduced in Australia in 1955 it is a very fine example of the variegated *Camellia japonica*.

'Winter Cheer'
Another Australian, having been introduced there in 1945, 'Winter Cheer' bears medium-sized semi-double to paeony form blooms with somewhat irregular petals in bright cherry red. It flowers rather late in the season on a fine, bushy plant.

'Yoibijin'
See 'Taro An'.

'Yours Truly'
Introduced in the United States in 1949, this sport of 'Lady Vansittart' is by far the finest. The deep 'Lady Vansittart' semi-double flowers of picottee crimson, edged white, are attractive in the extreme.

Like the 'Lady' herself, this plant is a dense, slow growing, upright bush and flowers quite late. It makes a fine container plant.

'Yukibotan'
Introduced from japan in 1895, but was recorded in that country nearly twenty years previously in 1877. It is a large white, single to possibly semi-double grower with beautifully waved petals and golden stamens. In the largest collection of camellias one would look at 'Yukibotan' more than once for it has a particular beauty and charm about it. It has fine leaves on a compact, bushy, upright shrub, flowering mid-season.

CAMELLIA RETICULATA

We have already seen that the earliest introductions of *reticulatas* were 'Captain Rawes', 'Robert Fortune' and the so called 'wild form'. The history of *reticulatas* goes back many centuries and there is good reason to believe that *reticulata* is not a distinct species but a hybrid with others. Many feel that *pitardii* is probably a parent although *pitardii* itself is thought to be a hybrid, possibly containing *japonica* blood.

For these reasons, there is good sense in listing varieties of *Camellia reticulata* (which assumes *reticulata* is a species) together with its hybrids.

Despite the above, many of us still think of the wild form, 'Captain Rawes', 'Robert Fortune' and the Kunming *reticulatas*, as they are generally known, imported in 1948 by Ralph Peer from China into the United States, as being varieties of *Camellia reticulata*.

Apart from the 'wild form', by which is meant the single flowered *reticulata*, the 'retics', outside the favoured gardens of the West, really need a wall or greenhouse protection to be seen at their best. True, in East Sussex, I have grown 'Captain Rawes' outdoors for over 20 years but, although it flowers and flowers quite well, it really needs additional warmth from a wall or conservatory. The same applies to the gorgeous 'William Hertrich' and, indeed, to all the original Kunming *reticulatas* (although 'William Hertrich' is not one of those). Apart from the one or two mentioned, including the wild form, I have no practical experience of growing the 'pure' *reticulatas*.

I do know from experience, however, that if grown on a wall they need maximum sunlight. Almost all are rather open, often straggly growing plants. It is in the size and beauty of their blooms that they excel, not in their shapeliness as garden shrubs.

The wild form, as usually seen, is interesting. It is perfectly hardy, makes a well-branched and well-furnished shrub and flowers freely. Strangely, though, it needs more warmth when in flower than we are able to provide outdoors in East Sussex. Given that warmth, the flowers open almost flat and are most attractive but, without it, they remain more trumpet shaped and less effective. Either way, it is an attractive rose colour. There is clearly more than one variety around for, at their stand at the RHS Camellia Show in 1990, the International Camellia Society in their display of camellia species showed quite a different plant with more open flowers and far smoother, less reticulated leaves.

The list below is probably a sufficient selection of 'pure' *reticulatas* for the average reader. There are several more which could be mentioned but it is unlikely that many will have greenhouse space or favoured walls to accommodate more than, say, four or five.

'Captain Rawes'

This is a late flowering plant, bearing large semi-double blooms of carmine pink. As we know, it was brought in from China in 1820. A late flowerer.

'Cornelian'

A vigorous, compact grower, bearing large paeony flowers with crinkled petals, turkey red striped and blotched white. Flowers mid-season.

'Crimson Robe'

One of the best of the Kunming *reticulatas*, 'Crimson Robe' bears very large, semi-double, carmine red blooms with crinkled petals. Flowers mid-season.

'Purple Gown'

A large to very large formal double to paeony form in dark purple red with pin stripes of white, borne on a plant of compact growth. Flowers mid-season.

'William Hertrich'

This seedling of *reticulata* 'Lion Head' bears very large, semi-double blooms with heavy irregular petals and smaller inner upright petals, intermixed with stamens in a most beautiful cherry red colour. It flowers mid-season and can make a fine, vigorous, bushy plant. We have not found it easy to please this variety outdoors.

Camellia Reticulata Hybrids

The next part of our list comprises cultivars which are, beyond doubt, hybrids containing *reticulata* blood. They range from plants which closely resemble the true *reticulatas* and which really need somewhat similar growing conditions, such as 'Lasca Beauty', to others, such as 'Inspiration' and 'Francie L', which are as easy going as the well-known *williamsii* hybrids and often hardier than many of them.

In making a list it is a difficult decision whether to list the hybrids which behave like, and need similar growing conditions to, the 'pure' *reticulatas* on the one hand or those which behave like *williamsii* on the other.

In this instance it is felt that, in order to keep together all the *reticulatas*, species, varieties (if they are that) and the hybrids, it is simpler to set out one list and to indicate how each behaves.

'Black Lace'

The opening petals have a lace-like edging which is the reason for its name. It is certainly not black, but a dark, velvet red in medium rose form to usually formal double blooms. It was introduced in the United Kingdom in 1968, flowers mid-season to late and in growth and hardiness resembles *C. williamsii*.

'China Lady'

The leaves on this *reticulata/granthamiana* cross are almost as unusual as those of 'Francie L'. Very, very long and narrow and deeply reticulated. It is a very hardy, vigorous, dense growing plant flowering from early to late and bearing very large single to semi-double orchid pink blooms with irregular petals. It was introduced in 1968 by Nuccio and is a thoroughly healthy, easy-going plant with outstanding flowers in its season.

'Dr Clifford Parks'

A hybrid between *reticulata* 'Crimson Robe' and *japonica* 'Kramer's Supreme' this cultivar resembles the *reticulatas*. It appears to be perfectly hardy outdoors, grows well, and makes a fine compact bush. It does appear to need plenty of sunshine and warmth to set flower buds and open them to the best advantage.

It bears very large semi-double to paeony form blooms of dark rose red with a hint of orange red. Due to its growth habit in early years, it trains extremely well on a wall.

It was introduced in the United States in 1971 and flowers mid-season.

'Dream Girl'

This is one of the 'three Girls' – 'Dream Girl', 'Flower Girl' and 'Show Girl' – all the result of crosses of *sasanqua* 'Narumi-gata' with *reticulatas*. All are perfectly hardy and behave like *williamsii* hybrids.

'Dream Girl' bears large semi-double rose pink blooms. These open early, between December, or even earlier, and March. In consequence, it needs a sheltered position with plenty of sun. It does well on a wall. It was introduced in the United States in 1965.

'Felice Harris'

Another *sasanqua* cross which behaves like a *williamsii* and bears many large, semi-double flowers in pale orchid pink. It makes vigorous, compact growth, wider than tall, and flowers mid-season to late. Introduced in the United States in 1960.

'Flower Girl'

Like 'Dream Girl', and very early flowering, but in colour the flowers are a lavender pink, shading darker in the centre. It was introduced in the United States in 1965.

'Forty-Niner'

We like this brilliant red very much. It grows quite satisfactorily outdoors but looks like a *reticulata* and needs plenty of sun to flower happily and produce its large paeony blooms in quantity. It was introduced in the United States in 1969 and flowers early to mid-season.

'Francie L'

This *saluenensis/reticulata* cross is one of the finest camellia hybrids of all time though it is doubtful if many would believe it when they first see a sparse, straggly, young plant, bearing leaves more like long, green, narrow straps than leaves and which can tend to hang disconsolately down.

Because of its habit, particularly in its early years, it is number one camellia for training on a wall – north, south, east or west. The branches can be trained like a peach but develop laterals which produce ample blooms.

In the open it forms a fine dense bush and flowers profusely, producing 5½in (13.75cm) deep crimson rose, semi-double flowers. These are of full *reticulata* quality and of very considerable hardiness. Indeed, after the very severest of winters when many camellias, including such well-known plants as 'Elsie Jury', drop every flower bud due to the intense cold, 'Francie L' comes through unscathed and produces its normal great crop of *reticulata* flowers.

Grown as a bush in the open, it really needs shelter and secure staking lest its great crop of leaves, buds and flowers prove to be more than the stem can stand if exposed to wind. It was introduced in the United States in 1964 and flowers mid-season.

'Grand Jury'

A *saluenensis*/'Salutation' cross by Les Jury in New Zealand in 1962. It makes a strong, spreading, pendant bush, equally satisfactory in the open or trained on a wall. It produces, mid-season to late, a fine crop of large loose paeony flowers, soft pink, tinted apricot. Although the large wavy petals make the blooms look a little soft they are, in fact, pretty tough and weather well.

'Howard Asper'

A *reticulata/japonica* cross raised in the United States in 1963 flowering mid-season to late which resembles *reticulata* in growth habit and bloom, producing very large, loose paeony form blooms in a beautiful salmon pink. It behaves extremely well in East Sussex outdoors in full sun where it survived three terrible winters without losing growth or buds.

'Innovation'

This is a fine *williamsii* × *reticulata* hybrid, raised in the United States in 1965. The medium to large flowers are paeony in form and of a rose crimson with a few golden stamens. They are long lasting and weather resistant borne on a very hardy, vigorous, but slightly open, bush. They open from early to late.

'Inspiration'

Raised in the United Kingdom in 1956 and flowering early to mid-season, 'Inspiration' ranks in hardiness with 'Donation' and many consider it a better plant. It is a neater, denser, more upright grower and its deep pink, semi-double blooms are of better formation and spacing than 'Donation'. In other words, one needs both!

'Lasca Beauty'

Raised in the United States in 1973, this camellia, with its very large, semi-double, flowers in clear deep pink, resembles *reticulata*, not only in its fine blooms, but also in its large leaves and stiff, open habit. It does well outdoors in East Sussex and flowers mid-season.

'Lila Naff'

A *reticulata* seedling from 'Butterfly Wings' introduced in the United States in 1967 which resembles *reticulata* in its large semi-double blooms of clear pink with a fine barrel of yellow stamens. It has the same stiff, open habit of most *reticulatas* and succeeds perfectly well outdoors in East Sussex. If flowers mid-season.

'Royalty'

The large, bright red, semi-double blooms 5 to 6in (12.5 to 15cm) across outdoors, make this look like a typical *reticulata* rather than a *japonica*, which was the other parent.

However, grown outdoors, it behaves more like a *japonica*, producing a good, compact shrub. It is excellent, too, for training on a wall. Introduced in the United States in 1968 it flowers mid-season.

'Salutation'

This is a large semi-double in delicate pale pink, the flowers borne on a large, somewhat open, shrub which, with us, needs plenty of sun if it is to maintain a good shape and regularly produce its copious crop of lovely blooms. Produced in Sussex in 1936, for years the argument raged whether it was a *reticulata/saluenensis* cross, as claimed by its raiser, or *saluenensis* × *japonica* like 'Donation', also raised by the same hybridist. It was ultimately proved beyond all doubt that the raiser's claims were true and it is a *reticulata* cross. It flowers profusely in mid-season.

'Satan's Robe'

A fine, hardy, red camellia with large, semi-double blooms and vigorous compact growth. It resembles the *williamsii* hybrids in flower and vigour and was introduced in the United States in 1965. It flowers mid-season.

'Show Girl'

In many ways, we call this the best of the 'Girls'. It bears large, semi-double, pink flowers on a strong, but somewhat open, bush. They are of good shape, freely borne and weather resistant. It flowers from December to March and its blooms under glass are scented. It was raised in the United States in 1965.

'Tristrem Carlyon'

One of Miss Carlyon's United Kingdom hybrids, introduced in 1972. It is a deep, rose madder, medium paeony form bloom, profusely borne on a vigorous, upright bush, flowering mid-season.

'Valley Knudsen'

In leaf and habit, this resembles the *reticulata* side of its family. Its large, semi-double, deep orchid pink blooms also resemble that parent but in their resistance to cold and minor frosts they by no means disgrace the name of *reticulatas*. It was introduced in the United States in 1958 and flowers mid-season to late.

NON-RETICULATA HYBRIDS

This list comprises those hybrids with other than *reticulata* parentage, known to us. Again the list is selective.

'Anticipation'
One of Les Jury's outstanding cultivars, 'Anticipation' bears large, full paeony flowers in a glowing rose crimson with great freedom.

It is extremely hardy and makes a very compact, upright bush, ideal for small gardens and containers. It flowers mid-season to late and was introduced in New Zealand in 1962.

'Beatrice Michael'
Introduced in the United Kingdom in 1954, this camellia has many of the attributes which 'J. C. Williams' lacks. 'J. C. Williams' tends to be an open, somewhat straggly, grower; 'Beatrice Michael' is compact, dense and spreading.

'J. C. Williams' bears blooms lacking somewhat in texture, 'Beatrice Michael' bears blooms of far more substance.

In woodland, 'J. C. Williams', due to its open growth, can look a bit sparse in flower; 'Beatrice Michael' smothers itself in a profusion of blooms. In this respect, the two are similar, although 'Beatrice Michael' is the earlier to flower.

'Bowen Bryant'
A 1959 Australian introduction, 'Bowen Bryant' makes a fine bush, taller than wide, and bears deep pink, large, semi-double flowers.

It flowers mid-season to late and is successful in Scotland as far north as Perth certainly up to Inverness and possibly beyond.

'Brigadoon'
This bears medium-sized, semi-double, rose pink blooms on a very hardy plant. Rather sparse in its early days, it ultimately makes a compact, upright shrub. Satisfactory for container culture. It flowers mid-season to late and was introduced in the United States in 1960.

'Charlean'
A large medium-pink, semi-double, with slight orchid overtones, pink filaments and lemon yellow anthers. It is a vigorous plant, making a sizeable bush.

It was introduced in the United States in 1963 and flowers mid-season to late.

'China Clay'

One of Miss Carylon's introductions of 1972, this is a fine camellia, bearing quantities of medium, semi-double, pure white blooms during mid-season.

'Citation'

Bears pale, silvery blush, large semi-double blooms and was introduced into the United Kingdom in 1950. It makes vigorous, slightly open, growth and in many ways is similar to 'Salutation' but perhaps a better grower. It flowers mid-season.

'Debbie'

For all-round excellence, 'Debbie' must rank amongst the finest of Les Jury's hybrids and, equally, amongst all hybrids so far raised. The glowing rose pink flowers of paeony form are always perfect in that form with little or no variation. They defy the weather. They drop when spent.

From the moment a cutting is inserted in the propagating tray to the time when the fine young shrub is planted in the garden, it seems to be impervious to setbacks or disease. 'Debbie' was raised in New Zealand in 1965 and flowers early to late. It received a well deserved Award of Merit in 1971. 'Debbie' is one of the really great camellias.

'Debbie' has a close relative in camellia 'Carnation'. This is so like 'Debbie' that many of us are unable to differentiate between the two, so that the current reference to 'Carnation' as 'Debbie Carnation' is, to us, eminently sensible. The great difference, we find, between the two is that 'Debbie Carnation' commences to bloom with us weeks earlier than 'Debbie'.

'Donation'

What can one say about 'Donation' which has not already been said? Perhaps we should concentrate on its bad points first. Perhaps its soft, pink blooms with carmine veins could be improved upon. Perhaps the form of its large, semi-double blooms could be better. Perhaps if it looked more like . . . and so on, we can go on. But it doesn't look like . . . and we have to take its soft pink blooms and their form as they are.

But, having done so, what do we have? I venture to suppose we have one of the greatest garden shrubs ever raised. One which, in the United Kingdom, will thrive from the south coast to way up to Scotland to Perth and beyond and one which, when other plants are producing a few better blooms in colour and form, will carry the whole garden under the mass of its flowers. One doesn't know the true meaning of 'flower power' until one has seem camellia 'Donation' in full bloom!

We know it was raised at Borde Hill in Sussex in 1941 and that it flowers early to late from February to May but what is not so well known or appreciated is that there are almost certainly several different clones available. Some are much better than others, so it is worth while making every effort to try to get hold of the best.

'Dream Boat'

This sister seedling of 'Waterlily' was raised by Les Jury's brother Felix. It is a fine plant, bearing pure pink formal double flowers in profusion. It was introduced in 1976 and flowers mid-season on a bushy plant wider than tall. A very fine camellia.

'E. G. Waterhouse'

Produced in Australia in 1954 by the late Prof Waterhouse, this lovely camellia is a first choice for small gardens and hedges as it grows in fastigiate form like an Irish yew. The flowers are formal double and of a pure, light pink, flowering mid-season to late.

Prof Waterhouse was the first President of the International Camellia Society and this chance seedling raised by him is a worthy memorial to him.

'Elegant Beauty'

A 1962 superb creation in New Zealand by Les Jury. It produces a prolific crop of rose pink, large anemone form blooms on long, arching growths which make it an ideal plant to train on a wall. In order to grow a goodly shaped, open ground bush, it may be necessary to prune back long growths hard so as to build up a compact shrub.

Time spent on training it on a wall or pruning it back to make a fine open ground plant is never wasted for 'Elegant Beauty' is one of the 'greats'. It has the added bonus that its young growth is bronze red. It flowers mid-season to late.

'Elsie Jury'

Another superb creation of Les Jury, introduced in 1964, it bears enormous clear pale pink blooms of full paeony form in profusion on a fine, upright, narrow bush. Excellent for small gardens, it flowers mid-season to late and appreciates plenty of sun to assist its great bud-making potential and then to ripen those buds and growth.

'E. T. R. Carlyon'

One of Miss Carlyon's hybrids introduced in 1972 and late flowering, it also has much to commend it.

The blooms are lime green in bud, opening to striking semi-double white flowers with yellow petaloids. It flowers late on a vigorous, upright growing bush.

'Francis Hanger'

For shape and profusion of bloom, one would have to go a long way to find a single white camellia which surpassed 'Francis Hanger' for it produces a mass of its pure white flowers on a fine spreading bush. The flowers drop even before they are fully spent, which makes it an ideal garden plant but a little frustrating for the flower arranger.

It needs a certain amount of shade to retain its dark green, glossy foliage for, grown in too much sun, this suffers from sunscald in bad cases, turning the leaves white, yellow and pale green.

'Francis Hanger' was raised in the United Kingdom in 1953 and flowers mid-season and over a long period.

'Freedom Bell'

This is a very hardy camellia, doing well in Scotland and excellent for small gardens as it makes a close, rounded bush.

It lives up to its name with a profusion of brilliant red semi-double blooms about 3½in (1.75cm) across. It flowers mid-season to late and rather resents too much fertilizer. It was introduced in the United States in 1963.

'Jenefer Carlyon'

Bred by Miss Carlyon in the United Kingdom, this 1972 introduction has much to commend it. The silvery, pink blooms are large, semi-double, borne in profusion, and the bush of spreading growth. It flowers from early mid-season to late.

'Jovey Carlyon'

Introduced by Miss Carlyon, 'Jovey Carlyon' is a fine, double white, sometimes flushed palest pink, and flowering mid-season to late. Growth is strong and the leaves of fine rounded form.

'Julia Hamiter'

A fine seedling of 'Donation', introduced in the United States in 1964. It bears very lovely, large, loose paeony flowers in white and palest apple blossom pink frilled petals. It needs plenty of sun to flower well and ripen its growth which is spreading and open. It flowers mid-season.

'Jury's Yellow'

A 1976 introduction. White petals around a most distinctive centre of yellow petaloids which seem to reflect back on to the white.

'Brushfield's Yellow' and 'Gwenneth Morey' are similar but, on the whole, we find 'Jury's Yellow' more prolific and its flowers seem to weather better. Perhaps this is because it contains 25 per cent *saluenensis* blood.

These three are the nearest we have to a hardy yellow camellia to date but, apart from this, 'Jury's Yellow' is a very fine camellia in its own right. From the cutting stage onwards, it always seems determined to grow into a fine well-branched shrub and, as a result, is a credit to any garden. In fact, it does not even need a garden for its fine, compact habit of growth and prolific flowering make it an ideal shrub for container culture.

'Jury's Yellow' flowers mid-season to late.

'Little Lavender'

We are very fond of this delightful little miniature anemone with blooms of pink, strongly tinged lavender, and often wonder why it is not better known and more popular than it is.

After all, miniature blooms have a strong following of supporters and anything in camellias with a mauvish or lavender cast is normally strongly sought after.

We have heard it said that it is not sufficiently 'self cleaning', that it holds on to its dead blooms too long, but feel that this is a totally unfair criticism. Probably the real reason is that it has never been sufficiently 'exposed' to the public. If the public rarely, if ever, see a plant it is hardly surprising if that plant is not sought after.

'Little Lavender' was introduced in the United States in 1965 and flowers mid-season on a vigorous, dense, compact shrub.

'Margaret Waterhouse'

The purest light pink, medium-sized semi-double blooms borne in utmost profusion on an extremely vigorous, upright, growing plant. That is 'Margaret Waterhouse', another introduction by the late professor.

It flowers early and makes twice the height and size of a normal vigorous grower, such as 'Adolphe Audusson', in the same number of years. Because of its upright growing habit, it is excellent in a hedge but will need some clipping.

This is yet another example of the old adage 'give a dog a bad name'. We have heard many 'experts' on their return from the United States deploring the flowering habit of 'Margaret Waterhouse'. This is because 'Margaret Waterhouse' is self-cleaning in the extreme and drops every spent bloom whilst it is still almost perfect. For us, this gives a beautiful carpet of pale pink beneath the shrub. For the Americans, that carpet is a potential source of flower blight – a disease virtually unknown in the United Kingdom.

It is no more logical to condemn 'Margaret Waterhouse' for that habit than it would be to condemn the Scots pine because it does not grow well in the Arizona desert!

'Mary Phoebe Taylor'

Another vigorous grower, though somewhat less so than 'Margaret Waterhouse', this camellia produces a profusion of large, light rose pink paeony form blooms on a fine, vigorous shrub.

It was introduced in New Zealand in 1975 and flowers early to mid-season.

'Mona Jury'

Les Jury named this beautiful hybrid after his second wife and considered it his best introduction.

Perfect paeony blooms with broad, waved petals in rich apricot pink, freely produced, make it a 'must' in any collection.

Although a bit 'floppy' for its first year or so, it grows into a vigorous, upright plant with quite large leaves. It flowers mid-season to late.

'Tiptoe'

One of the 'greats' for hedging due to its compact, upright habit, 'Tiptoe' bears a mass of semi-double flowers of silvery pink deepening to cherry pink at the edge of the petals. It is an Australian introduction of 1968 and flowers late.

'Waterlily'

The aptly named sister of 'Dream Boat' and introduced first in 1967 by Felix Jury, it bears superb medium to large formal double blooms of a lovely bright lavender pink on a fine, vigorous, compact, upright growing plant.

In recent times, 'Dream Boat' seems to have received all the limelight perhaps because it was second on the field but it is doubtful if it is better than 'Waterlily'. Both are superb and each is different from the other. 'Waterlily' flowers early to mid-season.

'Wilbur Foss'
Another Les Jury introduction in New Zealand in 1971, with large, full paeony flowers in a striking, rich claret colour on a vigorous, upright growing plant.

It is an excellent garden plant not dissimilar to 'Anticipation' in many ways and, like 'Anticipation', makes a good container subject.

'Yesterday'
This is another excellent plant, produced by Miss Carlyon, and received the Award of Merit in 1984. Its silvery pink blooms are medium-sized, formal double and produced mid-season. Growth is upright and vigorous.

Both 'Tomorrow' and 'Yesterday' (which is a 'Tomorrow' cross) are excellent plants. Who is going to produce 'Today' to complete the set?

Sasanqua and Allied Small-Leafed Camellias

These often neglected plants should not be ignored. The majority are as hardy as the *japonica* and hybrid camellias listed. The only difference is that they need a warmer site, fence or wall, porch, greenhouse or conservatory to bud up freely. We have grown a number outdoors for upward of thirty years and they flower freely year after year. When one considers that they flower from October to early January, what more can one want? We particularly recommend the following:

'Bettie Patricia'	'Mini No Yuki'
'Dazzler'	'Marumigata'
'Hugh Evans'	'Quintessence'
'Jean May'	'Scentuous'
'Jennifer Susan'	'Showa-Na-Sakae'
'Kenkyo'	'Sparkling Burgundy'
'Lucinda'	'Yuletide'

9

SPECIFIC PURPOSE CAMELLIAS

As, we hope, has been made clear throughout this book, camellias are versatile plants for which many uses can be found. Here we list some specific purposes.

HEDGING

The main problem here is what is meant by the term hedge – it may mean one thing to one person but something totally different to another. If one is thinking of a formal clipped hedge, almost like a piece of yew topiary work, then almost any fairly compact, upright growing camellia with good foliage will suffice and a mature camellia hedge of this type will certainly be the equal of clipped privet, euonymous, laurel, holly and so on.

Against this, though, there seems little point in planting for a hedge a beautiful flowering shrub such as the camellia if one is never going to see any flowers, for we must be quite clear that, if we clip our camellia hedge as fiercely as privet and holly is clipped, then we will only see the occasional bloom probably hidden behind foliage which shielded it in the bud stage from the shears.

Assuming, then, that we do want a flowering hedge, there is a choice between a formal hedge and an informal screen.

A Formal Hedge

By this we mean a flowering hedge which, for many years, will grow closely upright and require no clipping. For this we must choose carefully from such compact, upright growers as 'Tiptoe', 'E. G. Waterhouse', 'Margaret Waterhouse', 'Freestyle' and 'Joshua E. Youtz'. Additionally, provided one has a warm site to induce freedom of budding, the majority of *sasanquas* with their dense growth, small leaves and autumn/winter flowering habit, have much to commend them for every type of hedge, including little hedges under ground floor windows. All these will grow for many years with minimum trimming, although they may eventually require a little annual pruning or minor clipping. This should be carried out immediately after flowering. The plants should be installed not closer than about 2½ft (0.8m) apart; 3ft (1m) apart is actually better for the stronger growing ones but much depends on soil conditions, siting, exposure and so on.

The above suggestions are primarily made to produce a formal hedge requiring the minimum of clipping. There are very many other camellias which will make an excellent formal hedge, provided they are given a light annual clipping. For this purpose, many cultivars are suitable, in fact any camellia which has the natural habit of fairly dense growth coupled with an upright habit.

An Informal Screen

There are few shrubs which can make a denser barrier to screen off an unwanted view or to provide privacy than the camellia. It also flowers profusely, which gives one the best of every world.

The vast majority of camellias are ideal subjects for screens. If one wishes to cut out trimming almost entirely, then several cultivars mentioned earlier are admirable such as 'Tiptoe', 'E. G. Waterhouse', 'Margaret Waterhouse', 'Freestyle', 'Joshua E. Youtz', 'Anticipation', 'Brigadoon'. Where there is no objection to doing a little annual trimming or pruning, then one has a pretty free hand. Avoid the more open growers, such as 'Giganta' ('Kelvingtonii'), and try to match growth rates a little. In other words, it would be unwise to plant 'Juno' alongside 'High Hat' for in any given number of years, the former will have made more growth in yards than the latter in feet.

Installing a Hedge

Apart from choosing suitable subjects, the secret of all hedges is proper installation. Having set out the line the hedge is to follow, and more often than not this is strictly dictated by circumstances, the next thing is to dig it over amply wide, say 2½ft (0.8m) at least, at the same time incorporating all the peat, compost, leaf mould and well rotted manure plus general fertilizer which one can lay one's hands on. After all, left undisturbed, our camellia hedge will survive several human lifetimes so it does deserve a good start.

Having prepared the hedge area in general, the next thing is to further prepare the individual planting sites with even more peat, leaf mould and so on as described earlier.

Before doing so, one must, of course, decide on one's planting distances. Normally this should be about 3ft (1m) apart. For purely narrow, upright growers like 'Tiptoe' and 'E. G. Waterhouse', 2½ft (0.8m) may suffice although, in time, one may well regret not having made it wider, particularly if a mixed hedge, as opposed to one of all the same or groups of all the same varieties, is planted.

The question of planting distance must always be a compromise. After all, a planting 3ft (0.9m) apart means that each shrub can then expand to that total width. If it expands further, it is encroaching on its neighbour's territory. Many camellias can easily reach a width of 8ft (2.8m) or more but it would be ludicrous to suggest planting a hedge at that distance apart. As always, one must compromise, plant closer than one would like in order to obtain a screen or barrier in a reasonable time and then, if in due course the plants are clearly too close and spoiling each other, one must transplant some to another site.

Finally, remember that no amount of trouble is too much for the finished product. The camellia hedge, in or out of bloom, is incomparable and stands in a class entirely of its own.

WALLS AND FENCES

There are several different types of walls and fences. For instance, the walls of an inhabited house are warmer than free-standing walls elsewhere for, to some extent, house heating is dissipated through the walls. In consequence, house walls are often used to grow plants which are too tender to survive in the open ground.

Garden walls, not part of the house, also offer conditions considerably better than the open ground. This was well known to our forebears who utilized every foot of the often magnificent walls which surrounded the acre or so of their vegetable garden. On these walls many choice fruits such as peaches and nectarines thrived, although they would not have done so as bushes in the open ground.

Then there are fences. Whilst these are not in the same category as walls built of brick or stone they, nevertheless, offer growing conditions considerably better than the open ground. In addition, like a wall, they offer all that is required by a camellia for wall training – just like a peach.

There is more than one way in which one can plant to utilize a wall or fence. In the first place, the planting may be pretty near to the wall so that, in due course, the camellia may be tied in onto the wall or fence. One must never lose sight of the fact that camellias, if planted too close to a wall or fence, can end up by receiving virtually no rain at all. To guard against this one must be sure to select a site which offers some shelter and, above all, is far enough out from the wall or fence to ensure that an adequate share of rainwater is received when there is general rain in the area.

When selecting plants for walls and fences, bear in mind three main points. Firstly, if we are intending to physically train our plants on the fence or wall as opposed to planting a free-standing bush backed up by a wall, we should select one of the several camellias whose habit of growth makes them entirely suitable for this type of training, such as 'Francie L' and 'Elegant Beauty'.

Secondly, if the camellia is to be free-standing in front of a fence or wall, we should at least try to ensure that the plant's habit and rate of growth are such that it will remain in keeping with the wall or fence for as long as possible.

Thirdly, we must ensure that our chosen plants are suitable for the aspect available which may be north, south, east or west.

For south facing walls, many hybrids, *reticulatas* or *sasanquas* are suitable for these can bear full sun (many thrive on it) better than the *japonicas*.

Eminently suitable are hybrids such as 'Francie L', 'Elegant Beauty', 'Dream Girl', 'Flower Girl', 'Show Girl'. For a *japonica*, 'Grand Prix'; for *reticulatas* 'Dr Clifford Parks' or 'Royalty' and for the *sasanquas*, virtually any.

For east and west walls a whole range of suitable plants is available. Amongst many which would be eminently satisfactory trained on a wall or fence are 'Mary Phoebe Taylor', 'Elegant Beauty', 'Grand Prix', 'Francie L', 'Christmas Beauty'.

North walls and fences are suitable for 'Elegant Beauty', 'Francie L', 'Inspiration', 'Drama Girl', 'Donation', 'Debbie' and 'Daintiness'.

POTS AND CONTAINERS

Camellias will thrive in these. They can vary from a couple of litres to half large barrels and beyond but, whatever the size of container available, it is always best to select plants particularly suitable for container growing. One can enumerate certain basic principles to follow.

Firstly, the selected plant, if a *japonica*, will look better if it has heavier foliage in dark, glossy green rather than small pale green leaves. Next, its habit of growth is all important. It must not be too fast, straggly or ungainly in its growth pattern but should tend to make a dense, compact, well-furnished bush.

The following are all extremely successful: 'Anticipation', 'Wilbur Foss', 'Jubilation', 'Jury's Yellow', 'Mona Jury', 'Julia Hamiter' while, in the *japonica* range, 'Cecile Brunazzi', 'Janet Waterhouse', 'Joshua E. Youtz', 'Hawaii', 'Elegans Supreme', 'Elegans Champagne', 'San Dimas', 'Laurie Bray' and 'Conrad Hilton' provide a good all-round selection.

GREENHOUSES AND CONSERVATORIES

There have been quite a few references to growing in greenhouses and conservatories in somewhat general terms already, but now we have reached the point where we can consider this as a subject on its own.

Grown under glass, and flowering there in early spring, it must be apparent that the blooms are in a different class from those on outdoor plants flowering in poor weather conditions, possibly after a bad winter.

Occasionally, weather conditions are unbelievably favourable for camellias. For example, a long, hot summer may well cause most plants to form flower buds in profusion.

So does one learn anything from this? Only that camellias are some of the most rewarding and most beautiful shrubs we can grow but that, if one wants to enjoy superb, large blooms, seen at their best, year after year, then it is difficult to compete with those grown under glass or plastic.

It is fortunate indeed that so many gardeners, including many who have only very limited gardens in size, feel it advantageous to utilize a part of their available space for a greenhouse. For the raising of seeds, the growing on of young plants for propagation and many other purposes, it is useful in the extreme but, however great the use made of it, there is bound to be room for at least a few pots for camellias. Nothing could be more rewarding for, as mentioned above, camellias grown under protection are at their best not just this year, or last year, but every year.

The growing mixture or medium for containerized plants has already been dealt with in some detail (*see* Chapter 3) so need not be repeated here. Accordingly, the next and most important matters are the varieties and cultivars we should grow in that mixture in our available space.

The choice of plant is never an easy one. The vast majority of camellias is satisfactory when grown in containers so the best approach, for a start, is to eliminate the least satisfactory.

It has been mentioned several times already that warmer conditions tend to produce larger flowers. Accordingly, it follows that in normal circumstances it is pointless to grow under glass the miniatures such as 'Tinker Bell', 'Jingle Bells', 'Little Lavender', 'Little Bit' or the small doubles such as 'Pink Perfection' ('Frau Minna Seidel') whose main attraction is their buttonhole size and appearance. If we grow them indoors, then we may blow up their size until they start to equal many normal outdoor blooms.

Again, if a plant produces first-class weather resistant blooms outdoors, there is, in normal circumstances, no great point in molly-coddling it along in the balmy conditions of a conservatory. Better, by far, to choose one of the superb whites; for example, 'Nuccio's Gem' or 'Margarete Hertrich', which require really favourable weather outdoors to give a good account of themselves. Grown under glass protection, the perfect quality and unmarred beauty of their blooms leave one dumbstruck.

Hardly any of the 'pure' *reticulatas* are satisfactory as ordinary outdoor garden plants in the United Kingdom apart, possibly, from a very few very sheltered Cornish gardens. A number of the hybrids which resemble *reticulata* rather than the *williamsii* hybrids, such as 'Dr Clifford Parks', 'Forty-Niner' and 'Royalty' are, within limitations, perfectly satisfactory outdoor plants in the more favoured parts of the United Kingdom. Properly sited and installed, they grow, set flower buds and bloom perfectly well, so there should be no criticism or implied criticism of those gardeners who, lacking glasshouse protection, grow some of them outdoors. Having said all that, it must be conceded that what we can produce outdoors (and the author is one who does so) is quite insignificant when compared with the massive majestic blooms produced on the same cultivars under glass. There is just no comparison.

In addition, there is a large group of camellias which are simply better grown indoors than when grown outdoors and well worth the greenhouse space they take up. A typical example is *Camellia japonica* 'Magnoliaeflora'. This cultivar appears to exist in both a light pink and a white form. The classification 'medium semi-double' really does little to describe the particularly attractive form of its blooms. Outdoors, it is satisfactory to the extent that it grows well, sets flower buds freely and blooms quite profusely. The blooms would probably look better if they were just a little larger, they would have more impact but, that apart, the problem with

'Magnoliaeflora' outdoors is that, unless weather conditions are perfect, day and night, for days on end, it is virtually impossible to find one perfect bloom on a shrub bearing them in hundreds for, at the slightest hint of inclement weather, the simple perfection of 'Magnoliaeflora' is woefully marred. Given the protection of a conservatory it is perfection personified. There are many other perfectly hardy outdoor camellias which come into this category.

In the above few paragraphs, several groups have been mentioned which are either not satisfactory for greenhouses, such as the miniatures, or camellias which are superb as outdoor plants or which are particularly satisfactory in the conservatory, such as the *reticulatas* and various cultivars which rarely give of their best outdoors. To these we could well add a number such as 'Erin Farmer' and 'Twilight' whose colouring is so minimal that, outdoors, they look a rather dirty white whereas, indoors, the palest wash of pink produces a bloom of exquisite beauty.

Finally, there are the *sasanquas*. In general, perfectly hardy, scented or, at least, aromatic, flowering from October to January, they are exquisite grown under greenhouse or conservatory conditions. The scent of some, such as 'Scentuous' (a *lutchuenensis* hybrid) is superb but it does need winter protection whilst 'Quintessence', a somewhat similar cross, has the most beautiful, powerful scent of all – a cross between jasmine and jonquil. So far 'Quintessence' appears to be perfectly hardy outdoors but its winter blooms and scent will obviously benefit from greenhouse or conservatory conditions. Lastly, apart from the twenty or so *sasanqua* cultivars which we propagate and produce in our nursery, there is the wonderful strain of Australian Paradise *sasanqua* camellias. We have found these as easy to grow as any other camellia. They bud profusely and have a superb colour range, varying in form from single to semi-double, paeony to formal or rose form double. At the moment, we are growing seven different varieties and can only recommend them for the greenhouse or conservatory. Further trials may well find several of them perfectly hardy.

All one can do here is to give an indication of what many people feel about choosing camellias for indoor growing. Fortunately, we do not all have the same, or even similar, tastes, so many will disagree but whatever one's own views, it is never a waste of time to go round the shows, the gardens, the conservatories and the nurseries, to seek as many opinions as possible and then make up one's own mind as to what is to be grown inside, even if it is just one plant in a porch or extensive planting in a large conservatory.

So far in this chapter we have dealt with camellias most suited for specific uses such as hedging, wall and fence displays, for pots and containers and for greenhouses and conservatories. This brings us to that terrifying conclusion (terrifying to any author, that is) of setting out a list of the ten best camellias for general use. How easy that looks at first sight. How difficult it becomes, the more one thinks of it.

THE TEN BEST CAMELLIAS

Who is to say what is best and what is second best? It is all so much a matter of personal taste and, with camellias as much as with any flowers and more than with some, beauty, as ever, is in the eye of the beholder.

But does mere beauty make a plant the best? Clearly it does not, for there are many other factors to be put in the balance, freedom of flower, freedom from disease, ease of growing and many other considerations.

The more one thinks about compiling a list of the ten best camellias for general use, the more difficult the answer becomes until one is finally forced to concede that, however carefully one compiles such a list, however accurately and scientifically one weighs in the balance the various attributes and disadvantages, one ends up with a list which no one else, who has any knowledge of camellias, will agree with!

First, I must try to choose blooms of various forms and colours, of different habit and season of flowering and so on. That will certainly give me a 'list'. Then I'll walk round my garden and have a look at the 200 or so plants in bloom and say to myself: 'If I had to leave tomorrow, which ten plants would I take?'

No doubt the first answer would comprise a hundred and ten rather than ten but slowly, by a careful and painful process of weeding, I would end up with a list of just ten plants. They would not have been chosen scientifically. They would represent my personal choice which many would disagree with. However, of one thing I am certain and it is this. If any reader chose to plant my ten camellias they could not fail to give him or her much pleasure and if it were only a tenth of the pleasure I have had from those ten, then he or she would be well rewarded.

In making my choice, I am, of course, looking at the problem through the eyes of a gardener not the eyes of the grower of competition class blooms. I must always bear in mind the wise words of that great gardener, Michael Haworth-Booth, in his famous book *Effective Flowering Shrubs*. Although written a good many years ago, I would commend it to every shrub gardener for what we want with our shrubs is not the plants which bear a few show quality blooms, but shrubs which are effective, which stand out and demand to be looked at.

The Reds

My first choice is that fine old favourite, 'Adolphe Audusson'. In the middle reds I do not consider its colour has ever been surpassed. It is good natured, easy to grow, free flowering and produces blooms well up to any more modern competitor. Time and again in the nursery when one sees it in bloom alongside a couple of dozen other reds, many of them up to the minute triumphs, one is forced to say: 'Well, it may be a hundred and thirteen years old but it can still hold its own or surpass the vast majority of its competitors.'

I am not too worried about the form of my reds, more about their colour so, for my next choice, I am going for one of the really dark reds. For me, there are primarily four contenders: 'Dr Burnside', 'Bob Hope', 'Wildfire', and 'Midnight'. Each has its own particular qualities with 'Bob Hope', probably, the darkest of the quartet. However, for me, the choice is simple. I go for 'Dr Burnside' every time with its semi-double, more often paeony form, blooms. It is not the darkest of the quartet but it is still a very dark, pure red. It has excellent, strong, rather rounded foliage on a compact, healthy, strong-growing plant. It buds up well and flowers freely. For me, it is an outstanding plant in any colour. In the dark reds it is my favourite.

Finally, I will pick what I consider to be one of the finest of all camellias, namely, 'Miss Charleston', a deep red, large semi-double with a high centre to the blooms. It is a fine grower and bears a superb bloom. What, you may ask, is so particular about it? Well, 'Miss Charleston' starts to flower mid-season and carries on later than almost any others. Several camellias do that but the great thing about 'Miss Charleston' is that the last blooms are as fine as the first. Fine to look at, fine to last and even fine to pick. That makes it outstanding.

The Pinks

There are more pinks in camellias than any other colour so it is understandable if we include three in our ten best.

Many people say it is the finest camellia raised in the past 50 years. Some say it is outdated, over planted and several other uncomplimentary things but, for me, 'Donation' is a must. Until one has seen a good sized plant in full bloom one simply does not know the meaning of the phrase 'flower power'. 'Donation' is the most effective garden camellia ever produced. No other camellia can challenge it. It has already been quite exhaustively referred to and described in this book so repetition is unnecessary. Until some even more outstanding camellia comes along, 'Donation' must figure high on my list of ten.

'Leonard Messel' I rank very high indeed. Its rugged matt leaves and shapely compact habit of growth make it a most attractive shrub at all times and its shapely blooms, so freely borne and well presented, place it for me among the elite of camellias.

My final choice is something quite different and a *japonica* rather than a hybrid. 'Tomorrow Park Hill' has so many outstanding qualities. It makes a strong and shapely bush, it flowers late and so often escapes much of the worst weather and appears extremely resistant to disease and cold damage. Its flowers mirror in shape 'Tomorrow' itself, which is attractive in the extreme, but they are pale, soft pink and, to many of us, indescribably lovely. Their resistance to inclement weather is outstanding and, once again, 'Tomorrow Park Hill' is another example of those plants which never fail to surprise us, they look so delicate but are, in fact, extremely tough.

The Whites

Pride of place amongst the whites must go to 'Joshua E. Youtz', that great white formal double (outdoors) which we find more resistant to bad weather than any other formal double white. Its slow growth and narrow, upright form make it ideal for containers and also make it just the plant to fill that particular spot in the border which we have been looking for for so long.

'Hakurakuten' ('Wisley White') is a simple second choice. This semi-double to paeony form, with broad petals and a mixture of petaloids and stamens, is attractive in the extreme. In addition, after appalling winter weather, it still flowers perfectly normally and when its open or semi-open flowers are caught by frost or storm, it appears to suffer less damage than other whites.

'Francis Hanger', an early *williamsii* hybrid, is my third choice. It makes a fine, spreading bush, covered every year with a myriad medium-sized, pure white single blooms. It is so self-cleaning in habit that one occasionally feels that its flowers drop from the bush almost too soon. Of all the single whites, I know of none other which produces a crop comparable to 'Francis Hanger'. One word of warning though. It must be sited where it gets some shade. Planted in full exposure it flowers profusely and grows well but its leaves suffer from sun scorch more than almost any other plant. So give it a little shade and enjoy its dark green foliage as well as its flowers.

Bi-Colours

I was at pains to point out that anyone's choice of the ten best camellias is bound to be a very personal choice. As it happens, I am not terribly keen on the bi-colours and so I limit my choice to one only.

I think my vote must go to that fine old trouper, 'Contessa Lavinia Maggi'. Although raised in Italy 130 years ago, it remains the most popular striped formal double with white blooms boldly striped carmine and pale pink. It bears fine large blooms on a bush with fine round leaves.

It can revert to the rosy red double known as 'Contessa Lavinia Maggi Rosea' so, if pure red blooms appear, they should be cut out or the bush may revert to red.

There, then, is my list of the ten best camellias for general use.

Reds	'Adolphe Audusson' 'Dr Burnside' 'Miss Charleston'
Pinks	'Donation' 'Leonard Messel' 'Tomorrow Park Hill'
Whites	'Joshua E. Youtz' 'Haku Rakuten' 'Francis Hanger'
Bi-colours	'Contessa Lavinia Maggi'

10
HIGO CAMELLIAS

From what I have been told and from what I have read, the changes
which have taken place in Japan over the past forty or fifty years
have been more dramatic than those of any other comparable
country. To return there after an absence of, say, forty years must
surely be to return to an almost unknown land. In place of parks
and open spaces are houses and factories and, to a great extent, in
place of the old oriental values are Western values, ideas and ideals.

Over many, many centuries, Japanese culture in connection with
gardens, trees, and flowers – their creation, development, arrangement and preservation – has been totally different from that in
the West. So much of Japanese culture involved in the art of, say,
garden making, flower arranging, and flower and plant breeding
seems to have involved symbolic and religious aspects which have
played no part in their development in the West. For us, the
arrangement in which we place two or three plants is dictated
primarily by the desire to place them where they will grow best and
best complement, support and improve each other from a purely
practical viewpoint. Of course, we are trying to create something
of beauty but our values are practical values. In oriental countries,
and perhaps most in Japan, I understand the situation, particularly
in the past, has been totally different; the placing of a stone in a
garden or the planting of a shrub in a particular spot have either
symbolic or religious significance or both. Similarly, in the art of
flower arranging where so often there seem to be only three flowers
involved in an arrangement, symbolism plays a major part.

For my part, as an ordinary practical gardener and grower, I have
always had some doubts and reservations as to whether a study, in
any depth, of the symbolic and religious reasons and values
involved in the creation and layout of a Japanese garden, or flower
arrangement, is necessarily profitable. I am sure this will sound like
heresy to many, but until we are experts in our own spheres, in the
identification and cultural knowledge of our own plants and
gardens, and until we fully understand and appreciate the plan-
ning, the thought and the time (sometimes counted in centuries)
involved in the creation of many of our own famous Western
gardens, the study of such matters in, say, Japan or China, is

perhaps, relatively, not so rewarding. In a similar way, as a music lover, I feel that before I try fully to understand and involve myself in the intricacies of, say, Chinese or Indian music I could better spend my time in studying and listening to the works of, say, Beethoven, Sibelius and Rachmaninov. If our span of life was limitless we could do so much more but, as it is, none of us ever has time to acquire the knowledge or complete the tasks we set for ourselves so many years or decades ago.

Although there may be, or may have been, a different set of values for plants, flowers, gardens, their arrangement and so on in Japan and in our own country, one thing is common to both countries and that is that, just as in modern times people change their clothes according to fashion, there has always been a fashion with flowers and plants. For example, the Victorians adored their fernaries, which were damp dells in the garden that housed a collection of different species and cultivars. Today, ferns are not so highly prized but are, I believe, making a comeback. In my own lifetime, I have known the fuchsia highly rated and freely grown, only to become almost an outcast, and then to come bouncing back as a highly valued flower in the past few decades. The same can be said of many, many flowers. I could name a dozen or more which have been the victims or, equally, the favourites of fashion in flowers and garden plants. So it has been in Japan. Plants, including our beloved camellias, have been the victims of fashion.

In Japan, over the centuries, a mystique appears to have surrounded the camellia which has been slowly, tediously and painstakingly loved for certain characteristics often of a symbolic or religious flavour. I think much of this symbolism and love of it had already waned before the Japanese saw fit to involve themselves in, what was for them, the disastrous Second World War. Whether I am right in this conjecture or not is of no great relevance, for there is no doubt that the post-war emergence of Japan as a leading industrial nation with all the appurtenances of banking, finance, insurance, stockbroking and so on, and its consequent demand for land space, saw the demolition of parks, gardens and nurseries to a far greater degree than we have seen even in the United Kingdom. With their destruction, and rebirth as vast areas of factories, office blocks, railways, motorways, housing complexes and so on, it was inevitable that those once highly valued flowering cherries and camellias had to be destroyed. We have seen exactly the same thing happen in our own country where fine and carefully planned plantings of species and hybrid rhododendrons have been swept away by the bulldozers, like a field of wheat before the harvester.

At the time, as I understand it, the great change of scene from the old to the new, and the change of values too, did not cause too much concern to the average Japanese garden lover. In fact, at camellia shows, fine big American hybrid camellias or *japonica* cultivars would win first prize and the old Japanese singles, with a particular layout of petals and stamens, so greatly valued in former times, would be a poor second or third.

I suppose we all know the inevitable result of such a situation. It is a reawakening of interest in the old. We have had exactly the same situation here with, for example, the new-found fascination with old roses, and the formation of societies to search out and protect species and hybrids of many plants which were a commonplace in our gardens fifty or a hundred years ago but which are now lost, or nearly lost, to cultivation. Thus it is in Japan. For years now there have been enthusiasts searching for, finding and re-introducing the 'old' camellias so prized by their forebears. Their hunting grounds have been much the same as ours, including old houses and gardens, old cemeteries, old nurseries. In one or other of these, every now and then, the search is rewarded and something old but new and of exquisite value is discovered and re-introduced to an appreciative gardening public.

This phenomenon of fashion in flowers and plants is nothing new. It must have gone on for as long as man has populated the earth and, returning to Japan, it has often been said by far wiser heads than mine that an 'expedition' to Japan, to such places as its old nurseries, could well yield a far more valuable collection of plants for our gardens than is ever achieved by our modern expeditions to China and the Himalayas.

The reason I have dealt at some length with 'fashion' in plants and their consequent disappearance from gardens world-wide is because I think that this was the real reason for the creation of the Higo camellias. In the early nineteenth century there existed an association called the Hana Ren who were devoted to the collection, preservation, conservation and improvement of certain plants. It seems a reasonable guess that, just as today, as a result of fashion and the other influences referred to above, such a society or association carried out valuable work in the preservation and conservation of endangered plants. The brotherhood of Hana Ren already comprised camellia fanatics (camellia 'bugs' as I gather they are called in the United States) and they turned their attention to the breeding of a certain type of camellia in the province of Higo (pronounced 'Heego'). The area is now known as Kumamoto Prefecture on Kyusha Island.

Camellia japonica has always been known to produce plants from seed giving considerable variations in colour, form, size and so on, and frequently resembling the original wild form of *C. japonica* and, more often than not, bearing little resemblance to the original parents. Normally a high proportion are single and over the centuries the Japanese have selected various types which appeal most to them.

The Higo camellias were just such selected types, specifically bred to qualify as Higo camellias. In general, they are hybrids between *C. japonica* and *C. rusticana*. Other rarer species are probably involved in their breeding as well. They are, in fact, a type or style of flower rather than a particular hybrid or species, race or form. Generally, they have single blooms (although there are one or two exceptions that have a semi-double form) with normally five to nine thick, rounded, broad petals. They must have a profusion of stamens numbering 100 to 250, as they do not qualify as Higo if they have less than this. The stamens should be white, gold, pink or red, to match the overall colouring of the flower, and great store was put by their arrangement which could be in a dense columnar form or, ideally, like a plum blossom where the stamens are flattened out into a wide ring, leaving a solitary pistil projecting in the centre. It is this latter arrangement of stamens which one normally associates with the Higo. Colours have to be pure and brilliant, such as scarlet, crimson, white, pink or a brocaded pattern in which flecks and swirls of contrasting colour overlie the base tint. Because of their hybrid origin, Higos tend to sport freely, solid-coloured blooms appearing on plants of brocaded form, just as the true *japonica* 'Tricolor', which is basically white splashed with red and pink, sports to the solid red 'Lady de Saumarez'.

The brotherhood of Hana Ren must have wielded considerable influence, for they succeeded in getting laws passed to prevent the export of their plants from the Higo region and for the registration of them. They were reputed to guard their plants with tenacity and not to part with them, or propagating material produced from them, even to close relatives. I must confess that I have not seen many Higo camellias in the United Kingdom and have only grown two, namely 'Kyo Nishiki' and 'Kumagai', but have had the opportunity to spend some time studying the considerable collection in the Descanso Gardens in California.

Many do have, even to my untutored Western eyes, most beautiful individual flowers. The illustrations of two, 'Showa-No-Hikari' and 'Shiro Shintsukasa', in Col Tom Durrants' excellent book *The*

Camellia Story, with the typical great mass of stamens, supports this, as do many of the illustrations in Stirling Macoboy's great work *The Colour Dictionary of Camellias*. Many Higo camellias are, to some extent, scented and have been used in breeding programmes designed to produce fragrant camellias. A number of these are referred to in Chapter 11, Fragrant Camellias.

Generally, the Higos have thick rounded leaves, which is a foliage form highly rated in Japan, and tend to be rather small low-growing, rounded bushes. Great use of them is made in Japan for bonsai work. They are often grafted on to an old gnarled stock plant which is cut back hard so that the Higo scions make an effective display of their beautiful individual blooms on a plant with an ancient form. For those who like bonsai, this is a highly effective way of using the Higo camellia. For use in the ordinary garden, it is more a plant for the enthusiast than for the ordinary gardener. I think I cannot do better than quote from a letter recently sent to me by Charles Puddle, MBE, VMH, who was formerly the curator of Bodnant Gardens and is one of the world's greatest authorities on camellias, on the subject of Higo camellias:

'In the open, they appear to be rather sparse in bloom in my experience, and I have not seen many grown in gardens in Europe, Australia, New Zealand and the United States. Those I have seen appear to be small rounded bushes (I can only remember a few of any great size) and I think they are only for the enthusiast or for bonsai, in spite of the beauty of individual flowers.'

Where there is only a comparatively modest amount of space, three-tier planting should normally be introduced. By so doing, we treble the number of plants and, consequently, the amount of flower power, which we can obtain in any given area. The top tier consists of trees and, unless it is a woodland garden, these should be moderate-growing species and cultivars whose root systems, if at all possible, are not too competitive with those of other plants. In this respect, members of the legume family are ideal because, as has been mentioned before, they build up nitrogen in the soil instead of removing it. An excellent choice here would be the laburnum. The variety *vossii* has the finest racemes. If one can select (and they are easily grown from seed) a tree of the ordinary form (*anagyroides* or *alpinum*) but which flowers well on in June when flowering trees and shrubs are becoming scarce (hence the expression 'the June gap') then that is doubly valuable. There are others in the legume family also suitable such as *Genista virgata* now called *tenera*, or *Genista aetnensis* and several robinias. Flowering cherries and crabs make quite good neighbours and are superb in flower but the choice is extremely wide, for example, there are several styrax, halesias and hoherias that would be suitable, to name but a few. The styrax, particularly *S. japonica* and *S. hemsleyana*, and the halesias, *H. carolinianum* and *H. monticola*, flower in June which makes them better than the spring flowers and the hoherias such as *H. glabrata* and *H. lyalli* which wait till well on in July before producing their mass of white and, seen in the distance, almost cherry-like, blooms – which is a great asset.

So much for our top tier of trees. The next consists of the medium-growing shrubs, which are the backbone of the garden, namely rhododendrons, azaleas (many of these grow large enough for our purpose), camellias, hydrangeas and the shrub and larger-growing hybrid roses.

Our third layer which is, of course, forward of and, in some cases, partly under our second, consists of low-growing azaleas, dwarf rhododendrons, genistas, cytisus, ericas, leptospermum and innumerable other spreading dwarfs, so planted that they will grow into one another, a form of labour-saving planting so aptly described by Michael Haworth-Booth as 'close boskage'. Patches of early flowering bulbs, such as species crocus and others, which are happy to grow up through the dwarf shrubs, add extra colour and interest.

You may ask what all this has to do with Higo camellias. It is really that there will always be enthusiasts who will want to grow some of these beautiful plants but we must face the fact that they are not so free-flowering as other camellias, in the United Kingdom at least, and are generally much smaller than the normal *C. japonica* or hybrid camellia. However, the enthusiast can still grow them with very little loss of space if the three-tier system of planting just outlined is made, in effect, into a four-tier one by interspersing the Higos with, for example, lower-growing camellias in the second tier and the close boskage planting at the front. The fact that they are low-growing, rounded bushes makes this possible.

11
FRAGRANT CAMELLIAS

It must be a common belief that a beautiful flower will usually have a beautiful fragrance because, time and again, you see an admirer of a flower bend to smell it. The realization that there is no scent more often than not results in a look of surprise and disappointment. As far as camellias are concerned, these disappointments are unfortunately likely to continue for quite a long time to come for, generally speaking, they have no scent.

So far as I am aware, in camellia competitions in the United Kingdom, no points are given for fragrance, probably because it is so rarely present. I may be wrong, as I do not know whether our judges work to any particular code with points added for merits and deducted for demerits when judging each bloom. To expect them to do so in any real detail in the time available for judging quite a number of blooms might be asking too much. However, the American Camellia Society does suggest a points system based on the merits or demerits of the flowers, sprays or plants exhibited. These are decided from the consensus of opinions of experienced camellia growers in the United Kingdom, Australia and the United States. It could be helpful to exhibitors and growers if they knew that added points might be obtained for, say, distinctive or unusual leaves, as well as for quality of blooms.

Whether such a complicated points system would be of use to our judges is probably something of a moot point, particularly as they seem to manage pretty satisfactorily at the moment. However, it is worth giving it some consideration, if only as an aid to evaluating a camellia for both the amateur and professional grower. For these reasons, I feel it is helpful to set out the suggested merits and demerits but not complicating it too much by also setting out the number of points which are suggested as additions or deductions for each of these. The suggestions are given below.

MERITS

Vigour Disease resistance, hardiness, strength of root system and branches.

Growth Habit Plant form, symmetry, overall beauty as a shrub, density.

Foliage Amount, quality, glossiness, susceptibility to sunburn.

Flower Form Beauty and distinctiveness of petal and stamen formation, contrasts, perfection of petal layout.

Flower Colour Non-fading or non-purpling in reds, chalky in whites, delicate pleasing sheen, iridescence.

Substance Keeping quality, resistance to weather damage.

Size and Overall Effect Not necessarily largeness but rather whether it is in keeping with form and colour, to produce the most pleasing overall effect. Can be very large or very small, provided it is balanced.

Duration Length of blooming period, each flower and plant as a whole.

Garden Effect Value as a flowering shrub, self-cleaning, effec-,tiveness, flower power.

DEMERITS

Buds Fail to Flower Bud drop, 'balling', first flowers deformed.

Flower Distortion Weather damage to buds, tendency to deviate from the typical.

Undependability Does not perform consistently or set buds regularly.

Too Many or Too Few Buds Too few is common with *C. reticulata* and some very large flowers.

Flower Disintegrates Bloom shatters after it falls, garden neatness.

A premium can also be gained for special features. These include unusually early blooms, unusual hardiness, and a unique flower, whether because it is of gigantic size, has a very rare colour, form or fragrance, or has inflorescence.

I think the American tests cover every conceivable point we should have in mind when choosing, evaluating or judging a camellia, and the reader will notice that, under the Premium for Special Features, fragrance comes into its own. Rightly or wrongly, I rather think that when most of us are faced with a choice we fall in love with a particular bloom, its colour, form and so on and, smitten by this, tend to forget that the plant's growth is a bit leggy or that it flowers too early or too late. We tell ourselves we can correct and change the first by pinching and pruning and the latter by choosing a really warm sheltered spot. Perhaps we can do these things but it may not prove successful. Sometimes I think this confident belief that we can is much the same as that which so many have on entering into matrimony! They believe they can change their prospective partner so that in all respects he or she will become their ideal person. Unfortunately, in the vast majority of cases, they will sooner or later learn otherwise. How true it is that a leopard never changes its spots, be the leopard a person or a camellia plant.

FRAGRANCE

In this chapter, I shall concentrate on just one of the merits, fragrance. For many people, fragrance in flowers and also plants (for we must not forget that fragrance is not confined to flowers) is as important as beauty, and for some, such as the blind or partially sighted, it is all important. However, before discussing the matter further, it would be worth setting out one or two very simple terms which are usually used in connection with scent or fragrance:

Scent   A delicate, light, pleasing smell. Several camellias have this.
Fragrance   A more pronounced, pleasing smell. Trumpet lilies and *Rhododendron loderi* have this. As regards camellias, it is probably only *C. lutchuenensis* that has this.
Odour   A scent or fragrance that is not generally liked. The fox has a strong scent but because it is not generally liked we call it an odour. With camellias, the somewhat musty smell of several *C. sasanquas* is considered to be an odour.

The reason why a scent or fragrance is generally missing in camellias is something of a mystery. The smell of a flower or plant comes from a mixture of various oils present; the preponderance of one oil produces the fragrance of the carnation, the preponderance of another the fragrance of the rose. Camellias produce a large quantity of a wide variety of oils. Whereas in the West, we cultivate and cherish camellias for the beauty of their flowers, in the East, they were grown for their seeds, which yield a valuable oil. This oil was used in the East over the centuries for two basic purposes, as a cooking oil and for cosmetics, particularly for dressing the long hair of girls and women. According to Japanese statistics, nearly

100 tons of oil were produced in 1958 but this had declined to little over half that figure by 1962. Another example of a plant being grown in the East for its practical uses rather than its aesthetic qualities, is the glorious magnolia, which in some areas was grown only because it was generally thought (although I understand wrongly) that the oil from its seeds was a powerful aphrodisiac.

Returning to the camellia, I understand that in the production of cosmetic scents it is the most knowledgeable blending of various oils and other substances that creates the perfumes which sell at such crippling prices under various well-known names. Since the camellia produces so many basic oils, it does seem strange that, in general, camellias are not fragrant. Just as the blending of various oils and other substances is a major industry for the cosmetics market, with persons of great skill creating all the different subtle or even shocking 'scents', so expert breeders and hybridizers are blending various camellia scents and fragrances with the aim of endowing a new generation of camellias with a fragrance pleasing to virtually all and of sufficient strength to be easily detected and appreciated by all, or almost all.

Unfortunately, fragrance in flowers, as in almost everything else, is an extremely subjective matter. It is strange that a number of people who rave about the scent of a rose or a trumpet lily may be oblivious of the fact that many other plants can emit fragrance or odours, which are pleasant to some, from parts other than their flowers. I remember when I was weeding in a bed of candelabra primulas that time and again I wondered from where a most delicious scent came. None of the plants were in bloom so it could not be their flowers. For a long time I assumed it must be coming from further away; then, finally, I traced it. It emanated from the leaves of *Primula helodoxa*, one of the few evergreen candelabras. The leaves of many plants have much to offer. Rhododendron leaves, particularly the *lepidotes*, can produce some delicious scents, as can some varieties of *R. cinnbarinum*, whilst others have a musky or tangy scent which most people find extremely pleasant.

The human nose is a pretty poor instrument when compared with that of a dog. To watch a trained dog as it sets about the task of locating drugs or explosives really is something of a lesson. In fact, many dogs will use their noses where human beings would use their eyes. I once owned a massive golden retriever, the finest dog I ever had. If I walked out into my garden and then down a long sloping path through the woodland leading to the vegetable garden, Mac, if he was in the house, would almost immediately twig that he had been left behind and bark to be let out. He would then follow me, purely by his nose. By the time he reached the sloping path he would have worked up a good speed. Unfortunately, as he had his head down following his nose, he would not see me a few yards ahead and so would crash into me. The effect of many stones of dog against the back of my knees was to knock me flying and I took many a tumble before I schooled myself to expect this pantomime and to wait till the last moment and then side step, to let him go tearing by.

I suppose that for Mac my 'smell' was one of the great odours of the world, however unpleasant many others might find it. It is said, and rightly I believe, that smell plays a great part in sexual attraction in human beings, not the smell of some artificial scent or aftershave lotion but the actual animal smell of the body. As is always the case, what is attractive to one may be totally unattractive to the vast majority. So it is with flowers. To one person a flower may have superb fragrance, to another a pleasant but weak scent, to another an unpleasant one and to yet another, no scent or odour at all. *Camellia japonica* 'Kramer's Supreme' is a typical example of this. It is reputed to be scented. One or two customers who have bought it from us say they are delighted with its delicious fragrance which, for them, perfumes the air, others claim to detect a slight scent whereas I am unable to detect any at all even from plants flowering indoors. All, of course, are propagated from the same stock plant.

Whether a camellia is flowering inside or outside is of the very greatest importance, so far as the fragrance or scent emitted by it is concerned. Just as the size of bloom is greatly affected by the temperature in which a camellia grows, and obviously it is warmer inside, so is the strength of the fragrance of a scented or fragrant camellia similarly affected. The time of day affects the fragrance as well. Some scented rhododendrons, such as the *loderi* hybrids and the hybrids with *R. fortunei* or *griffithianum*, emit their most powerful scent in the evening when large areas around them are filled to capacity with their delicious fragrance. Similarly, those who visit Mediterranean areas will know that the typical smell of the maquis, be it from flowers, leaves or stems, is never stronger than in the full heat of the day.

Hybridizing for fragrance in camellias began in about 1960 and the fact that some success has been achieved is apparent by the names given to some of these new plants, such as 'Fragrant Star', 'Fragrant Pink', 'Scented Treasure', 'Scentsation'. Hybridizing between so called fragrant *japonicas* proved disappointing on the whole but, meanwhile, *C. lutchuenensis*, the most highly fragrant of the species, was introduced and a range of interspecific hybrids (which are hybrids produced from crossing two different species) bred for scent has followed. Although *C. lutchuenensis* is undoubtedly the most fragrant species introduced so far, a number of other species also have some fragrance including *C. fraterna, C. kissi, C. oleifera* and *C. sasanqua*. In addition, there are other fragrant species in existence, in China in particular, and now that freer access to that country can be obtained and relationships have improved, many of these will undoubtedly be introduced to the West.

We must not expect miracles overnight. From the time a cross is made to the time a plant flowers may well take five or seven years. If that cross was only made to produce a parent to breed from, ten to fifteen years may pass before this second generation is produced. Science, which has produced micro-propagation, will no doubt also find a way of speeding up the flowering of a new cross but that is still for the future.

The earliest efforts to breed fragrant camellias were made in the United States but this project has since become world-wide. The ultimate aim is the same for all, namely a show quality bloom with real fragrance produced on a good garden plant. To date, some 30 years have been expended in trying to achieve that aim. It is nearer to achievement now than back in the 1960s but there is still a long way to go. However, I think it is inevitable that, in due course, the dedication and persistence of breeders will produce camellias that can equal the fragrance of the old-fashioned rose, *Rhododendron loderi, Azalea pontica* and the trumpet lilies. When that is achieved, what more could the camellia enthusiast want? But ask a silly question and you get a silly answer for he will immediately want camellias in a colour range of true blue, deep yellow, orange, apricot and so on, and to produce these, I am convinced, will take far longer than the production of fragrant blooms. It is a sobering thought that if all the money which has had to be spent on armaments in the last forty or so years had been spent on breeding better and different crops and flowers we would already have our deep yellow, fragrant camellias and this world of ours could have been turned into a veritable Garden of Eden.

In his superb book *The Colour Dictionary of Camellias*, Stirling Macoboy lists a large number of camellias that are, or are reputed to be, fragrant:

Japonicas 'Beauty of Holland' (a sport of 'Hikaru Genji'), 'Beni Botan' (another sport of the same), 'Benten' (with variegated leaves), 'Billie McCaskill', 'Blood of China', 'Cara Mia', 'Carter's

Sunburst', 'Erin Farmer', 'Fragrant Star', 'General Eisenhower', 'Grand Slam', 'Kingyo Tsubaki' (the fishtail camellia), 'Kokuryu', 'Kramer's Supreme', 'Mrs Bertha Harms', 'Odorotissima', 'Orchid Pink', 'Party Girl', 'Scented Treasure', 'Scentsation', 'Spring Sonnet', 'Temple Incense', 'Violet Bouquet'.

Hybrid Camellias 'Alice Cutter', 'Fragrant Pink', 'Fragrant Pink Improved', 'Virginia Cutter'.

Higo Camellias 'Akatsuki No Kaori' ('Fragrant Dawn'), 'Nioi Fubuki' ('Scented Storm'), 'Kosmi' ('Fragrant Pink'), 'Koon' ('Fragrant Cloud'), 'Odairi Kaori' ('Odaira's Fragrance'), 'Tama Ikari' ('Precious Anchor'). Most, if not all, the Higos mentioned have been used in hybridizing programmes.

News does not always travel fast so that in countries such as the United States, Australia and New Zealand, it is by no means easy to keep up to date with the most recent successes in the quest for fragrant camellias. The most exciting introduction to date is Camellia 'Quintessence', a cross between *lutchuenensis* and *japonica*. As mentioned under Greenhouse and Conservatory Camellias in Chapter 9, its scent is supreme, a cross between jasmine and jonquil. It is of dwarf, dense, spreading habit with small *sasanqua*-like leaves. It seems that its ultimate height is unlikely to be more than 1½–2ft (45–60cm), but its spread very considerable. It is undoubtedly outstanding for ground cover or even as a plant for a hanging basket. It flowers profusely with smallish blooms of white which are at first flushed pink, and has performed perfectly satisfactorily outdoors in the south of England over several winters and could well be suitable outdoors elsewhere. We have now displayed it for several shows at the RHS Westminster fortnightly shows, where its freedom of bloom and superb scent (we think the finest so far) has caused very considerable comment. It is certainly true that if you walk past it on a show stand or in the nursery where it is grown, you are immediately entranced by the exquisite perfume.

As I have said earlier, I have great doubts whether hardy true yellow and its derivative colours such as orange-flowered camellias will be produced in the reasonably near future. However, turning to the optimistic side, I am absolutely confident that truly fragrant, hardy, large-flowered camellias will be bred in the not too distant future and will be freely planted to fill the air with their sweetness.

Some of us may not have the time to wait for that day but must make do with and plant what we have got, and what we have are our world's greatest beauties. We need only look at our cities, towns and too often bespoiled villages to see a treeless, colourless, ugly land created by man alone, in his wisdom. Light-industrial sites, in rural areas, are frequently no better. How vastly improved all could be by literally massive tree and shrub planting schemes; nothing less would be enough. It often appears that the only planned plantings on any effective scale are the tree planting schemes alongside some of our motorways. None of this is going to change overnight and it is the gardener, from the suburban amateur to the forester, who must show the way. Remember that every time we plant a flower-bed, a tree or a shrub, be it for this year or next year or for posterity, we have made this world a slightly better place and, surely, we were all sent here for that purpose. Perhaps there should be one more beatitude added to those we know so well:

'Blessed are the gardeners for they shall beautify the Earth'.

APPENDICES

I CULTIVARS OF INTER-SPECIFIC ORIGIN

Table 1: first generation hybrids

(a) *C. saluenensis* × *C. japonica* (*williamsii* hybrids)
'Anticipation'　　　　　'Gay Time'
'Beatrice Michael'　　　'George Blandford'
'Bowen Bryant'　　　　'J. C. Williams'
'Brigadoon'　　　　　'Jenefer Carlyon'
'C. F. Coates'　　　　'Margaret Waterhouse'
'Caerhays'　　　　　'Mary Christian'
'Charles Michael'　　　'Mary Jobson'
'China Clay'　　　　　'November Pink'
'Citation'　　　　　　'Phillipa Forwood'
'Debbie'　　　　　　'Shocking Pink'
'Donation'　　　　　'St Ewe'
'E. G. Waterhouse'　　'Tregrehan'
'Elegant Beauty'　　　'Wilbur Foss'
'Elizabeth Rothschild'　'Waterlily'
'Elsie Jury'

(b) *C. japonica* × *C. saluenensis*
'Angel Wings'
'Apple Blossom'
'Francis Hanger'

(c) *C. reticulata* × *C. japonica*
'Arbutus Gum'　　　　'Howard Asper'
'Descanso Mist'　　　'Lasca Beauty'
'Dr Clifford Parks'　　'Otto Hopfer'
'Forty-Niner'　　　　'Pink Sparkle'

(d) *C. japonica* × *C. reticulata*
'Diamond Head'　　　'Harold L. Paige'
'Fire Chief'　　　　　'Royalty'

(e) *C. saluenensis* × *C. reticulata*
'Barbara Clark'　　　'Phyl Doak'
'Dr Louis Polizzi'　　'Salutation'
'Fluted Orchid'

(f) *C. reticulata* × *C. saluenensis*
'Inspiration'

(g)   *C. saluenensis* × *C. cuspidata*
     'Cornish Snow'

(h)   *C. cuspidata* × *C. saluenensis*
     'Winton'

(i)   *C. sansanqua* × *C. reticulata*
     'Flower Girl'   'Show Girl'

(j)   *C. reticulata* × *C. granthamiana*
     'China Lady'   'Lois Shinault'

(k)   *C. japonica* × *C. lutchuenensis*
     'Fragrant Pink'

(l)   *C. japonica* × *C. fraterna*
     'Tiny Princess'

(m)   *C. japonica* × *C. heterophylla*
     'Belinda Carlyon'

Table 2: second and back-cross generation hybrids

(a)   *C. williamsii* × *C. japonica*
     'E. T. R. Carlyon'   'Little Lavender'
     'Gwavas'   'Rose Parade'

(b)   *C. japonica* × *C.* × *williamsii*
     'Charlean'   'Tiptoe'

(c)   *C.* × *williamsii* × *C. reticulata*
     'Black Lace'   'Innovation'

(d)   *C. reticulata* × *C. williamsii*
     'Leonard Messel'

(e)   *C. saluenensis* × (*C. saluenensis* × *C. reticulata*)
     'Grand Jury'

(f)   (*C. japonica* × *C. saluenensis*) × *C. reticulata*
     'Francie L'

(g)   (*C. cuspidata* × *C. saluenensis*) × *C. japonica*
     'Bonnie Marie'

(h)   *C. sasanqua* × (*C. reticulata* × *C. pitardii*)
     'Dream Girl'   'Felice Harris'

(i)   *C. saluenensis* × (*C. reticulata* × *C. pitardii*)
     'Valley Knudsen'

(j)   *C. japonica* × (*C. rusticana* × *C. lutchuenensis*)
     'Ack-scent'

II BIBLIOGRAPHY

American Camellia Society, *The Camellia*, (American Camellia Society, 1978).

Bean, W. J., *Trees and Shrubs Hardy in the British Isles, 8th edition*, (John Murray, 1970; Supplement, 1988).

Durrant, T. *The Camellia Story*, (Heinemann, 1982).

Haworth-Booth, M., *Effective Flowering Shrubs*, (Collins, 1987).

International Camellia Society, *The Camellia Register*, (Fine Arts Press, Australia, 1993).

Macoboy, S., *The Colour Dictionary of Camellias*, (Lansdowne Press, 1981).

Treseder, N. and Hyams, E., *Growing Camellias*, (Nelson & Sons Ltd., 1975).

In addition, The Southern California Camellia Society publishes *Camellia Nomenclature* every four years.

INDEXES

I INDEX OF SPECIES AND CULTIVARS

II GENERAL INDEX